P9-EEH-394

Pageantry in the Shakespearean Theater

Pageantry in the Shakespearean Theater

Edited by David M. Bergeron

The University of Georgia Press   Athens

© 1985 by the University of Georgia Press
Athens, Georgia 30602
"Making Greatness Familiar" © 1981 by Stephen Orgel
All rights reserved

Designed by Kathi L. Dailey
Set in 11 on 12 Linotron 202 Garamond No. 3

The illustrations on the title and part-title pages are sketches
by Inigo Jones of costumes for the royal entertainments
of James I and Charles I.

The paper in this book meets the guidelines for permanence
and durability of the Committee on Production Guidelines
for Book Longevity of the Council on Library Resources.

Printed in the United States of America

89 88 87 86 85   5 4 3 2 1

Library of Congress Cataloging in Publication Data
Main entry under title:

Pageantry in the Shakespearean theater.

Includes bibliographical references.
 1. English drama—17th century—History and criticism—Addresses,
essays, lectures.   2. Pageants in literature—Addresses, essays,
lectures.   3. Shakespeare, William, 1564–1616—Criticism and
interpretation—Addresses, essays, lectures.   4. Shakespeare, William, 1564–
1616—Dramatic production—Addresses, essays, lectures.   5. Pageants—
Great Britain—History—Addresses, essays, lectures.   6. Masques—
Addresses, essays, lectures.   I. Bergeron, David Moore.
PR658.P25P33 1984   791'.6'0942   83-24221
ISBN 0-8203-0716-5 (alk. paper)

Contents

Pageantry in the Shakespearean Theater

Introduction

David M. Bergeron

At the International Shakespeare Association Congress meeting in Stratford-upon-Avon in August 1981, one of the seminars focused on the topic "Pageantry in the Shakespearean Theater." These essays are an explicit outgrowth of that seminar, though they do not attempt to reproduce precisely its events or comments. The present volume provides the developed essays of several of the seminar participants along with other, invited papers.

By happy coincidence, the session marked a full decade since the publication of my *English Civic Pageantry 1558–1642* (1971). The decade of 1971–81 was fruitful indeed for studies of pageantry, including both civic and court entertainments. This period saw important book-length studies by Gordon Kipling, Roy Strong, Stephen Orgel, Glynne Wickham, and others. The year 1981 also offered another installment of Wickham's *Early English Stages* (volume 3), a book that specifically explores "drama and occasion" and "emblems of occasion," written by a theater historian who since 1959 has been directing our attention to the importance of pageants in the development of Renaissance drama.

As will be obvious in these essays, the term *pageantry* is a multifaceted, sometimes elusive idea that has several different meanings. These essays range over several categories of its meaning: tournaments, royal entries, Lord Mayor's Shows, funeral processions, progresses, and court masques. We interpret "Shakespearean theater" generically; thus what is said here is not exclusively about Shakespeare's drama. Part of the richness of this collection is, I think, its diversity, which nevertheless starts from a shared assumption about the emblematic tradition in English Renaissance theater.

Sir Dudley Carleton, writing about the production of Jonson's first masque, *The Masque of Blackness,* reported in 1605: "At night we had the Queen's Maske in the Banquetting-house, or rather her Pagent."[1] Stephen Orgel has ably explored the possible implications of Carleton's choice of words, suggesting that the remark is "both a characterization of a perfectly familiar form as something that looked quite different to the casual spectator and a critique of its relevance to the function for which it was designed."[2] That is, Carleton may have sensed a familiarity in the pageant devices of the masque, and he may have found the entertainment "empty." On the latter meaning one recalls words from the Venetian Senate conference about the threat of the Turks in *Othello.* After a Sailor reports that the Turks are bound for Rhodes, the First Senator says:

>   This cannot be
> By no assay of reason. 'Tis a pageant
> To keep us in false gaze.   [I.iii.17–19]

—an empty show, in other words.

Meanwhile, Anthony Munday in his civic pageant of 1615, the Lord Mayor's Show *Metropolis Coronata,* characterizes the evening processional thus: "The way being somewhat long, the order of march appeared the more excellent and commendable, even as if it had been a Royall Maske, prepared for the marriage of an immortall Deitie, as in the like nature we hold the Lord Maior."[3] By the 1630s Thomas Heywood was creating in his mayoral pageants scenes that have no verbal content and serve only to amuse spectators. For example, in *Londini Emporia* (1633) Heywood describes the third show on land by saying that it "consists onely in motion, agitation and action." He provides a rationale: "And without some such intruded Anti-maske, many who carry their eares in their eyes, will not sticke to say, I will not give a pinne for the Show."[4] Antimasque, an idea and term first used by Jonson in *The Masque of Queens* (1609), now finds its way into street pageants. At such moments the usual distinctions between civic pageants and court masques blur.

The regular drama itself clouds the ordinary distinctions made about kinds of entertainment. Armado, for example, informs Holofernes and Nathaniel in *Love's Labour's Lost* "that the king would have me present the princess, sweet chuck, with some delightful ostentation, or show, or pageant, or antic, or fire-work" (V.i.98–100). In the preceding scene Berowne urges his fellow lovers, all fresh from having rationalized their oathbreaking:

>   In the afternoon
> We will with some strange pastime solace them [the women],
>
> . . . .
>
> For revels, dances, masks, and merry hours
> Forerun fair Love, strewing her way with flowers.   [IV.iii.371–75]

Given the setting in the park of Navarre and the concluding "Pageant of the Nine Worthies," the play at moments resembles progress pageants that greeted Queen Elizabeth on her summer tours. In Shakespeare's last plays we find episodes of self-conscious spectacle: the vision of Diana in *Pericles*, the descent of Jupiter in *Cymbeline*, the restoration of Hermione in *The Winter's Tale*, the wedding masque in *The Tempest*, and Katherine's vision in *Henry VIII*. All bear a relationship to masque and pageant traditions. Perhaps the culmination of the intermingling of forms comes in Middleton and Rowley's *The World Tost at Tennis* (1620), a "courtly masque" intended for performance in a regular theater.

In order to illustrate something further about the interrelationship of masque and pageant, I focus on the year 1605 and the careers of Jonson and Munday. This year marks Jonson's first masque, *The Masque of Blackness*, and Munday's first extant Lord Mayor's Show, *The Triumphes of Re-United Britannia*. Strange as it may seem, given Jonson's prominence in writing masques, up to the end of 1604 his pageant career had concentrated on outdoor and street entertainments. But for the first court employment in 1605, Jonson might have continued to write civic pageants. For the delectation and entertainment of newly arrived Queen Anne and Prince Henry, Jonson wrote an outdoor show performed at the home of Sir Robert Spencer at Althorp in late June 1603. Nearly a year later, in May 1604, Jonson presented a pageant for King James and Anne at the home of Sir William Cornwallis at Highgate. Both entertainments, allowing for certain differences, resemble Elizabethan progress pageants.[5]

In March 1604 Jonson in collaboration with Dekker and Middleton prepared an opulent royal entry pageant for James. Here on seven triumphal arches the city of London offered its grand compliment to the new king. For the first time in royal entries major dramatists of the public theater devised the entertainment. Jonson wrote the scenes that took place at the first and last arches, plus a show in the Strand.[6] Late in 1604 Jonson tried his hand at writing a Lord Mayor's Show; unfortunately, the text does not survive. Records of the Haberdashers reveal a payment of twelve pounds "to Beniamyn Iohnson for his device, and speech for the Children."[7] Despite his satiric scorn directed at Munday in *The Case Is Altered*, Jonson nevertheless apparently collaborated with Munday in this October mayoral pageant, for the same guild records show a payment of two pounds "to Antony Mundey for his paines." After this busy 1604, Jonson wrote no more civic pageants; he turned to court masques instead.

Munday, by contrast, had a hand in fifteen Lord Mayor's Shows from 1602 to 1623; in addition he wrote a street pageant celebrating the investiture of Henry as prince of Wales in 1610. Is there, however, some point of contact between what these one-time collaborators, Munday and Jonson, were doing from 1605 onward? Allowing for inherent and obvious differences, both masque and civic pageant were "occasional" drama, involving considerable sums of money, actors, properties, machines, and elaborate costumes. While Jonson negotiated with the Master of the Revels and received payments from the court, Munday dealt with the Masters and Wardens of the London guilds. Jonson had his Inigo Jones and Munday his John Grinkin and others to assist with the design and construction of the entertainments. Jones's drawings give special life to Jonson's masques, as do the drawings for Munday's 1616 show, *Chrysanaleia*—the only extant drawings for a Jacobean Lord Mayor's Show. Jonson's texts are displays of his immense learning; so to a lesser extent are Munday's, especially his 1605 pageant text. Professional actors performed in Jonson's masques, as they did occasionally in Munday's pageants: three members of the King's Men appeared in his 1610 and 1611 pageants. The two dramatists also share a number of similarities in subject content. A substantial common ground therefore exists in the work of Munday and Jonson, one entertaining the city and the other, the court.[8] We may thus better understand Sir Dudley Carleton's use of "masque" and "pageant" when describing a performance of *The Masque of Blackness*. Though he may have sensed a distinction in the terms, many of his contemporaries found them interchangeable.

Spectators attending masques, pageants, and plays in the regular public theaters may not have discerned any significant differences in the staging; such is Glynne Wickham's contention. Wickham suggests that the Jacobean playgoer "would not have been aware of many material differences between the stage conventions that met his gaze on these several occasions."[9] Insofar as this observation is valid, all the more reason exists for discussing pageantry in the Shakespearean theater. We must, as Wickham argues in his first volume, banish "our present-day ideas that the exclusive purpose of stage spectacle is to represent . . . we must anticipate a whole language of signs and learn to read it."[10] To explore several manifestations of pageantry, as the essays in this volume do, is to focus not on mimesis but on emblematic representation in the Renaissance theater.

Offering insight into the "language" of pageant dramatists and revealing something of the process of creation, Dekker writes in his part of the 1604 royal entry: "By this time Imagine, that *Poets* (who drawe speaking Pictures) and *Painters* (who make dumbe Poesie) had their heads and hands full; the one for natiue and sweet Inuention: the other for liuely Illustration of what the former should deuise: Both of them emulously contending (but not striuing) with the proprest and brightest Colours of Wit and Art, to set out the beautie of the great *Triumphant-day.*"[11] Later in the same civic pageant Dekker describes the allegorical figures located on one of the arches. Of Justice he writes: "Hauing tolde you that her name was *Iustice,* I hope you will not put mee to describe what properties she held in her hands, sithence euery painted cloath can informe you" (2:295). Dekker obviously believes that spectators readily apprehend the emblematic language of representation. Throughout his pageants Munday uses such terms as "emblems," "imprese," and "conceits"; in practice he presents many of his figures with appropriate symbolic properties. In the discourse of the pageants these emblems are signs of additional meaning. This may be what in part Jonson has in mind at the beginning of his masque *Hymenaei:* "Though their voice [that of the inventions or devices] be taught to sound to present occasions, their sense or doth or should always lay hold on more removed mysteries."[12]

Jonson had in 1604 written similarly when describing the function of the first triumphal arch of James's royal entry: "The nature and propertie of these Deuices being, to present alwaies some one entire bodie, or figure, consisting of distinct members, and each of those expressing it selfe, . . . yet all, with that generall harmonie so connexed, and disposed, as no one little part can be missing to the illustration of the whole." With a mixture of emblematic methods, Jonson says, "the garments and ensignes deliuer the nature of the person, and the word the present office." Under such circumstances it will not be necessary to write, *"This is a Dog;* or, *This is a Hare:* but so to be presented, . . . they might, without cloud, or obscuritie, declare themselues to the sharpe and learned."[13] That is the ideal.

More than a decade later Munday says much the same thing in the text of his 1618 Lord Mayor's Show: "For better vnderstanding the true morality of this deuise, the personages haue all Emblemes and Properties in their hands, & so neere them, that the weakest capacity may take knowledge of them; which course in such solemne Triumphes hath alwaies beene allowed of best obseruation: both for avoiding trouble to the Magistrate, by tedious and impertinent speeches, and deuouring the time, which craueth diligent expedition."[14] Munday consciously refers to an emblematic tradition in the pageants, a mode or representation inseparable from court and civic entertainments.

Having examined some concepts of dramatic pageantry, I turn to focus briefly on some of the critical work done on this subject in the twentieth century. The 1920s constitute a convenient starting point, for two pioneering works appeared during that time: Robert Withington's *English*

Pageantry (1918–20) and Enid Welsford's *The Court Masque* (1927). Though Withington touches on tournaments and masques, his primary concern is a historical survey of folk mummings, royal entries, progress entertainments, and Lord Mayor's Shows. In his two-volume study Withington even explores some pageants of the late nineteenth and early twentieth centuries. Revealing his evolutionary perspective, Withington writes: "Like all dramatic, or semi-dramatic forms, the pageant is a growth. . . . Utilized by the Church, developed by the guilds, this form of entertainment grew with more and more elaboration until the pageant, as we know it, came into existence."[15] Rather bluntly he writes: "The pageant is the lowest form of dramatic expression; but it is a form deeply rooted in the heart of the people" (p. xx). These two views guide much that Withington does; therefore, valuable as his study is, it did little to rescue pageants from the oblivion to which theater historians had assigned them.

Welsford's book is also mainly historical as she traces the origins and development of the court masque. For her the masque is but "sophisticated mumming."[16] That partial view has been supplanted in more recent years by a fuller understanding of what the masque is. Like Withington, Welsford has some difficulty taking the masque seriously as drama. She writes: "The story of the masque is the tale of how the magic of the mummers was transformed into a noble pastime and only just failed to become an enduring form of art" (p. 18). Two hundred pages later she observes: "In spite of all the efforts of the dramatists it [masque] was never really turned into art; it was always a form of amusement" (p. 244). Her zeal in discussing the influence of the masque on the drama shines through in one of her conclusions: "The chief justification of the masque influence and the special lyrical moment is that they made possible the diffused lyricism of Shakespearian tragedy" (p. 297). I do not think that anyone writing today about either Shakespeare or the masque would make such a claim. Welsford exaggerates the influence of the masque by finding it somehow constitutive of Shakespeare's achievement.

The scholarly contribution of Withington and Welsford is, problems aside, substantial. They remain starting points for serious investigations of pageantry, and one returns to them regularly with a genuine sense of reward. One large area that receives scant attention from them, however, is politics, that is, the political circumstances and the effect of what seem to be insubstantial pageants: they are clearly more than simple amusement. Later criticism has turned its attention to this problem and others. At the risk of considerable violence to the scholarship of intervening decades, I want to focus on the contribution of the past fifteen years.

Had we world enough and time, a full-fledged historical survey would necessarily examine George Kernodle's *From Art to Theatre* (Chicago: University of Chicago Press, 1944), in which the author attempts to link the public playhouses with the street tableaux, insisting that the Elizabethan stage was more closely related to the street theaters than to any other form. Alice Venezky Griffin in *Pageantry on the Shakespearean Stage* (New York: Twayne, 1951) provides the first full-length exploration of pageantry within Shakespeare's plays, a subject that Bruce Smith examines in this collection of essays. The 1960s witnessed, in addition to part of Glynne Wickham's *Early English Stages,* two important studies of Jonson's masques: John Meagher's *Method and Meaning in Jonson's Masques* (Notre Dame, Ind.: University of Notre Dame Press, 1966) and Stephen Orgel's *The Jonsonian Masque* (Cambridge, Mass.: Harvard University Press, 1965). Meagher primarily examines the philosophical meaning of Jonson's masques, arguing that it is as "a humanistic poet that we must finally view Jonson the masque-writer" (p. 186). Orgel explores the Jonsonian masque in terms of its tradition, its audience, and its theater, with emphasis on the importance of the monarch or honored guest in the masque experience. He also suggests that the Jonsonian masque shows us Jonson's "humors theory applied to universals" (p. 198), and that the idea of theater that Jonson conceived could be perfected only in the masque (p. 200).

Many pageant studies of the last fifteen years have explored the political significance of such entertainments, whether court or civic. This emphasis certainly characterizes Sydney Anglo's *Spectacle, Pageantry, and Early Tudor Policy* (Oxford: Clarendon Press, 1969). Anglo sees a twofold political significance in the pageants: "they were related to a European tradition of the magnificence expected of a potentate"; and "many festivals were political, either through the desire to enhance great diplomatic occasions, or because they actually included specific comment on an international situation" (p. 2). He therefore examines festivals, disguisings, masques, plays, tournaments, and royal entries, beginning with Henry VII and closing with Elizabeth's royal entry pageant of January 1559. After Katharine of Aragon's 1501 pageant, Anglo finds nothing new in the remaining Tudor royal entries; but he does find distinctive new elements in the tournaments and court disguisings. He also sees Burgundian influence in the court entertainments, a point later developed by Kipling. Because he is a historian in search of political significance, Anglo occasionally overlooks the artistic importance of the pageants.

Working independently of Anglo, I pick up where he had left off in *English Civic Pageantry 1558–1642.* In my historical survey of civic entertainments from Elizabeth's 1559 entry to the closing of the theaters, I

focus on progress pageants, royal entries, and Lord Mayor's Shows. I see
the 1604 pageant for James as a turning point, unlike those that had
preceded it and determinant of the form for those that follow. About the
same time, the Lord Mayor's Show acquires a complexity unknown in the
Elizabethan period. Though I examine the political and historical contexts
of these pageants, my emphasis is on these shows as drama. I explore
themes—political, moral, and personal—that pervade the pageants; I
both chronicle and analyze the work of the craftsmen, the artificers, who
assisted the pageant dramatists by lending substantiality to the pageants.

In 1973 Stephen Orgel and Roy Strong published the magnificent *Inigo
Jones: The Theatre of the Stuart Court,* which includes in its two volumes all
of Jones's theatrical drawings. The editors suggest that the "Stuart masque
as a form was largely the creation of a unique collaboration in the history
of the English stage, that of Inigo Jones and Ben Jonson."[17] These volumes give vivid testimony to that collaboration. The introductory essays
include one on the politics of the masque and its royal connection. Strong
and Orgel conclude: "The masque is for the monarch and about the monarch, the more directly in the reign of Charles I because the King himself
played the leading part in his spectacles" (1:50)—unlike his father. Orgel
pursues some of these matters in his *The Illusion of Power,* a brief book rich
in implications. Stated simply, his thesis is that "court masques and
plays . . . were recognized to be significant expressions of royal power,"[18]
idealizations of the monarch as an exemplary figure. Orgel writes further:
"Masques were essential to the life of the Renaissance court; their allegories gave a higher meaning to the realities of politics and power; their
fiction created heroic roles for the leaders of society" (p. 38). The illusion
of power was, of course, eventually at odds with the reality of power, as
Charles I learned. Orgel and others have taken us a long way from the idea
that a masque is sophisticated mumming. It is, but it is also much more.

What Anglo hinted at, Gordon Kipling develops: namely, the Burgundian influence on court and civic entertainments of the early Tudor period.
In his *The Triumph of Honour* (Leiden: Leiden University Press, 1977) Kipling traces this influence through many literary forms, ranging from tournaments to poetry and including royal entries and disguisings. He offers
an antidote to the arguments of those who insist on Italian influence every-
where. Katharine of Aragon's 1501 entry receives much attention as Kipling documents its use of Burgundian tradition. Its narrative plot and its
form of medieval dream-vision make it unique. Kipling also argues that
"while the English masque thus stands indebted to Italy for its name, it
owes its basic structure and spectacular form to Burgundy."[19] His arguments, convincingly made, call for certain revisions in the work of
Welsford and Withington, among others.

I return finally to an author and book invoked several times already: Glynne Wickham and his *Early English Stages,* the most recent volume published in 1981. Since 1959 Wickham through these volumes has done much to increase awareness among theater historians of the vital importance of masques and civic pageants and of the emblematic tradition. In the forthcoming final volume Wickham will specifically discuss entertainments, masques, and civic pageants of the seventeenth century. Here in volume 3 Wickham returns to an examination of the nature of occasion and its dramatic expression and the major shifts of emphasis "that caused old forms to decay and new ones to take their place."[20] Masques and pageants, for example, part company from the regular drama when it ceases to be celebratory. Wickham observes, "The homogeneity that is so marked a characteristic of medieval and Tudor audiences, finally crumbled in the period 1576–1642 to be replaced by new structures closely allied to social self-consciousness and the growing educational and economic divisions in English society" (p. xxi).

But, of course, in some ways the drama appropriated techniques and devices from the pageant theater, and that is part of Wickham's concern as well. He writes: "The problem that confronted the devisers of all these occasional entertainments was to achieve a satisfactory balance between static tableaux, set speeches and the combative, processional or choreographic actions which they adorned and explained" (p. 79). These disparate components, if coherently linked, lead to an emblematic whole. The persistence of this emblematic technique goes far, Wickham says, in explaining "why English drama, despite strong pressures to make it conform to principles derived from classical antiquity, remained so stubbornly loyal to native, medieval traditions of play-construction and theatrical conventions" (p. 82). As we move from Withington to Welsford to Wickham, we perceive the profound imagination and knowledge that have gone into the study of pageants, and we see the considerable changes that have come about in our understanding of this subject.

What, to ask the obvious question, remains to be done? For one thing, court masques have received perhaps a disproportionate share of critical attention, leaving civic pageants often ignored. I have wondered at this disparity. Partly it may be the result of the awesome importance of Ben Jonson (with his meticulously prepared masque texts); no corresponding single major dramatist is so prominent in writing civic entertainments. Some critics have had difficulty in taking the street pageants seriously as drama, but surely these entertainments share many ingredients of the masque. What we need, of course, is a full-scale study of the relationship of the masques and pageants. Essays here by Gail Paster and Leah Marcus show how fruitful and exciting such investigations can be. If such a study were undertaken, it would not be done merely to add prestige to the civic shows, but rather it might help us see more clearly than we do at present how each influenced the other. Setting and occasion probably account for the major differences between them. But the mythical, historical, allegorical, and symbolic worlds they have in common suggest a comparable poetic imagination informing them. We know that at times they shared properties and costumes as, to cite one instance, in the case of the Master of the Revels' providing costumes for Elizabeth's glorious coronation civic pageant in 1559. From such practical but interesting matters one can explore further the similar poetics and theatricality of the masque and pageant.

Most of the essays in this volume examine the connection of pageants and the regular drama. Here, too, much needs to be done. Is the drama of Shakespeare and his contemporaries indebted to the pageants? Clearly the answer is yes. The issue is how that influence works and what its significance may be. What about staging techniques and machinery as one moves from Shakespeare to civic pageants to court masques? We know, for example, that members of the King's Men performed not only at the Globe but also in court masques and in an occasional civic entertainment. Might different styles of acting be required by these different forms? Did anybody even think of them as being particularly different? Did it matter to Richard Burbage that he performed in a street pageant celebrating Henry's investiture as prince of Wales in 1610? We know that, except for Shakespeare, the principal dramatists of the time wrote plays and pageants or masques. Did they think one form slighter than another, or was all playwriting a commercial enterprise? Did they write Lord Mayor's Shows merely because the pay was good? These teasing questions compel us to think seriously about the nature of theater and of pageants and masques in particular.

Inherently, pageantry is rich in visual display and appeal. Fortunately, Inigo Jones's drawings for the masques survive so that we can appreciate something of the visual impact of those shows. Precious few drawings are extant for the civic pageants and nothing on the scale of Jones's sketches. Thus we are left to infer from the surviving texts what civic entertainments might have looked like, a matter more troublesome than for the regular drama since so much in the pageants hinges on spectacle. The relationship of the verbal text and the visual display is another area needing investigation. Closely allied to this issue is the matter of iconography, the rich, symbolic significance of the visual rendering. Only scattered efforts have thus far explored the iconography of civic shows; yet a writer like Middleton demonstrates acute awareness of iconographic traditions in his Lord Mayor's Shows, rivaling Jonson in the masques. Obviously, dramatists made assumptions about what audiences would understand from the emblematic properties and representation. Without some such understanding, audiences would have found the pageants and masques virtually incomprehensible.

Thanks to the work of Andrew Sabol, we know much about the songs and dances of the court masque; we do not have a comparable study of the civic pageant. Song and music fill the shows, ranging from a "noise of instruments" to the singing of the children of Saint Paul's. Several of the songs are crucial to the thematic presentation of the shows, especially from the estate progress pageants. At least two quarto texts of Lord Mayor's Shows include musical notation for songs; so far as I know, neither has ever been discussed musically. Are there any connections—in words, music, style, or purpose—among the music of the regular theater, the masques, and the civic pageants? We do have guild records for some entertainments that document the participation of well-known musicians, such as William Byrd, John Bull, Orlando Gibbons, and Nathaniel Giles.

Though we are blessed with excellent editions of court masques—I think of the Jonson masques edited by Stephen Orgel and earlier by Herford and Simpson—we lack adequate editions for a number of civic pageants. For example, at present we have no sound critical editions of the pageants of Anthony Munday, Thomas Middleton, or Thomas Heywood, though these three dramatists of considerable renown are the most prolific writers of Lord Mayor's Shows. (An edition of Munday's pageants is forthcoming.) The edition of Thomas Dekker's pageants by Fredson Bowers and the commentary notes by Cyrus Hoy are a model of the kind of attention pageant writers deserve. Also, texts need to be made readily available in forms appropriate for classroom use; one would be hard pressed to find an anthology of Renaissance drama that includes any civic pageant. Merely trying to round up texts of pageants for serious study is a formidable task; doubtless good editions would encourage further study of the civic shows.

The present collection of essays meets at least some of these needs. The essays explore the interconnections of masque, pageant, and regular drama; techniques of pageantry; themes; and the impact on Shakespeare's drama, both practical and theoretical. Like a summer progress, this collection wanders over the landscape of pageantry but, like Queen Elizabeth on such a tour, always with a clear purpose: our destination is to gain fuller understanding of how and in what ways Shakespearean theater encompassed pageantry. The essays therefore range from Orgel's suggestion that pageantry is theater miming greatness to Bruce Smith's explanation of how Shakespeare incorporated pageantry into the plays.

We begin with Stephen Orgel's broad perspective of what constitutes pageantry. Seeing it as an essential ingredient in all Renaissance drama, Orgel demonstrates how it reflects and imitates court life. He wisely comments on how much we do not understand about the theater of that time: so many curious and inexplicable things go on, especially the relationship of the court to drama. Pageants and masques clearly serve political purposes, a point also made by Leah Marcus in her essay on Jonson's *Golden Age Restored*. As she has skilfully done in other published essays, Marcus here reveals the crucial importance of the effect of occasion on the shaping of the masque. What is startling is the realization that Jonson seems to be responding explicitly to Munday's 1611 Lord Mayor's Show. Linking several pageants and masques, Gail Paster explores how these dramas represent the concept of London as a city. At times the writers of civic pageants idealize the power and wealth of the city, making it rival the court. The emphasis on city history underscores a heroic tradition, and the pageants thereby minister to the city's self-esteem. One of the pageants that consciously idealize London is the 1604 royal entry for James I. In the last essay in this group I examine how this particular pageant influenced Middleton in writing his comedy *No Wit, No Help*. He had written but one speech for the pageant, collaborating with Jonson and Dekker, but the whole experience lingered in his artistic consciousness. One wonders how many other dramatists imitated or parodied specific episodes from pageants.

Several of the papers at the Stratford conference focused on Shakespeare's history plays; some are represented here. In the first essay in this section Gordon Kipling examines the 1392 civic pageant in London honoring Richard II, a pageant that seems to have established a pattern to be followed for the next 150 years, evident in the royal entries of Elizabeth (1559) and James I (1604). Kipling particularly explores the liturgical influence on this royal entry, in which Richard II comes to the holy city of London as its Christ-king. Kipling's rich study opens several possibilities for the study of other entertainments. It also may suggest why Shakespeare developed religious imagery in association with Richard II: perhaps the dramatist was being historical, since in fact London had received Richard in such terms. The ideal of Christian polity functions in both pageants and plays. Turning to the dramatically realized Richard, James Black explores the theme of the beggar and king in *Richard II*. The supposedly farcical scene of Aumerle (V. iii) may be likened to an antimasque, countering the "woeful pageant" of Richard's deposition (IV.i). As in the court masque, such an episode does not diminish the value of the whole but rather enhances and reinforces it. Through the pageant-king Richard, Shakespeare may also be glancing at the mysteries of the fourteenth century. Like insubstantial pageants, the authority of the king is little and brief. Barbara Palmer examines the use of pageantry in the second tetralogy of history plays, demonstrating how and why it varies from *Richard II* to *Henry V* but always underscores the image of kingship that Shakespeare wants to depict. Looking at the other side of the coin, Palmer also discusses the role of the commons in pageantry and in creating and sustaining the position of king; her perspective grows in part from civic records that illustrate the community's involvement in preparing pageants. Hal's "becoming" a prince is the focus of Gerard Cox's essay; much in *1 Henry IV* links Hal to traditional chivalric pageantry—the challenge to single combat, for example. At his greatest moment, when he kills Hotspur, Hal becomes the emblematic figure of the knight *sine pluma,* thereby demonstrating that his nobility transcends mere show; pageant appearance becomes actuality.

The final group of essays encompasses a broad sweep over Shakespeare's canon, as the discussion moves from the tragedies to the romances. Citizens of London in particular were familiar with great funeral processions—for example, the one for Elizabeth in 1603, and for Prince Henry in 1612. Michael Neill demonstrates how these funeral pageants find their application in tragedies by Shakespeare and others. Neill explores what no one else has done by discussing the crucial importance of the placement of the funeral pageant in the play. In some plays such a pageant becomes the iconographic and emotional center of the drama, paradoxically reminding us of a scheme of earthly order and of the process of death that sweeps all order away. In his essay James Yoch links civic and court pageantry and landscape design to three of Shakespeare's pastoral plays, illustrating the change that Shakespeare's drama undergoes as we move from *A Midsummer Night's Dream* to *The Tempest.* Like the outdoor pageants themselves of the Elizabethan period, Shakespeare's early plays show little concern for unifying landscape; instead, it remains eclectic with discrete parts. By *The Tempest,* however, Shakespeare offers Prospero, who has a commanding and unifying vision of the landscape of his island, reflecting a change in the display of royal power in pageants. Bruce Smith's complementary essay traverses some of the same ground but with a different perspective. In fact, perspective is part of his concern: How does the audience see the pageant images in the plays? Smith suggests that Shakespeare confronts the artistic problem with three solutions that differ according to the period of his writing. Like the landscape to which Yoch refers, the pageants within the early plays maintain a separate and subordinate identity. In the second period, however, they fuse with the drama, offering a single perspective view; and in the final period, that of the romances, the pageant elements coordinate the drama, providing a reality more compelling than the fable itself.

As Jaques says, "All the world's a stage, / And all the men and women merely players." If we take "merely" to mean "entirely," we appreciate the full scope of the familiar metaphor. In his *Renaissance Self-Fashioning* Stephen Greenblatt has brilliantly explored the richness and seriousness of this metaphor for everyday life. Obviously Elizabethans took the concept to heart in ways that we only vaguely understand. Before Jaques summed up succinctly what we have come to take more as a proverb than an actuality, Richard Mulcaster in the text for Elizabeth's 1559 royal entry into London had likened London that day to a vast stage. So Dekker, in the text of the 1604 pageant for James, likens London to James's "Court Royall": "So now at his [James's] going from her . . . She lost that honour: And being (like an Actor on a Stage) stript out of her borrowed Maiestie, she resignes her former shape and title of Citie" (2:301). This is possible, Dekker says, because "such Vertue is begotten in Princes, that their verie presence hath power to turne a Village to a Citie, and to make a Citie appeare great as a Kingdome."

With a theatrical flair that characterizes her reign, Queen Elizabeth responded to the events of her London royal entry pageant, receiving, for example, the English Bible from Truth, kissing it, and promising to read daily therein—to the great delectation of the audience. At such a moment the crucial, determinate role of the honored guest in a pageant or masque is transparent. If all the world is a stage, then not only are there no private places, as Jonathan Goldberg has observed, but the performers may include members of the audience as well. Certainly the spectators in the streets of London or at the Banqueting House in Whitehall are there to see the sovereign or mayor as much as to see planned dramatic activity. The rare modern-day performance of a masque—I know of no performances of civic pageants—is by definition lacking an essential ingredient, namely, the sovereign for whom it was designed. As a London citizen wound his way from Holborn or Milk Street through the dirty, narrow, cold streets of London, a light snow falling, to take his place in Cheapside to watch Elizabeth's 1559 pageant, he must have come with keen anticipation of seeing the new queen. That he was participating in a theatrical experience can be of little doubt. Theater histories that ignore pageants, as many do, provide at best an incomplete view of what drama was like in this its richest era and on the largest stage in England. Our focus on Shakespeare and the drama of the public and private theaters should not blur our vision of a time and place in which all the world was a stage. Theater did not occur merely in formal structures designed to be theaters: it happened in

London and other cities and in elegant chambers at court. Infinite variety is the hallmark of English Renaissance drama.

The essays contained herein capture some of that variety. Unable to resist but not wishing to distort, I nevertheless suggest that this collection is somewhat like a pageant itself: rich, colorful, entertaining, varied, multidimensional, visual and verbal. This volume will, I hope, provide much satisfaction but also make us eager for the next pageant, perhaps giving rise to other attempts to explore such issues and venture in yet uncharted areas. One issue, however, radically separates these essays from my pageant analogy: they are substantial. These essays are not to be dismantled and carted off immediately after the show, causing our memories to evaporate into air, into thin air. Rather, they provide a foundation to which we may return many times and on which we may build.

Notes

1. John Nichols, *The Progresses, Processions, and Magnificent Festivities of King James the First* (London: J. B. Nichols, 1828), 1:473.

2. Stephen Orgel, *The Jonsonian Masque* (Cambridge, Mass.: Harvard University Press, 1965), p. 115.

3. Anthony Munday, *Metropolis Coronata* (London, 1615), sig. B4ᵛ.

4. Thomas Heywood, *Londini Emporia; or, Londons Mercatura* (London, 1633), sigs. B3ᵛ–B4.

5. For a brief discussion see my *English Civic Pageantry 1558–1642* (Columbia: University of South Carolina Press, 1971), pp. 70–71, 89–91.

6. Bergeron, *English Civic Pageantry*, pp. 71–89.

7. Jean Robertson and D. J. Gordon, eds., *Collections III: A Calendar of Dramatic Records in the Books of the Livery Companies of London 1485–1640* (Oxford: Malone Society, 1954), p. 63.

8. This point is explored in the introduction to my *Pageants and Entertainments of Anthony Munday: A Critical Edition* (New York: Garland, 1984).

9. Glynne Wickham, *Early English Stages 1300 to 1600* (New York: Columbia University Press, 1959–), vol. 2, pt. 1, p. 7.

10. Ibid., 1:85.

11. Thomas Dekker, *The Dramatic Works of Thomas Dekker*, ed. Fredson Bowers (Cambridge: Cambridge University Press, 1955), 2:257.

12. *Ben Jonson: Selected Masques*, ed. Stephen Orgel (New Haven, Conn.: Yale University Press, 1970), p. 48.

13. *Ben Jonson*, ed. C. H. Herford, Percy Simpson, and Evelyn Simpson (Oxford: Clarendon Press, 1925–52), 7:90–91.

14. Anthony Munday, *Sidero-Thriambos; or, Steele and Iron Triumphing* (London: Nicholas Okes, 1618), sig. C1ᵛ.

15. Robert Withington, *English Pageantry: An Historical Outline* (1918–20; reprint ed., New York: Benjamin Blom, 1963), 1:84.

16. Enid Welsford, *The Court Masque: A Study in the Relationship Between Poetry and the Revels* (Cambridge: Cambridge University Press, 1927), p. 4.

17. Stephen Orgel and Roy Strong, eds., *Inigo Jones: The Theatre of the Stuart Court* (Berkeley and Los Angeles: University of California Press, 1973), 1:1.

18. Stephen Orgel, *The Illusion of Power: Political Theater in the English Renaissance* (Berkeley and Los Angeles: University of California Press, 1975), pp. 44–45.

19. Gordon Kipling, *The Triumph of Honour: Burgundian Origins of the Elizabethan Renaissance* (Leiden: Leiden University Press for Sir Thomas Browne Institute, 1977), p. 115.

20. Wickham, *Early English Stages,* 3:xix.

Part One

Making Greatness Familiar

Stephen Orgel

One of the chief attractions of the Elizabethan popular theater was clearly its pageantry, conceived in the broadest sense: its ability to mime the spectacle of courts and aristocratic enterprises to an urban, predominantly middle-class audience in a society that had grown relatively (contemporary critics said dangerously) mobile. Ironically, the attraction was especially powerful when the pageantry was presented in the service of a nostalgic medievalism, expressing the traditional values of an established hierarchy and a chivalric code, since that was precisely the Elizabethan courtly mythology. It was a mythology consciously designed to validate and legitimate an authority that must have seemed, to what was left of the old aristocracy, dangerously *arriviste*. Indeed, it must have seemed so to Elizabeth herself, the granddaughter of a prosperous London merchant, faced with continual questions about the sources of her authority and the very legitimacy of her birth.

The chivalric code, with its attendant social forms and public displays, had been a crucial element in Tudor policy from the beginning. Gordon Kipling has shown how consciously Henry VII imported Burgundian chivalric models as the basis of a broad cultural program to project the image of a noble and honorable court.[1] The image, for this monarch, was everything, since Henry reigned without even a doubtful claim to the English throne. Chivalry here was a mask for the inelegant realities of military power on the one hand and the mundane details of administrative efficiency on the other. For his son Henry VIII, as quickly became apparent, chivalry served as a mask for the lack of either: the splendid fantasies of the Field of the Cloth of Gold were universally admired, but nobody, least of all the French king whom they were designed to impress, was deceived into thinking that they represented real power.

Elizabeth redefined Tudor chivalry to create a mythology that was peculiarly her own. In it, the essence of knighthood was service to a lady, and when the lady was a version of the queen, frustration was indissoluble from heroic achievement. Spenser's epic sums up and embodies decades of royal image-making, accurately expressing not only the ideal but its powerful ambivalence—for example, in the endlessly delayed or aborted marriages, and the narcissistic paradox of the lady-knight.

Chivalric ideals and their expression in courtly spectacle, in Accession Day tilts, royal entertainments, and court protocol generally, constitute a good instance of the utility of symbolic fictions—of pageantry and poetry in the largest sense—within a society. It is clear that Spenser grew increasingly dubious about the values implicit in his chivalric metaphor, and that Elizabethan society did so too. Recent criticism has tried to see in Elizabethan chivalry an effective cultural mediator, a social trope that allowed for the channeling and sublimation of potentially dangerous energies.[2] Ceremonials and their attendant fictions certainly *can* function in this way, as the work of Clifford Geertz amply demonstrates, and Elizabeth clearly had something of the sort in mind; but it is also clear that, by the last two decades of the reign at least, a strong sense of impatience and disillusion with the royal mythology was being felt. The mythology had become increasingly private, a way for Elizabeth to see herself, and its rhetoric was adopted only by those who had a vested interest in mirroring her self-image. People whose livelihood did not depend on court patronage adopted quite a different tone in addressing her—for example, the tone of John Stubbs's *Gaping Gulph:* scolding, impatient, affectionate, familial, commonsensical. We surely err in taking the queen's version of herself as a working model for the life of the commonwealth. King James's son Prince Henry, in 1609, saw himself as the center of a chivalric revival: chivalry had to be *revived* in 1609, having been dead, in Henry's mind, not for the six years since Elizabeth's time but since the Middle Ages.

The program that Prince Henry proposed, militaristic and aggressively Protestant, involved a very different notion of chivalry from that of Elizabeth. It is the same notion that thirty years earlier had informed Sidney's pleas for royal employment, and that were responsible for his aborted career. Sidney's version of chivalry was antithetical to the queen's, and dangerous to it. Henry's, in the same way, was energetically resisted by a large and powerful court faction, including both his father the king and his poet Ben Jonson.[3] This will not seem anomalous if we recall how dubious a moral principle chivalric courtesy becomes in Book VI of the *Faerie Queene.* The age's attitude toward chivalry is part of a larger attitude toward poetry as a whole, toward the relation of symbolic fictions to effective action—that is, to real life. There is a remarkable touchstone in Book V, in the trial of Mary Queen of Scots as Duessa. After a prosecution by Zeal seconded by Artegal, the knight of Justice, "she was guilty deemed" by the court, and Elizabeth as Mercilla is appealed to for judgment. Here is Spenser's account of what happened:

But she, whose Princely breast was touched nere
With piteous ruth of her so wretched plight,
Though plaine she saw by all, that she did heare,
That she of death was guiltie found by right,
Yet would not let iust vengeance on her light;
But rather let in stead thereof to fall
Few perling drops from her faire lampes of light;
The which she couering with her purple pall
Would haue the passion hid, and vp arose withall.   [V.ix.50]

Allegorized as Mercilla, what else can Elizabeth do? Four stanzas into
the next canto, after lavish praise of the queen's incomparable mercy,
Spenser does acknowledge that Mary/Duessa was in fact executed, though
even here he cannot quite bring himself to say so: the death is referred to
as Duessa's "willful fall," thereby effectively exonerating Elizabeth from
making the decision. This was a clear mirror not of events but of the
queen's mind: Elizabeth had devised a similar fiction for her own conscience, by signing Mary's death warrant but refusing to send it. It was
sent by her privy councillors—on her tacit instructions, of course—and
they thereby bore the direct responsibility for Mary's execution. A less
shrewd poet would have undertaken to justify Elizabeth's actions, and
would have offended her as deeply as Spenser's account of Duessa's fall
offended King James. The poet's own attitudes here remain utterly obscure: the poem is expression not of the poet's mind, but of the patron's.
The moment, however, is a dangerous one—Spenser is not playing it safe.
Obviously the queen cannot be criticized in an epic celebrating her greatness, especially in the Book of Justice; but why does Spenser want to
include the episode at all? This is not an isolated example: in the latter
books of the *Faerie Queene* Spenser repeatedly confronts the realities of his
society with his poetic mythology, and keeps making the same point: it
doesn't work.

The choice of this particular myth, and its extraordinary elaboration
under Elizabeth, are not difficult to understand. The idea that knighthood
consists of service to a lady is surely the most *disarming* of fictions; but
Spenser himself testifies to how little it expressed the realities of Elizabethan society, even within the courtly circle mirrored by Calidore or by
Colin Clouts Come Home Againe. And for James I, chivalry was a *dangerous*
myth. His favored personae were instead biblical or classical—Solomon,
Aeneas, Neptune. When his son undertook to revive the chivalric mythology in the interests of his own military ambitions, he was firmly put
down—disarmed—as much because he had got the point of the myth
wrong as because, in the king's terms, it was the wrong myth.

The ambiguities of chivalry are insistently present on Shakespeare's stage, throughout the Lancastrian tetralogy, for example, or in the account of the Field of the Cloth of Gold that opens *Henry VIII,* or in Hamlet's yearning for a time when kings settled their differences by single combat and honored their compacts, or in the fairy-tale first scene of *King Lear,* or in the subversive career of Bertram, the antihero of *All's Well That Ends Well.*

If the mythology is evident, the realities of courtly spectacle are insistently present too, whether chivalric, Roman, or simply opulent. The richness of the costumes surprised and impressed foreign visitors, and the inquisitive Swiss traveler Thomas Platter investigated and found that they were real court clothes, the slightly used suits and dresses of genuine aristocrats. At a theater like the Blackfriars, where one could, for a relatively high price, buy a seat on the stage, the distinction between spectacle and spectator would have all but disappeared. At court masques, those quintessential instances of Renaissance pageantry, the audience was as much on display as the performers, and contemporary accounts tend to dwell at greatest length on the spectators, not the players. This, of course, was entirely appropriate, since the center of the spectacle was not the entertainment but the entertained, the monarch.

The interchangeability of spectacle and spectator does not end here. When the Lord Chamberlain's Men became the King's Men they became gentlemen, the king's servants, technically members of the royal household, and entitled to wear the royal livery. Thus clothed, they were in fact part of the pageantry of Jacobean royal power, outward and visible signs of James's sense of his office. Shakespeare himself registers the same ambitions as his audience by reviving his father's application for a coat of arms. To do this is not simply to move up into—or in this case back into—the gentry: it is to become a part of that same courtly mythology of romantic medievalism. And—fortuitously no doubt, but the fact must have pleased the Shakespeares—the shield designed by the College of Heralds bore a recognizably chivalric symbol, a lance, the spear of the family name, but one that looks, in the extant drawing, more ceremonial than serviceable. The motto, which would have been devised by Shakespeare, not by the Heralds, asserted his right to the honor he claimed in an appropriately antique French: *non sanz droict.*

The pageantry of the Elizabethan stage went deeper than displays of courtly magnificence. At the beginning of the reign, *Gorboduc* entertained the queen with a historical drama that spoke directly to her own problems, an exemplum specifically for her. Her presence was part of the meaning of the play, and the other spectators must have made this connection. Like the king at a masque, she was not merely part of the spectacle but an essential element in its significance. At Cambridge in 1565 the scholars of King's College made a similar point in a more visible way by placing her on the stage for the production of Plautus's *Aulularia* they had devised to entertain her. George Peele's *Arraignment of Paris* made her part of the action as well, bringing indoors to a court theatrical the specific conventions of civic pageantry—the climax of Peele's drama is the device of a triumphal arch.

The relationships I have been describing sound fairly cozy, but in fact they are distinctly uneasy and involve a good deal of tension. Theatrical pageantry, the miming of greatness, is highly charged because it employs precisely the same methods the crown was using to assert and validate its authority. To mime the monarch was a potentially revolutionary act—as both Essex and Elizabeth were well aware. Elizabeth, indeed, in her moving and baffling expostulation to William Lambarde, transformed the drama of *Richard II* into a piece of very dangerous civic pageantry, an allegory of her own reign performed, she said, "forty times in open streets and houses."[4] Forty times is doubtless an accurate enough perception, if somewhat hyperbolically expressed, of the play's popularity, and the houses may reasonably be assumed to include theaters as well as Essex's palace in the Strand; but the "open streets" must be the queen's invention, a fantasy whereby the whole city became a stage for a continual performance in which, in the person of her ancestor, she was mimed and deposed.

When Ben Jonson mimed the queen openly, in *Every Man Out of His Humor,* the theater was considered to have overstepped its bounds, making the monarch subject to the whim of the playwright. Only Jonson would have presumed so far, using the power of royalty to establish the authority of his fiction, but the case is exceptional only because Jonson's egotism is involved. *Sejanus* and *Eastward Ho* were *presumed* to be miming—and thereby undermining—the royal authority, even though Jonson insisted (from prison in the latter case) that this time he had no such intention. Such examples place Richard Venner's famous fraud *England's Joy,* a play about Elizabeth to be performed, so the advertising asserted, "only by certain Gentlemen and Gentlewomen of account,"[5] in a rather different light from the one we are used to. Venner's genius lay in claiming to have created a stage that would at last present not impersonations of courtly life, but the real thing. The conception actualizes one of the deepest corporate fantasies of the Elizabethan theater and its audience.

In fact, in the period the alliance between court and theater works both ways. King James wanted the theatrical companies under royal patronage because he believed in the efficacy of theater as an attribute of royal authority; and no doubt when the actors, poets, designers, and musicians provided court masques celebrating his wisdom and glory, the investment looked like a good one. But the theater is too anarchic to be so confined, and often enough the protection of the crown was interpreted by the actors to be protection *from* the crown. Take for example the strange case of the Children of the Revels producing plays satirizing the king's Scottish knights, and producing one play in particular attacking his favorites and depicting James himself, as the French ambassador put it, "ivre pour le moins une fois le jour"—drunk at least once a day.[6] This play so enraged the king—understandably—that he swore he would never have the company play before him again and would make them "beg their bread." The players were in fact back at court within the year: the incident reveals how little we really understand what must have been a very complicated and ambivalent relationship. Why did the company produce such plays to begin with? They pitted the prejudices of the Blackfriars audience, or at least of a significant part of it, against the wishes and authority of their own patron: how was this in their interests? Why did they not anticipate the king's displeasure, or if they did, why were they willing to risk it— what was in it for them? Where was the censor: why did the lord chamberlain allow such a production? And surely most baffling of all, why did the king cool down? Consider a few dates: the play satirizing the favorites and depicting the king drunk was produced in March 1608—the French ambassador's letter about the king's fury is dated March 25. The boys next played at court on January 1 and 4, 1609, the Christmas season of the same year. But their *last previous* appearance at court had been in the season of 1604/5: they were not a company that regularly played before the king. The invitation to perform at New Year's 1609 was therefore extraordinary, a mark of special favor.

What are we to make of all this? James was used to being attacked and insulted to his face by ministers preaching in his chapel, but surely neither he nor the players could have believed that theatrical companies, like preachers, served a higher law. Jonson, characteristically, regretted the fact: he told Drummond that "he heth a minde to be a churchman, & so he might have favour to make one Sermon to the King, he careth not what yʳafter sould befall him, for he would not flatter though he saw Death."[7] Like the Children of the Revels, Jonson dreamt of attacking with impunity; and the target of the attack in both cases is not the playhouse audience but the king. The relationship between the Renaissance stage and the crown was a complex mixture of intimacy and danger.[8] Given this context, Queen Elizabeth's performance for William Lambarde sounds less like a paranoid fantasy.

Sir Henry Wotton's remarks on the first performance of Shakespeare's *Henry VIII,* that celebration of kingship all of which (as the contemporary subtitle assures us) is true, may be taken as paradigmatic. The play was, he wrote, "sufficient in truth within a while to make greatness very familiar, if not ridiculous."[9] For this spectator, to mime nobility on the stage was to diminish it. And yet Elizabeth and James could not remain aloof, for this was precisely how they saw themselves: both regularly employed the metaphor of the player-monarch. "A King," James told his son, "is as one set on a stage, whose smallest actions and gestures, all the people gazingly doe behold."[10] "Stage" in the first edition of the treatise had read "skaffold"; the king's emendation of the ambiguous word surely reveals something of the danger James must have felt to be inherent in the royal drama. Elizabeth was undoubtedly a better performer than her successor; but whether the pageant constituted celebration or satire lay ultimately not in the power of the actor or the intentions of the inventor, but in the eye and mind of the beholder.

Notes

1. See Gordon Kipling, *The Triumph of Honour: Burgundian Origins of the Elizabethan Renaissance* (Leiden: Leiden University Press for Sir Thomas Brown Institute, 1977), and "Henry VII and the Origins of Tudor Patronage," in *Patronage in the Renaissance,* ed. Guy Fitch Lytle and Stephen Orgel (Princeton, N.J.: Princeton University Press, 1982), chap. 5.

2. E.g., Frances Yates, *Astraea* (London: Routledge and Kegan Paul, 1975), and Daniel Javitch, *Poetry and Courtliness in Renaissance England* (Princeton, N.J.: Princeton University Press, 1978).

3. See Norman Council's excellent analysis, "Ben Jonson, Inigo Jones, and the Transformation of Tudor Chivalry," *ELH* 47, no. 2 (Summer 1980): 259–75.

4. The incident is recounted in the Arden edition, ed. Peter Ure, p. lix.

5. E. K. Chambers, *The Elizabethan Stage* (Oxford: Clarendon Press, 1923), 4:500.

6. Ibid., 1:326–28, 2:53.

7. *Ben Jonson,* ed. C. H. Herford, Percy Simpson, and Evelyn Simpson (Oxford: Clarendon Press, 1925–52), 1:141, ll. 330ff.

8. For important explorations of this theme, see Steven Mullaney, "Lying like Truth: Riddle, Representation and Treason in Renaissance England," *ELH* 47 (1980): 32–47; Louis Adrian Montrose, "The Purpose of Playing: Reflections on Shakespearean Anthropology," *Helios,* n.s., 7 (1980): 51–74; Stephen Greenblatt, "Invisible Bullets: Renaissance Authority and Its Subversion," *Glyph* 8 (1981): 40–61.

9. Chambers, *The Elizabethan Stage,* 2:419.

10. *Basilicon Doron,* in *The Workes of the Most High and Mighty Prince James* (London, 1616), p. 181. This is a revised edition; the work was first published separately in Edinburgh in 1599.

City Metal and Country Mettle: The Occasion of Ben Jonson's Golden Age Restored

Leah Sinanoglou Marcus

Ben Jonson's masque *The Golden Age Restored* was a great success at court, "so well liked and applauded that the king had yt represented again the sonday night after, in the very same manner."[1] Jonson himself seems also to have thought well of it: he disrupted the chronological order of the masques in the 1616 folio edition of his *Works* to give *The Golden Age Restored* significant final place, so that the *Works* end in exalted praise for James I as the restorer of England's Golden Age. And the masque is significant in another sense: it inaugurates an important shift in the pattern of Stuart masques that hinge on a contrast between rural simplicity and city or court sophistication. Before *The Golden Age Restored* the rural gives way to the urban; in *The Golden Age Restored* and later productions, by contrast, a corrupt civilization in the antimasque yields to a vision of pastoral perfection in the main masque, so that an idealized countryside, not an idealized court, becomes the goal of the masque's transformation.[2] Despite its importance for Jonson, however, *The Golden Age Restored* has aroused little twentieth-century commentary, perhaps because its subject seems tired and worn. Queen Elizabeth had regularly been hailed as England's Astraea and the bringer of a lost Golden Age. James I's first speech before parliament claimed some of the same imagery for himself; in poetry and civic pageantry he too was lauded as a reviver of the First Age. But such imagery, oft repeated, tends to lose its luster: in Jonson's masque, we may see only a restatement of "lofty commonplace."[3]

To study Jonson's masque in terms of its contemporary social and political context, however, is to revive some of its luster and to recognize that it is richer and more interesting than we have supposed. Jonson claimed that he "taught" the "voice" of his masques "to sound to present occasions";[4]

he made use of "lofty commonplace," but shaped it to accord with specific events and royal policies, and to serve as commentary upon them. *The Golden Age Restored* is one of Jonson's middle masques, written for James himself rather than some other member of the royal family and, like all the other masques from that period, immersed in the policies and problems of the king. Jonson offers a vision of James as restorer of the Golden Age, but sets that off against another more cynical Jacobean commonplace—that the times were no Golden Age but an age of gold, of intense preoccupation with money.

One of those most intensely occupied with money during the years before the performance of *The Golden Age Restored* had been James I himself: he was constantly out of it, widely known already for his conspicuous consumption of it, involved in numerous controversial projects to get it, and committed to specific programs for improving its quality and regulating its supply. Not all of the money problems of the second decade of his reign could be blamed on James's personal extravagance. In addition to a shortage of royal income, there was a genuine and serious scarcity of gold and silver coins in England during the years before *The Golden Age Restored*. The Chronicler of London for 1611 noted that "from the second yeere of his Maiesties raign and for six yeares after, here was more plenty of golde than euer was before: and so would haue continued, if it had not beene so much exported" by merchants and financiers who flouted the strict laws against such activity. While "English gold was verie plentifull in forraine Nations" it had begun to "waxe so scant in England, that for the space of almost two yeres here was not any vsuall payments made in golde."[5] *The Golden Age Restored* weighs and contrasts two sets of royal activities in the years between 1611 and the beginning of 1615: the king's new programs to create an "age of better metal" (p. 224) by improving the currency, limiting the export of gold, and increasing the money supply; and related to that, his efforts to create an "age of better mettle" (to use Jonson's own spelling, which makes the double meaning clearer)—an age of better courage and spirit—by ordering the nobles out of an overcrowded and overcommercialized London and back to their country estates, where they were to revive and sustain a Golden Age of traditional English values. In Jonson's masque, mettle triumphs over metal—the king's efforts to strengthen the English countryside are preferred over and presented as a transformation of his earlier efforts to improve English money.

At the same time, a study of the masque's "present occasion" will alert us to a fascinating interplay between court entertainments and rival civic pageantry. David Bergeron and others have demonstrated a gradual separation and alienation of royal entertainments from civic ceremonies like the London Lord Mayor's Shows—a separation brought about in part by James's dislike for crowds and his reluctance to put himself on public display, but symptomatic of a political rift between crown and city centered on questions of law, prerogative, and money. In keeping with his strong views on royal absolutism, James I often tried to use his own prerogative to override laws and local ordinances. He would attempt to raise revenue by extending his authority into a new area through "illegal" royal proclamations; the city would protest in the name of common law; the king would then try to override the law and, in effect, govern by proclamation.[6] In *The Golden Age Restored,* Jonson adopts materials from a pageant of three years earlier, Anthony Munday's *Chruso-thriambos: The Triumphes of GOLDE* (1611), in honor of the inauguration of Sir James Pemberton, Goldsmith, as Lord Mayor of London. Jonson's masque recasts the earlier pageant in order to undo its high praise for the Goldsmiths and its implied criticism of the king. Through the superiority of his own work over Munday's, Jonson demonstrates the superiority of royal policies, poetry, and pageantry over the industrious but menial arts of London. Again mettle triumphs over metal. London's devotion to gold, a substance afforded much adulation and gaudy display in *Chruso-thriambos,* is shown to be petty and divisive, a hindrance to the implementation of James's proposals for restoring the nation to balance and pastoral harmony.

Chruso-thriambos had its own "present occasion": its praise of gold and the assay-masters who test it commemorates a notable honor accorded the Company of Goldsmiths earlier in 1611. To inaugurate his new policies in reform of English money, James I had performed an unprecedented ceremonial act. In May 1611 the king and the prince of Wales had proceeded in great pomp to the royal Court of Star Chamber to witness the testing of his money. The Wardens of the Mint and other officials "caused the pixe to be brought from the mint thether, where in the presence of the King they with their seuerall keyes opened the pixe, and powred forth the gold and siluer, to be assayed and tryed by their seuerall Standardes, according to the forme of the indentures made betweene the King and the masters, and workers of his Maiesties moneys." This event was routine, but the place where it was carried out and the number and rank of those in attendance were not. It was "beyond all memory and mention, for an hundreth yeeres space, that euer any King or Queene, came in proper person to see any of these tryalls." Finally, the king constituted a group of Goldsmiths as the judges of his money: "At this time his Maiestie in person gaue a Jurie of sixteene of the most honest, skilfullest, and best reputed Goldsmiths their oathes, and charge for tryall of the moneyes, and the Jurie proceeded in al things according to their Charge, and they gaue vp their verdict the same day, at the Court of Whitehall, and the King shewed them great grace and fauour." Ten days later, having "examined the abuses of the Common Wealth, practised by very many persons vpon all sorts of moneys," James I "made Proclamation the eighteenth of May" for the preservation of moneys.[7]

James I probably intended his ceremonial encounter with the Goldsmiths to serve as much as a warning as an honor. His proclamation for the preservation of moneys noted the scarcity of money in England, outlawed "melting or conueying out of the Kings Dominions of Gold or Siluer, coined or currant in the same" and specified goldsmiths and merchants as chief offenders: for "their priuate lucre and gaine," Goldsmiths were culling out the heaviest gold and silver coins for melting down into plate for export to "forreine parts for priuate mens particular gaine, whereby there is a great scarsity of good Money likely to ensue."[8] Jacobean Goldsmiths were much more than artisans. Some of them served as bankers and lenders on a large scale; as a result of their activities in national and international finance as well as the more traditional aspects of their trade, many were immensely wealthy. By personally giving them their "oathes" within the Court of Star Chamber, the king offered the Goldsmiths a reminder of his power, a strong hint that they would do well to abandon certain aspects of their search for "priuate lucre" and heed his proclamation for the preservation of money.

That is not, however, the interpretation of the 1611 events given in the October Lord Mayor's Pageant. *Chruso-thriambos: The Triumphes of GOLDE* celebrates the Goldsmiths, not the king, as the custodians of law and money. The pageant has three major parts. The first depicts the arts of the Goldsmiths in geographic perspective: it is a water pageant which shows the carrying of gold not *out* of England, but *into* it, in accordance with James's own policy: from the "rich and Golden *Indian* Mines" Chioroson the "Golden King" and his queen are "(at their owne entreatie) brought into England, with no meane quantity of *Indian* Gold, to behold the Countries beauty, and the immediate day of sollemne tryumph." Their gallants perform sea fights and skirmishes, each gallant "hauing his *Indian* Page attending on him, laden with Ingots of Golde and Siluer, and those Instruments that delued them out of the earth."[9] The second part of the pageant shows the honor of the Goldsmiths in historical perspective through a visit to the tombs of favorably inclined monarchs and particularly notable members of the company, including Nicholas Faringdon, four times Lord Mayor of London, who is resurrected from the dead in order to behold the Triumph of Gold. The third part and the most crucial for our purposes displays the origin of gold itself, and therefore of the other two sections of the pageant. The *"Orferie, or Pageant"* proper depicts a "Rocke or Mount of Golde" and the activities connected with its mining, refining, testing, and manufacture: "The Pioners, Miners, and Deluers, doe first vse their endeuour and labour, to come by the Oare of gold and Siluer hidden in the Rock; which being (from them) conuaied to the industrious Finer, it is by him framed into Ingots of diuers formes, . . . applyed to most necessary vses, as likewise is apparantly discouered, in the Mint-Maister, Coyners, Gold Smithes, Ieweller, Lapidarie, Pearle-Driller, Plate-Seller, and such like, all liuely acting their sundry professions." Finally, in clear reference to the honor done the king's assay masters and other Goldsmiths in May of the same year, the mount shows "an ingenious Say-Maister, with his Furnaces, Glasses of parting each Mettall from other, his Table, Ballance, and Weightes, euen to the very smallest quantitie of true valuation, in Ingots, Iewelles, Plate or Monies, for the more honour of the Prince and Countrey, when his Coynes are kept from imbasing and abusing" (sig. A4).

The Mount of Gold must have been rather crowded: in addition to all the artisans, it held allegorical personages who establish the relationships between gold itself, the various activities of the Goldsmiths, and the ideal of justice. Since, as Munday informs us, the motto of the Honorable Company of Goldsmiths is *"Iustitia Virtutum Regina,"* the figure of Justice, Queen of Virtues, sits atop the mount of gold, with her "two precious Daughters, *Chrusos* and *Argurion*" linked to her chair of state with a chain of gold. The artisans and assay masters on the lower parts of the mount are her "golden Sonnes": they commend their gold to her while her daughters Gold and Silver "bountifully hurle abroad their Mothers treasures, after she hath (yet once againe) tried them by the *Touch*[stone] of undeceiueable perfection" (sig. C1ᵛ). Somewhat confusingly, the queen atop the mountain also represents *"Chthoon,* or *Vesta* (Mother to *Saturn,* and called likewise *Terra,* the breeding and teeming Mother of al Golde," so that in two ways she is associated with the Golden Age—as Justice (Astraea) and as the mother of Saturn. The rock of gold delved industriously by the miners represents herself, Terra, out of whom her daughters Gold and Silver are dug and refined for the benefit of humankind. Munday's pageant honors the Company of Goldsmiths as bringers of a Golden Age—the agents by which gold is made available to the kingdom—which they were to a considerable degree, not only as artisans and importers of gold but as moneylenders and bankers to the wealthy. But, transcending that, the Pageant of the Orferie commemorates the just dealings of Goldsmiths: their rectitude in general, but also the particular "justice" of their actions in the Court of Star Chamber earlier that year, when the jury of Gold-smiths had been sworn by the king himself, shown "great grace and favour," and allowed to proceed with gravity and exactness to their verdict in the "tryall of the moneyes."

Considered in itself, the 1611 Lord Mayor's Show may appear in-nocuous enough. In its contemporary context, however, it can be seen as an assertion of independence from the king. During the early years of James I's reign, we find that the subject matter of the Lord Mayor's Shows often parallels the court masque in celebration of royal policy. In 1605, for example, the Lord Mayor's Show centered on "Royall King *James*" in his role as "second *Brute*" (the first Brutus, of course, having been the legend-ary founder of Britain), in order to commemorate his efforts to create Great Britain by uniting England and Scotland; Ben Jonson's *Hymenaei*, performed at court a few months later, in January 1606, celebrates the same policy.[10] By 1611, however, court and city were seriously at odds over money. In the parliament of 1610–11 there had been sharp criticism of James's extravagance and considerable reluctance to offer him the sub-sidies needed to carry on the work of government. The king had dissolved parliament in anger at the near-traitorous behavior of some of its members and sent out requests for forced loans under the privy seal. But that tactic had met with widespread balking on the grounds that his forced loans were an illegal usurpation of parliamentary authority. His proclamations the same year outlawing new building in London created additional re-sentment: city lawyers and justices argued that the king could not use his proclamations to outlaw something which had been legal before, and be-fore long it was to be rumored about London that the king's policy was only a way of increasing his revenue through fines on the illegal struc-tures. In several areas over which he claimed authority, he and the courts of common law were caught in a struggle over the legality of his claims.[11] Questions of royal financing all too frequently came down to the issue of law versus prerogative.

By the autumn of 1611, money was very scarce at court: the Twelfth Night masque for that holiday season was Ben Jonson's *Love Restored*—a barebones affair by comparison with the usual court production and based on an acknowledgment of the severe shortage of money.[12] *Chruso-thriam-bos*, by contrast, had been a celebration of wealth. At a time when James was strapped for funds and stymied in his efforts to extract financial sup-port from the city, the city itself appeared, at least from the perspective of James I's supporters, to be arrogantly luxuriating in its own prosperity. *Chruso-thriambos* is not unmitigatedly materialistic in its values: the pag-eant admonishes the new Lord Mayor to help the poor and keep generous hospitality: "You are a Gold-Smith, Golden be / Your daily deedes of Charitie" (sig. C4ʳ). But the gold of these good offices is so closely associated with the metal itself that the two are hard to separate: the metal becomes a virtuous means by which other virtues are furthered. And the pageant itself is less than reticent about the matter of its own financing. Munday's text places unusual emphasis on the great cost of the show, its lavishness a manifestation of the splendid wealth of the Goldsmiths who had sponsored it, and the pageant proper depicts Goldsmiths as happily surrounded with the stuff of their trade.

Moreover, the king receives short shrift in the allegorical scheme of the pageant. Munday need not have introduced the subject of kingship at all: many of the Lord Mayor's Pageants did not, and without implying any slight toward the monarch. But *Chruso-thriambos* keeps returning to the subject of kingship in ways that subtly denigrate James I and his high notion of royal prerogative. The show's emphasis falls not on James I, who was at that moment attempting to curtail city liberties through proclamations and other means, but rather on those monarchs who had graced the city with its liberties in the first place: Richard I, who originally "gaue London the dignity of a Lord Maior" (its first provost having been Leofstane, a Goldsmith, according to Munday's erroneous information)[13] and King John who "(most graciously) gaue the Cittizens of London absolute power, to elect a Lord Mayor amongst themselues, in which worthy condition it hath euer since continued" (sig. A4ʳ). Then too, the Indian king and queen who come in the first part of the pageant to wonder at the glories of London are, for all their wealth and status, clearly inferior to the city. And the third part of the pageant includes a very damaging possible reference to the king. The figure of Justice (Vesta) who sits in "cheefest Soueraignetie" atop the Mount of Gold explains the source of the touchstone by which she "tries the vertue of her Ingots, Iewels, [and] Monies": that "greedy and neuer-satisfied *Lydian* King, who desired, that whatsoeuer he toucht might turne to Golde, [evidently Midas, though he was from Phrygia and King Croesus, from Lydia] finding his own couetousnesse to be his ruine, & he (imaginarily) Metamorphozed into a Stone: Our *Chthoon,* finding this *Lydian* Stone fit for her vse, tearmed it *Lithos;* and because (in his life time) the King was so immeasurably affected to Golde, shee imposed this vertue on the Stone, that it should (for euer after) be the Touch-Stone and Trier of both Gold and Siluer, to warne other Worldlings of the like auaritious folly" (sig. B1ʳ). We will remember that this section of the pageant commemorates the Goldsmiths' ceremonial trial of moneys before the king only a few months before. Then, it had been James I who had been the source of the "Touch-Stone" of Justice in that he had symbolically granted the jury of Goldsmiths the authority to try gold and silver. Given these parallels, it is all too easy to identify the Lydian king with James himself, who had been brought to fiscal disaster by his insatiable appetite for magnificence and who was "immeasurably affected to Golde" in the view of many of his subjects. Of course, the identification of the Lydian king with James is blurry, but it is not counterbalanced by any very positive depiction of the monarch and his virtues. The figure of Justice herself can hardly represent James because she is the embodiment of the motto of the Goldsmiths.

The pageant's only references to King James by name come in the final blessing of the new Lord Mayor: Munday interprets his name Pem-ber-ton to signify head-shining-town: so Pemberton will be a "bright-shining Head vnder his Soueraigne." James Pemberton is admonished to "Consider likewise, *Iames* thy gracious King, / Sets *Iames* (his Subject) heere his Deputy." But even at this point royal notions of prerogative are subtly undermined. The emphasis falls not on the "high power" James claimed for himself, but on the "absolute" power he has granted the Lord Mayor (and cannot legally retract):

> When Maieste doth meaner persons bring
> To represent himselfe in Soueraignty,
> I'st not an high and great authority?   [sig. C3]

James I was even then challenging the authority of the mayor and Common Council of London; in *Chruso-thriambos,* the authority of the Lord Mayor, once granted, is depicted as absolute in the areas under his jurisdiction, and the mayor, as a surrogate for the king.

Jonson's character of Plutus in *Love Restored* caricatures city and parliamentary criticism of the monarch like that which had been aired in the 1610–11 House of Commons and given visual embodiment in *Chruso-thriambos.* Plutus, the personification of wealth, speaks in the legalistic and puritan cadences of James's 1611 opposition, railing against masquing and other "vanities in these high places" as the prodigal "ruin of states." But he himself is a major cause of the present disharmony at court. The masque cannot go forward because he, the god of money, has usurped the position of Cupid, god of love; he will allow the king nothing, but hoards all the wealth for himself: "I cherish and make much of myself, flow forth in ease and delicacy, while that [the spirit of poverty, but by extension the English court] murmurs and starves." Plutus is finally unmasked as the "god of money, who has stol'n Love's ensigns, and in his belied figure reigns i' the world, making friendships, contracts, marriages and almost religion . . . holding the nearest respects of mankind, and usurping all those offices in this age of gold which Love himself performed in the Golden Age" (pp. 192–94). Jonson's handling of Plutus is clearly intended to glance at the "Golden Age" of *Chruso-thriambos,* a display of fantastic wealth at a time of financial dearth for the king. To the poet, an "age of gold" like that represented in the pageant was not a paradigm for justice, but a perversion of it, based on blind avarice and deficient loyalty to the king.

During the time between *Chruso-thriambos* and Jonson's *Golden Age Restored,* James's financial situation and his relations with London and Parliament grew, if anything, worse. Since it had almost immediately become "visible and notorious" that his May proclamation for the preservation of money was being flouted, he issued a new proclamation in November of the same year to discourage the export of gold by raising its domestic value against that of silver and other currency. Later he took other measures to create a "golden mean" in prices and attract money into government coffers.[14] Since his 1611 proclamation outlawing new building in London had also had little effect, he published a new proclamation ordering the gentry and aristocracy with no necessary business in London to retire to their country estates; he also created a commission to exact fines against those who had defied his earlier proclamations against building. But that plan, along with several other revenue-raising schemes, encountered stiff resistance and was challenged in the courts. Again, law against prerogative. By the end of 1613 it was reported that the court suffered a "great lack of money" and that "projects abound."[15]

The time had come to call another parliament, and one was elected, but amidst strong antigovernment feeling in London and the counties. The "addled Parliament" of 1614 sat for only two months before James dissolved it in exasperation. Some of its members were unusually outspoken in their criticism of the king, his prodigality, and many of his major policies: the lawmakers would grant him money only at the price of his ceding vital areas of his prerogative. Some of their assaults on his power James himself termed "trayterous"; upon the dissolution, he had several of its members imprisoned.[16] And again, as in 1611, he was left with the pressing problem of money. He asked the city of London for a loan of one hundred thousand pounds but was refused: many previous loans were still outstanding, which did not improve the city's zeal for the king. Eventually the City Corporation made an outright grant of ten thousand pounds. The government also requested "benevolences" from the more affluent subjects—gifts to help meet his pressing financial needs. But, as with the earlier privy seal loans, James encountered widespread resistance, mutterings about Magna Carta and the ancient liberties of Englishmen.[17] Anyone surveying the king's 1614 financial and political situation from the perspective of the court might well despair at the predicament of the king. He claimed in most cases to act upon principle and could show plausible reasons for many of the "illegal" policies which he was attempting to impose. But the seriousness of his financial plight colored everything else: the higher values he unquestionably possessed were overshadowed by his unseemly search for money. Gold outshone his other virtues, much as it had the virtues of the Goldsmiths in the pageant of 1611.

James himself was quite aware of the problem: in a proclamation of October 24, 1614, he attempted to reestablish the lost balance between pocketbook and principle in one important realm of controversy by extending his policy against new buildings into an area which few were likely to call self-serving. His earlier proclamations had mustered numerous arguments in support of his policy: the overpopulation of London would create "infinite inconveniences," shortages of food and other commodities, increased disease, a decline in the beauty and spaciousness of the capital at a time when she needed to improve her appearance, especially for foreign visitors. But, as he himself was to acknowledge publicly later on, these plausible reasons had been taken as a mere cover for "profit": "We would have Our Loving Subjects understand, that it shall well appeare by Our resolute and constant restrayning of all future private Buildings without all Dispensation, Tolleration or Connivence, that it was not profit that was the scope and end of Our said Commission, but the reformation of the abuse."[18] In 1614, in accordance with the principle of mettle's replacing metal, he issued the proclamation which forms the immediate occasion of Jonson's *Golden Age Restored:* "A Proclamation commanding the repaire of Noblemen and Gentlemen into their severall Countreys, at the end of the Terme," Royston, October 24, 1614. Since this proclamation forms the basis for the structure of the masque, it is worth quoting in detail:

> IT is Our Princely Office and care to provide that all parts, Estats and Degrees of our People bee sustained and cherished, and that they may receive mutuall comfort the one by the other, especially where the need is most: And that the ancient and lawdable customes of this Our Realme be continued and observed, and new inconveniences (which the times doe dayly breed) repressed and prevented; Whereas therefore We are given to understand, That there is a great repaire and confluence, aswell to the Cities of London and Westminster, and the Suburbs of them, as to other Cities within Our Kingdome, of Noblemen and Gentlemen, who are Our principall Ministers for the government of the

severall Counties of Our Kingdome, in respect of Our Commissions of
Lieutenancie and the Peace: And that their comming is with purpose to
live and abide in the said Cities and places with their families for this
whole Winter, or at least during the Christmas time; whereby the
government of the Countreys will be weakened, Hospitalitie and the
reliefe of the poore (especially at such a time) decayed, and the said
Cities, and places surcharged and pestered, and the prices of Victuals
there, and all other provisions and things excessively raysed and
inhaunsed: Wee doe by these presents will and command, aswell all
Our Lieutenants and Noblemen (except such as be of Our Privie Coun-
cell, or beare any Office about the Person, or Court of Our selves) . . .
That they and every one of them doe immediatly upon the end of this
present Tearme, being the Nine and twentieth day of November, from
the said Cities and places, repaire unto their severall Countreys to
attend their service there, and to keepe House and Hospitalitie, as
appertaineth to their place and degree, upon paine of Our high displeasure, and such punishment as is due for the contempt of Our
Royall commandment. [19]

The parallels between proclamation and masque are obvious. In the
proclamation James declares his intention that the "ancient and lawdable
customes" of the realm be "continued" while "new inconveniences" are
suppressed: Jonson's antimasque presents the "new inconveniences" of the
Iron Age, Evils associated with parliamentary wrangling and city commerce and manufacturing, who conspire to defeat their enemy Jupiter
(James I); Pallas conquers and "metamorphoses" them merely by showing
her shield, and then introduces a Golden Age of restored rural values. The
main masquers are English nobles—"semigods" revived from torpor by
the lightning of Pallas's shield and shown an idealized countryside which
is their proper sphere of action. James called upon his nobles and gentry to
return to the country in order to keep county government operating properly, to provide traditional hospitality and relief for the poor; in the
masque, the semigods are the ones that "justice dare defend, and will the
age sustain" provided that they return to their proper realm. Pallas shows
them the rich and fertile landscape prepared for them and admonishes:

> Behold you here
> What Iove hath built to be your sphere;
>   You hither must retire.
> And as his bounty gives you cause,
> Be ready still without your pause
>   To show the world your fire. [p. 231]

By giving up London and the court and retiring to shine in the country
"like lights about Astraea's throne," they will set in motion a reciprocal

process by which both they and justice herself will be increasingly sustained and nurtured, so that the Golden Age shown them by Pallas will take root and grow "forever." As government officials for the "severall Countreys" the gentry and nobility referred to in James's proclamation and Jonson's masque were the chief middle administrators of the kingdom: they were to serve as conduits for His Majesty's enlightened authority so that Astraea's perception will become a perpetual English reality:

> I feel the godhead! nor will doubt
> But he can fill the place throughout,
> Whose power is everywhere.   [p. 232]

Jonson's masque even takes into account a chief complaint of the upper classes against James's policy to reduce the size of London: the city was attractive to them because it was fashionable, but also because it was cheap. In the country the nobles were expected to keep house on a grand scale with a splendid complement of retainers; in London they could avoid such obligations and live much more simply and privately. Astraea and the Golden Age complain,

> But how without a train
> Shall we our state sustain?

But Jove has provided for that difficulty through his transmutation of metal to mettle: instead of mere money, they will have a train of poets to wait upon them—Chaucer, Gower, Lydgate, and Spenser all having praised or written from within the traditional values James was attempting to restore. Jonson's language converts cold words associated with the manufacture of money to vital, organic functions within a renewed society: virtue, not coins, "pressed" shall grow; buried arts (not ore) shall emerge and flourish; "all" will "be gold" not in Midas's sense but in terms of a newly awakened spirit of harmony; instead of coining money, the country aristocracy will coin families and chaste pleasures, just as in the Golden Age

> The male and female used to join,
> And into all delight did coin
> That pure simplicity.   [p. 230]

By the end of the masque, the word *gold* has been redefined to mean country virtue. It is only in terms of such a redefinition that Astraea will remain among humankind,

> And in the midst of so much gold
> Unbought with grace or fear unsold,
> The law to mortals give.   [p. 232]

The Golden Age Restored is structurally different from the usual Jonsonian masque in that the same figure, Pallas, presides over its entirety. More characteristically in Jonson's works, the world of the antimasque is introduced by its own set of partial or negative deities, who are banished or transformed as part of the transition to the main masque, while the agents of that transformation are absent or quiescent at the beginning of the antimasque. *The Golden Age Restored,* by contrast, begins with the descent of Pallas and, in the version performed at court, ended with her reascent (p. 484n.). She presides over every stage of the masque, first calling for the "age of better metal," then vanquishing its enemies in the antimasque, and finally, summoning Astraea and the Golden Age to earth and awakening the nobles who will sustain the new age in the countryside. As a daughter of Jove sprung from his forehead, Pallas clearly represents on one level the wisdom of James himself, the Jove of the masque, whose power pervades the landscape. But Pallas Athena was a goddess traditionally associated with the city—a bringer of urban peace and prosperity symbolized by her act of planting an olive tree on the Acropolis.

It is in terms of Pallas's multiple functions in *The Golden Age Restored* that we can, I think, understand Jonson's masque as not just praise for James's proclamation of October 1614 but a more extensive commentary upon the recent history of the reign and a critique of city values. The three sections of the masque correspond with the three stages of royal policy already outlined above in their interaction with the king's opposition. Just as James I in 1611 had announced with fanfare his plans for reforming the currency, Pallas at the beginning of the masque, apparently not fully aware of the conflicts she is about to unleash, proclaims that Jove has decided to "let down in his golden chain / The age of better metal." At this point, she seems to see no conflict between metal and virtue. Her comments about the great invading the less refer to James's proclamation and its expression of the hope that all "Degrees of our People bee sustained and cherished, and that they may receive mutuall comfort the one by the other," and can be taken to refer to a general social problem or specific rivalries at court.[20] But her language also applies to the condition of English money in 1611: heavier newly minted gold coins had driven down the value of older coins, and James's policies were intended to create a new equalization.[21] The same terms describe all levels of an unbalanced situation: restoring the gold and restoring a Golden Age of justice are part of the same proposal. Pallas, albeit with different intent, is making the same mistake the Goldsmiths had made in their pageant of 1611 when they confused virtue with money.

In light of the clamorous challenges that follow upon her announcement, however, Pallas's proposal for better metal seems overly simple and optimistic, just as James's policies in 1611 had failed to take fully enough into account the power and ambition of the city. Jonson's antimasque of the Iron Age may appear to bear little resemblance to the Goldsmiths' earlier show: it can and should be taken as a much more general depiction of disorder. But Jonson shaped his antimasque to heap scorn on the low artistic and commercial values glorified in *Chruso-thriambos*. To understand that specific functioning of the antimasque is to recognize additional reverberations of wit and harmony in the construction of Jonson's masque as a whole. To begin with, there are Pallas's cryptic remarks about Jove's golden head (based on the mythological idea that Saturn's head was golden):

> That even Envy may behold
> Time not enjoyed his head of gold
> Alone beneath his father.

These lines can be taken as a reference to Munday's clumsy explication of the name of James Pemberton, Goldsmith, as the shining head of London. Jove wants "envy" of the sort represented in Munday's analysis to be reminded unequivocally of the true origin of the power the city calls its own, for Pemberton's head "shines" only with the reflected light of the king—a glory that has proceeded through the generations of royal succession and is not so easily usurped by beings of lesser stature. The notion of the gold-headed Goldsmith seems to have piqued Jonson: we find it treated again with similar scorn in *The Devil Is an Ass* (1616), in the character of Thomas Guilt-head, Goldsmith, usurer, schemer, and close ally of a corrupt city judge.[22] But Pallas's warning against the overadmiration of borrowed glory goes unheeded. Her proposal for better metal precipitates not an age of gold but an Iron Age of pride, avarice, and rebellion, just as the royal favor offered the Goldsmiths in 1611 had "erupted" into a pageant which seemed from the viewpoint of the king's supporters to be a proud display of avarice, insolently disrespectful toward the authority of the king. By demoting the city rebels to the Iron Age, Jonson follows the analysis in James's proclamation—places their newfangled ideas where the king would agree they belonged—but he also makes a shrewd point about the city's capacity for mythography.

Munday's praise of gold is indeed a strange muddle if considered from the standpoint of even the most elementary classical scholarship, in that he associates the refining, manufacture, and coining of gold with the Golden Age, whereas all of those activities are characteristic of later ages of man, particularly the Iron Age, by which time justice had fled the earth. Munday's revision of myth was probably quite deliberate, but it boomerangs against him since, according to Ovid's account, it was only in the Iron Age that men were so unnatural as to demand wealth of the earth:

> Nec tantum segetes alimentaque debita dives
> poscebatur humus, sed itum est in viscera terrae;
> quasque recondiderat Stygiisque admoverat umbris,
> effodiuntur opes, inritamenta maiorum.
> Iamque nocens ferrum ferroque nocentius aurum
> prodierat; prodit bellum, quod pugnat utroque,
> sanguineaque manu crepitantia concutit arma.[23]

The digging and delving of *Chruso-thriambos* are thus prototypically Iron Age activities, and display the true nature of the Goldsmiths' achievement to be the hurt and corruption of mankind; appropriately, the evils of Jonson's Iron Age echo the pageant by issuing from a cave: first Avarice, then Fraud and Slander (especially of the king), then "Corruption with the golden hands" and other political evils. Their intent is nothing less than to destroy Jove and become themselves

> masters of the skies,
> Where all the wealth, height, power lies,
> The scepter and the thunder   [p. 226]

—precisely the interpretation of opposition motives made by King James and his closest supporters.

Jonson's description of this particular antimasque is brief and schematic: it is tempting to speculate that in performance it may have included mimicry of some of the actual activities celebrated in *Chruso-thriambos*— particularly the testing of gold and silver coins. Then the mimicry of coining in the antimasque would balance the main masque's adaptation of the vocabulary of coining to the organic riches of the countryside, just as the foul cave of the antimasque balances the dreamy bower in the main masque from which the semigods emerge to dance. Perhaps Jonson wished to deemphasize the particularity of the antimasque's attack in his printed text, for the Lord Mayor's Shows in the years since 1611 had shown no comparable disrespect for the king.[24] But, speculation aside, Jonson's antimasque does demonstrate the fallacy not only in the allegorical scheme of *Chruso-thriambos*, but of any city claim to the mythography of the Golden Age. London's citizens are fallen, Iron Age men by the very nature of their professional activities, and therefore unlikely to serve as protectors for the golden goddess Astraea. And the fact that they are silenced and metamorphosed by Pallas, traditional patronness of cities, suggests that their pride and divisiveness have gone against their own best interests, if only they could stop wrangling long enough to notice.

During the years immediately preceding *The Golden Age Restored,* the city had claimed law and justice as the foundation for its challenges of royal prerogative: so, in *Chruso-thriambos,* the figure of Justice is given sovereignty and associated with the Lord Mayor, Goldsmiths, and city magistrates. But in the real Golden Age, there had been no judges, for there had been no need for them. Jonson's antimasque makes all too clear the danger of associating money with virtue, particularly with the virtue of justice. In *The Golden Age Restored* justice belongs to the king and his wise plans for England. The main masque offers a compelling argument for submission to the royal proclamation, since Astraea is willing to remain on earth only insofar as the king's policy is honored by his subjects. Surveying the rural landscape charged with the power of James's plans for reform, she vows:

> This, this, and only such as this
> The bright Astraea's region is,
> Where she would pray to live. [p. 232]

The many transformations of terminology from coining in the main masque also serve to buttress the king's claim to justice against the rival claims of the advocates of common law, since coinage was the absolute prerogative of the king: even James's severe critics did not challenge his power to coin money as he saw fit, and his supporters habitually used his undisputed power over the coinage to reason to other disputed powers.[25] In a similar way, Jonson's main masque adopts the language of coinage in order to confer the same absolute status upon the king's proclamations for restoring the countryside.

If James I has the power, he also has the poetry. As numerous readers have noted, *The Golden Age Restored* is far more lyrical, more melodious, than most of Jonson's other masques. The sheer beauty of its main masque—all harmony in its intricate interweaving of many voices, all afire with Ovidian feeling and the "quickening" energies of James's new Golden Age, in which nature and art produce their honeyed products without base money or machines—displays Jonson's poetic art and court art generally as dazzlingly superior to the low poetry of London. In *The Case Is Altered* Jonson had satirized Munday and city taste through the character of Antonio Balladino, "*Pageant* Poet" to the city of Milan: "I supply the place sir: when a worse cannot be had sir,"[26] and Munday's depiction of the age of gold does indeed stand up badly against Jonson's Golden Age. Good poetry comes relatively cheap. It requires not metal, but mettle—a virtue and judgment sufficient to recognize and cherish it when found. James I possesses that mettle, while his London rivals do not.

Jonson's masque does not exempt James from criticism: like Pallas, he has in the past been willing to assume more compatibility between gold and virtue than his experience has borne out. But given the rhetorical scheme of the masque, a continuation of such confusion becomes logically untenable. *The Golden Age Restored* itself is an example of conspicuous consumption, bought with much gold. But the masque does not insist upon its own costliness, and spends itself wisely to lessen the court's dependence on gold. Like the archconservative he was, Jonson praises the king for his efforts to restore a traditional pattern of society, not for his attempts to come to terms with the new commercial interests which were in the process of altering that pattern. Yet the poet was as much reformer as conservative: even as he celebrates James's shift from metal to mettle, he cautions the king against a return to his earlier trust in money.

The king's financial problems did not, of course, disappear (as though metamorphosed by the lightning from Pallas's shield) upon the implementation of his new policies. But art is more malleable than life: James's greater emphasis on the virtues of the countryside did bring about an important shift in the pattern of the masque. After 1614 the king regularly issued proclamations ordering the nobility back to their rural estates, and the masque followed suit, presenting the city environment as an unwholesome alternative to the pastoral harmony of the country. Jonson's masque for 1617, *The Vision of Delight,* is very closely related to *The Golden Age Restored* in that it reworks some of the same ideas in praise of James. As *The Golden Age Restored* reflects the specific features of the 1614 proclamation, so *The Vision of Delight* follows the more elaborate analysis made in the king's 1616 speech in Star Chamber again ordering the gentry and aristocracy to "get thee to the country."[27] The king's 1616 speech was a particularly pivotal one, chastising his upstart judges as a prelude to the removal of Chief Justice Edward Coke from office, upholding the binding force of royal proclamations, and then moving on to a new analysis of the imbalance of the nation and his renewed order for the gentry to retire to the country. That speech is given the important final position in the 1616 folio edition of the *Works* of James I, just as Jonson's depiction of James as the reviver of Astraea in *The Golden Age Restored* appeared last in the 1616 folio of the *Works* of Ben Jonson. This parallel placement of a statement of policy and a masque commemorating the policy was surely not accidental, but carefully arranged by the poet: Jonson violated the chronological order of the masques only in this one case, in order to bring it about.

Not only the masque's position but the text itself was altered. Editors of *The Golden Age Restored* have suggested that Jonson transposed Astraea's speech to the end of his masque for the published version (and apparently only once the volume was in press) "for literary reasons" in order to leave the "final word" with Astraea: "returning to a transformed earth, she found a heaven there and wished to stay in it. *Iam redit et Virgo, redeunt Saturnia regna,* for James was on the throne."[28] But Jonson's reasons can be pushed further than that. The change was almost certainly made after James's 1616 speech and its projected place in the volume of the king's works were known to the poet: the alteration emphasizes the connection between Jonson's 1615 masque and James's 1616 speech and creates an echoing between them, so that both folios end in a harmonious vision of the English countryside restored by the proclamations of James I, and both culminate in a reaffirmation that justice belongs to the king. Considered in itself, *The Golden Age Restored* is a dazzling vindication of court art, its own poetry depicted as arising out of the quickening power of the king. Considered as the final entry in the volume of Jonson's *Works,* it becomes an offering of all the learning and formidable poetic talent displayed in that volume to the wise uses of the king. One could scarcely imagine a finer tribute from a poet to his monarch.

As for the city and its metal, they seem to have prospered quite nicely despite the blasts from court. Although the intervening Lord Mayor's Shows may contain useful materials for the study of the competitive interaction between court masques and city pageantry, Anthony Munday's 1618 pageant for the Ironmongers is particularly interesting in terms of our present focus on gold, metal, and mettle. Munday's *Sidero-Thriambos; Or, Steele and Iron Triumphing* is unabashed in its support for the city Iron Age, by contrast with Munday's 1609 pageant honoring the same company, which had had as its main device an island of happiness depicting the golden world of "true Majesty" and celebrating the amity between the Lord Mayor and James I.[29] In Munday's 1618 pageant the device of the island appears again, but this time it is the island of Mulciber, "the God of *Mynes* and *Mettals,*" and contains a mine which he and the Cyclopes are delving industriously. The four corners of Mulciber's island are graced with nymphs representing the Four Ages, but former ages give way to the Iron Age, the age "wherein wee liue." The pageant's second device is a mount (like that of *Chruso-thriambos*), only this is the Mount of Fame. An ancient British bard leads the way to the mount, addresses the mayor in deliberately archaic language, and offers the mayor his poetry, hallowed by reverend age.[30]

Munday had no choice about the metal he was to celebrate, but he and the pageant's organizers presumably had considerable latitude when it came to mythological motifs. And they chose again, with deliberate incongruousness, to use motifs associated with the Golden Age. The return of the mount was surely no accident: Munday did not reuse the central motif from *Chruso-thriambos* out of imaginative impoverishment, but with the express intent of recalling the earlier pageant to the minds of his spectators and reengaging its political themes in a new way. It is almost impossible not to regard this pageant as Munday's response to *The Golden Age Restored* and *The Vision of Delight.* While Jonson disparaged the city and its metalworking activities as Iron Age corruptions, Munday boldly reintroduces motifs from his earlier pageants (except that the metal is iron now, not gold) and makes a virtue of necessity by exalting city business and manufacturing for what they actually are. While Jonson portrayed the Iron Age in the Ovidian manner as marked by war and rebellion, Munday's Mulciber is honest and peaceable, his potential for violence carefully contained. The new mayor is shown Hope and other allegorical figures "treading downe those vile Incendiaries, *Ambition Treason,* and Hostility, which seeke the Subuersion of all estates, by Bribing, Corruption, and smoothing insinuation, or else by open Fire and Sword" (C1^r); Mulciber's Iron does not incite rebellion, but manacles it. Jonson brought a train of revered English poets into his masque and displayed his own verse as an aspect of royal "state"; Munday, not to be outdone, introduces his Bard, a figure yet more ancient and therefore more worthy of respect, raised up by the "spirit of poetry" to pay verse tribute to the mayor. Munday's 1618 pageant is considerably more deferential toward King James than his 1611 production had been: Fame presents the new Lord Mayor to Sovereign Majesty, and although the mayor is again presented as a figure of the monarch, Munday makes it much clearer that the Lord Mayor's bright beams are borrowed from James I (B4^r). *Sidero-Thriambos* assimilates and answers Jonson's critique of the earlier *Chruso-thriambos,* tempering its sturdy assertion of city virtues with conciliation instead of continuing to needle the king.

And so our study of the parallels and transmutations could continue. The memory for earlier masques and pageants, at least in the minds of their chief devisers and participants, would appear to stretch much longer than we might have believed. And their main symbolic devices appear to have constituted a common stock of politically charged motifs which could be traded back and forth, echoed and reechoed with significant differences, in accordance with shifts in the contemporary situation and a corresponding alteration in the political statement to be made through a given masque or pageant. To examine these ephemeral forms carefully in terms of their "present occasions" is to recognize how much we have left to learn about the kinds of meaning they were capable of generating for their audiences; it is also to gain new respect for their freshness and complexity as art.

Notes

1. Quoted from a January 12, 1615, letter by John Chamberlain in *Ben Jonson*, ed. C. H. Herford, Percy Simpson, and Evelyn Simpson (Oxford: Clarendon Press, 1925–52), 10:553. Chamberlain reports that it was the dancing, not the show or device, which made the masque a success. Since Jonson's text presents the dancing as an outgrowth of the poetry of the main masque, he probably would not have been upset.

2. The observation is Stephen Orgel's, *The Illusion of Power: Political Theater in the English Renaissance* (Berkeley and Los Angeles: University of California Press, 1975), pp. 48–50. Based on my reading of *The Golden Age Restored*, however, I date that masque as the beginning of the new trend, rather than the 1616 *Mercury Vindicated*, which is identified as the first by Orgel. In doing so, I am revising an earlier statement made in my " 'Present Occasions' and the Shaping of Ben Jonson's Masques," *ELH* 45 (1978):201–25, in which I followed Orgel.

3. The phrase is Herford and Simpson's, *Ben Jonson*, 2:299. For James as the restorer of the Golden Age, see *The Political Works of James I*, ed. C. H. McIlwain (1918; rpt. ed., New York: Russell and Russell, 1965), pp. 272–73; and W. Todd Furniss, "Ben Jonson's Masques," in *Three Studies in the Renaissance: Sidney, Jonson, Milton* (1958; rpt. ed., Archon Books, 1969), pp. 100–102.

4. *Ben Jonson: The Complete Masques*, ed. Stephen Orgel (New Haven, Conn.: Yale University Press, 1969), p. 76. Subsequent quotations from Orgel's edition, to which I am greatly indebted, will be indicated by page number in the text. I have argued more generally for the importance of "present occasions" in the interpretation in Jonson's masques in two earlier studies, that from *ELH* cited above, n. 2; and "Masquing Occasions and Masque Structure," *Research Opportunities in Renaissance Drama* 24 (1981): 7–16.

5. Edmvnd Howes, *Annales; or, A Generall Chronicle of England. Begun by Iohn Stow: Continved and Augmented . . . vnto the end of this present yeere, 1631* (London: Richard Meighen, 1631), p. 1001.

6. On the separation of court and civic entertainment, see David M. Bergeron, *English Civic Pageantry 1558–1642* (Columbia: University of South Carolina Press, 1971), pp. 5, 66; and Paula Johnson, "Jacobean Ephemera and the Immortal Word," *Renaissance Drama*, n.s., 8 (1977): 151–71, esp. 157–58. My statement of the political aspects of the rift is, of course, a vast oversimplification of a complex set of oppositions. The present discussion will be based on the general analysis in Margaret Atwood Judson, *The Crisis of the Constitution* (1949; rpt. ed., New York: Octagon, 1964); David Little, *Religion, Order and Law: A Study in Pre-Revolutionary England* (New York: Harper and Row, 1969), esp. chap. 6; John D.

Eusden, *Puritans, Lawyers, and Politics in Early Seventeenth-Century England* (1958; rpt. ed., Hamden, Conn: Archon Books, 1968); Robert Ashton, *The Crown and the Money Market 1603–1640* (Oxford: Clarendon Press, 1960); and on the wonderfully detailed accounts of week-to-week events in Samuel R. Gardiner, *History of England from the Accession of James I to the Outbreak of the Civil War,* vol. 2 (London: Longmans, Green, 1904).

    7. Howes, *Annales,* pp. 1000–1001.

    8. James I, *A Proclamation against melting or conueying out of the Kings Dominions of Gold or Siluer,* May 18, 1611, in *A Booke of Proclamations, published since the beginning of his Maiesties most happy Reigne* (London, [1613]), p. 242.

    9. A[nthony] M[unday], *Chruso-thriambos: The Triumphes of GOLDE* (London: William Iaggard, 1611), sig. A3ᵛ. Further quotations from this edition will be indicated by signature number in the text.

    10. Bergeron, *English Civic Pageantry,* p. 144; D. J. Gordon, *The Renaissance Imagination,* ed. Stephen Orgel (Berkeley and Los Angeles: University of California Press, 1980), pp. 168–79; Marcus, "Masquing Occasions," pp. 9–11.

    11. Gardiner, *History of England,* 2:104–11; *Calendar of State Papers Domestic, James I,* vol. 2 (lxvii), 102 (December 24, 1611); (lxviii), 114 (January 27, 1612) and 117 (January [n.d.], 1612).

    12. *Love Restored* has no visions of elaborate transformation in its main masque; Inigo Jones was not involved in the production. It cost only £280 as opposed to £1087 for *Oberon* in the previous year; *Ben Jonson,* ed. Herford and Simpson, 10:522, 533.

    13. Bergeron, *English Civic Pageantry,* p. 151.

    14. James I, *Booke of Proclamations,* pp. 250–59.

    15. *Calendar, James I,* vol. 2 (lxxv), 214 (December 9, 1613).

    16. Gardiner, *History of England,* 227–49; William Cobbett, ed., *Parliamentary History of England,* vol. 1 (London: Bagshaw, 1806), col. 1156. For a different interpretation of the addled parliament, see Thomas L. Moir, *The Addled Parliament of 1614* (Oxford: Clarendon Press, 1958), esp. p. 59; Moir argues that the major problem of the parliament was not the discontent of its members but a failure of leadership in the court party.

    17. Gardiner, *History of England,* pp. 260–70; *The Letters of John Chamberlain,* ed. N. E. McClure, Memoirs of the American Philosophical Society, no. 12 (Philadelphia: Lancashire Press, 1939), 1:546, 568.

    18. James F. Larkin and Paul L. Hughes, eds., *Stuart Royal Proclamations,* vol. 1, *Royal Proclamations of King James I, 1603–1625* (Oxford: Clarendon Press, 1973), pp. 346–47; Gardiner, *History of England,* 2:305–6.

    19. Larkin and Hughes, eds., *Stuart Royal Proclamations,* 1:323–24.

    20. Mrs. Thomson, *The Life and Times of George Villiers, Duke of Buckingham* (London: Hurst and Blackett, 1860), 1:87–88.

    21. James I, *Booke of Proclamations,* p. 242; Stephen Leake, *An Historical Account of English Money,* 2d ed. (London: W. Meadows, 1745), pp. 276–80.

    22. Herford and Simpson, however, take his name to refer to a variety of fish; *Ben Jonson,* 10:217–18.

23. Ovid, *Metamorphoses,* 1. 137–43: "Nor was it only corn and their due nourishment that men demanded of the rich earth: they explored its very bowels, and dug out the wealth which it had hidden away, close to the Stygian shades; and this wealth was a further incitement to wickedness. By this time iron had been discovered, to the hurt of mankind, and gold, more hurtful still than iron. War made its appearance, using both those metals in its conflict, and shaking clashing weapons in bloodstained hands." *The Metamorphoses of Ovid,* trans. Mary M. Innes (Baltimore: Penguin, 1955). Munday was not the only dramatist popular in London to see the Golden Age in such violent terms: Jonson may also have had in mind Thomas Heywood's *The Golden Age* (London, 1611), which is a strife-torn muddle narrated by Homer, who speaks in Heywood's less-than-golden verse.

24. Bergeron, *English Civic Pageantry,* pp. 153, 164–65, 182–85.

25. Judson, *The Crisis of the Constitution,* pp. 25–27, 145.

26. *Ben Jonson,* ed. Herford and Simpson, 3:107 (I.ii.29–31); Bergeron points out that Munday was sneered at by other dramatists (*English Civic Pageantry,* pp. 140–43).

27. *Political Works of James I,* pp. 326–45; Marcus, "Present Occasions," pp. 203–13.

28. *Ben Jonson,* ed. Herford and Simpson, 7:420.

29. Bergeron, *English Civic Pageantry,* pp. 146–47.

30. Anthony Munday, *Sidero-Thriambos; Or, Steele and Iron Triumphing* (London: Nicholas Okes, 1618), sig. B1ᵛ. Further quotations will be indicated by signature number in the text. See also Bergeron's discussion, *English Civic Pageantry,* pp. 158–61. As Bergeron suggests, Munday may also have been influenced by Thomas Heywood's poor but very popular plays on the Four Ages of Man.

The Idea of London in Masque and Pageant

Gail Kern Paster

I t will surprise no one to be told that, in Renaissance England, civic pageantry and court masques have much in common. The conventions of public panegyric—for praising a king, a newly elected Lord Mayor, a visiting foreign prince—impose an emphatic similarity of tone and rhetoric upon the two forms, while the emblematic and decorative heritage that they share creates a marked similarity of allegorical content and visual effect.[1] In the Jacobean period, however, the relation between the civic pageant and court masque takes on a new interest for several reasons. One is that because James disliked public shows far more than his politically canny predecessor, the number of civic pageants throughout England declines after his accession. Even in London, the once-varied displays of pageantry begin to concentrate almost exclusively on the yearly installation of the Lord Mayor on October 29.[2] The particular significance of James's withdrawal from public display, moreover, is that it seems to correspond so closely to his encouragement of the introverted adulation of the court masque. The increasing elaborateness of the London Lord Mayor's Shows during these years is usually regarded, therefore, not merely as compensation for the lack of other occasions for civic entertainment, but as an emulous response to what was going on at court—conspicuous display matching conspicuous display. Glynne Wickham even sees the growing opulence of both forms as manifestations of aggression comparable to the military parades of rival nations and symptomatic of the political crises to come.[3]

It may or may not be justified to find such a strong, partisan political motive in the London civic pageantry of the Jacobean period, particularly since the city fathers themselves differed about religious matters and attitudes to the crown.[4] Gordon Kipling has qualified such a political interpretation, at least implicitly, by suggesting that civic pageantry in

London during the sixteenth century absorbed the concentration and effort expended elsewhere on the Corpus Christi plays. Later development of pageantry in London, while stimulated by state suppression of cycle drama, had its own internal coherence and momentum.[5] His demonstration of London's special devotion to pageantry is particularly appealing, furthermore, because its development may be linked to the sharp rise in the early seventeenth century of an urban self-consciousness brought about by such factors as London's growth in size and population, the expansion of international trade and finance, the establishment of a London social season, and the success of commercial theater. The population of Stuart London, it may be useful to remember, numbered around a quarter million, while the populations of Norwich and Bristol, contending for second place, were well below fifty thousand. Jonson mocks London self-congratulation in the prologue to *The Alchemist* when he declares, "No clime breeds better matter, for your whore, / Bawd, squire, imposter, many persons more" (ll. 7–8).[6] But Jonson, like Middleton, Dekker, and others, found London no less fertile a subject for praise than for satire, as the evidence of the pageants suggests. The eagerness with which they competed for commissions as well as the care they took in publishing their pageant texts underscore the prestige attached to civic ceremonial and those involved in it.[7] Just as the masque tells us not what the king was but how he liked to see and understand himself, so the civic pageant tells us how London liked to see and understand itself.

The emphasis that the city placed on its pageantry as a source of civic pride and self-definition may seem even more significant if we first consider the somewhat belittling portrait of London to be found in many of Jonson's most accomplished masques. As Stephen Orgel has argued, a major change in the Jonsonian masque occurs when Jonson starts to replace such fanciful antimasque creatures as the hags in the *Masque of Queens* or the satyrs of *Oberon* with more realistically drawn characters from the city or the belowstairs world at court. His motives for doing so, aside from the pure pressure of novelty, were probably to give the masque more comic potential and to make it socially far more expressive than a simple moral contrast between good and evil could be.[8] With actors from the King's Men regularly at his disposal, it is difficult to imagine Jonson resisting the temptation to invent, and write idiosyncratic dialogue for, characters as lively as deaf mother Venus from Pudding Lane in *Christmas His Masque;* the printer, chronicler, and factor in *News from the New World;* or the brewers, alewives, and bear-wards from Saint Katherine's in *The Masque of Augurs.* Of course he does not single out the city in his choice of antimasque characters. Ireland provides the footmen and the dialect in *The*

Irish Masque, Wales delivers three gentlemen with full Welsh dialect in *For the Honor of Wales,* and characters like the Cook in *Neptune's Triumph* come from the king's own household.

The fact remains, however, that after 1612, the year that saw the production of the first prose antimasque in *Love Restored,* Jonson looks more and more to the lower orders, particularly in London, for comic characters and comic language to make up the antimasque. The prevailing geniality of masque decorum and the goal of social harmony to which the masque moves prevent these citizen antimasquers from suffering anything worse than mild ridicule. It is even possible to argue that, despite the eccentricities of their language, the lower-class characters participate in the general idealization of the occasion, especially if they are contrasted with their greedy and corrupt counterparts in Jacobean city comedy. Citizens here err out of eagerness to see, entertain, and be near the king; they intrude where they do not belong. Such eagerness is particularly true of the Irish footmen in their desire to bless the king's sweet face, but it also explains the invasion from Saint Katherine's in *The Masque of Augurs.* The citizens sneak in, aware that "there is as much danger [in] going too neere the King, as the Lyons" in the Tower (ll. 12–14), yet determined to "shew our loves, sir, and to make a little merry with his Majesty to night" (ll. 62–63) by bringing him a masque of dancing bears. When the brewers realize that the bears and the Dutch artist Vangoose whom they have also brought along are appropriate only for making up the antimasque, they accede to their place in the entertainment and thus in the social order as well: "Sir, all our request is, since we are come, we may be admitted, if not for a Masque, for an *Antick-mask;* and as we shall deserve therein, we desire to be returned with credit to the Buttry, from whence we came, for reward, or to the Porters Lodge with discredit, for our punishment" (ll. 148–52).

In *Neptune's Triumph* the Cook and the Poet quarrel over which art—cookery or poetry—better pleases the palate of the guests. The Cook's antimasque, a stew of persons to represent the meats, turns out to contain a kitchen boy, the king's forester, a poulterer's wife, Hogrel the butcher, and a fruiterer "with a cold red nose, / Like a blue fig" (ll. 319–20). Such characters—cooks, footmen, brewers—are fully alive to the ethos of the masque world. Their consuming devotion to the pleasure and service of the king is never in doubt because it motivates most of their indecorous behavior in the hall. Their devotion anticipates, in a lower mode, the lyric expressions of loyalty, obedience, and wonder in the masque proper. And there can be no doubt of these citizens' usefulness to the court, which can hardly do without footmen, cooks, or suppliers of food and drink. The contrast between the antimasque and masque thus expresses the ideal political reciprocity of a class-based social hierarchy. The antimasque serves to place and to celebrate those members of the community who take care of the ongoing physical life of the court and whose reward is comically epitomized by credit at the buttery.

But, while the antimasquers are absorbed in the general atmosphere of social harmony that climaxes the masque, they are largely excluded from the aristocratic celebration of power that Stephen Orgel has also taught us to see there. The masque projects a world where natural law has been understood and brought under human control, where the range of human action has been radically expanded to bring the dead back to life or to recreate the Golden Age.[9] But the antimasquers themselves, however essential in maintaining the physical life of the court, have no part to play in the major assertions of royal power in the masque lyrics. The citizen antimasquers are, after all, identified by occupation in an aristocratic world from which labor—though not the fruits of labor—is barred. The masquers themselves have only to dance as gracefully as possible in order to fulfill their roles perfectly. And while Jonson occasionally calls attention to the intricacy of their movements (as in *The Masque of Queens,* ll. 749–56), he does so to insist not upon their hard work but rather upon their beauty and the tight social discipline to which they so easily submit. In masques with maritime motifs, like *The Fortunate Isles,* Jonson and Jones celebrate the nation's naval power in lyric and scenic presentations of the fleet. But even here, where the city's contribution to the crown might easily be mentioned directly, the two artists define that power solely in terms of the king, for whom all maritime venture is apparently conducted:

> See, yond', his Fleete, ready to goe or come,
> Or fetch the riches of the *Ocean* home,
> So to secure him, both in peace, and warres,
> Till not one ship alone, but all be starres.
>
> [*The Fortunate Isles,* ll. 624–27]

The king's power engenders paradox as the only means for expressing such effortless use and perpetual renewal as in the wonders of the deep, "where all is plough'd, yet still the pasture's greene, / New wayes are found, and yet no paths are seene" (ll. 582–83).

This emphasis on ease, this hierarchical division of social function implicit in a structure where antimasques concern the life of the body and masques celebrate the life of the spirit, yields to a very different ethos in the civic pageant. The pageants, as we turn to them, will demonstrate that the city was no less studious of its magnificence than the court, no less aware of its power. But, in a status-conscious age that continued to exalt birthright gentry over the merchant class, the image of its ideal self must have seemed less readily available to the city than it was to the court. This may have been particularly true in the difficult economic circumstances after 1615, when the city's merchant princes were "worried merchant princes caught between the discontent of the city poor on one side and the exactions and monopoly grants of a spendthrift court on the other."[10] Furthermore, while the court could and obviously did regard playing at masques as an efflorescence of its very nature, the city seems to have been identified with the spirit of work—with everyday, not with holiday. Dekker, for instance, so completely associates the idea of a city with work that he finds London during the 1604 ceremonial entry of the king to be no more a "Citie, (because that during these tryumphes, shee puts off her formall habite of Trade and Commerce, treading even Thrift it selfe under foote,) but now becomes a Reveller and Courtier."[11]

Celebrations of the city, furthermore, do not automatically carry with them the inherent moral importance that the obligation to praise the sovereign bestows on the masque. The court, thanks to its immediate relation to the king, does not have to acknowledge the city in the same way that the city has to acknowledge the court. The pageants make clear how much of London's traditional importance derives from the presence of the king, without whom London would not be the center of the kingdom. Dekker constructs an elaborate conceit describing the city's loss of "borrowed Majestie" as James passed out of London on his processional day:

> And thus have wee (lowely and aloofe) followed our Soveraigne through
> the seaven Triumphal gates of this his Court Royall, which name, as
> *London* received at the rysing of the *Sunne*; so now at his going from her
> (even in a moment) She lost that honour: And being (like an Actor on a
> Stage) stript out of her borrowed Majestie, she resignes her former
> shape and title of Citie; nor is it quite lost, considering it went along
> with him, to whom it is due. For such Vertue is begotten in Princes,
> that their verie presence hath power to turne a Village to a Citie, and
> to make a Citie appeare great as a Kingdome. [*The Magnificent Enter-*
> *tainment,* ll. 1534-43]

Yet, like the masque poet, the pageant poet tried to insist upon the symbolic centrality of his community and its location. Frequent references to London's ancient title of *camera regis* seem intended not only to remind the city that its centrality derived ultimately from the king but to remind the king of the power and protection which only London could offer. This kind of reciprocity seems to underlie Dekker's simile in the 1604 entertainment of the city as royal court. Each stop at a city landmark repre-

sented a different part of the royal palace, the Little Conduit for example
becoming the Privy Chamber, the device at Saint Mildred's in the Poultry
signifying the Presence Chamber, and so forth. In his 1613 mayoral show,
The Triumphs of Truth, Middleton emphasizes the religious implications of
London as *camera regis.* A "reverend mother" personifying the city reminds
the newly installed mayor:

> This place is the king's chamber; all pollution,
> Sin, and uncleanness, must be lock'd out here,
> And be kept sweet with sanctity, faith, and fear.   [p. 238][12]

The Recorder of the City welcomed James in 1604 with a similar trope,
drawn from Revelation, inviting him to "come, therefore, O worthiest of
Kings, as a glorious bridegroome through your Royall chamber."[13]

In the 1626 *Triumphs of Health and Prosperity,* the first Lord Mayor's
Show after the accession of Charles, Middleton uses a figure personifying
government to redefine the proper relations of city and king, city and
kingdom. The Platonic correspondence between the human body and the
body politic becomes proof of London's centrality:

> With just propriety does this city stand,
> As fix'd by fate, i' the middle of the land;
> It has, as in the body, the heart's place,
> Fit for her works of piety and grace,
>
> . . . .
>
> And as the heart, in its meridian seat,
> Is styl'd the fountain of the body's heat,
> The first thing receives life, that last that dies,
> These properties experience well applies
> To this most loyal city, that hath been
> In former ages, as in these times, seen
> The fountain of affection, duty, zeal,
> And taught all cities through the commonweal;
> The first that receives quickening life and spirit
> From the king's grace, which still she strives t'inherit,
> And, like the heart, will be the last that dies
> In any duty toward good supplies.   [pp. 408–9]

The speech is a particularly good example of the recurrent tension between
acknowledging how much London owes to the king and how much the king
owes to London—the very issue that the masque, as we have seen, carefully
skirts. In its emphasis on loyalty, the speech may well have been intended to
reassure Charles of the city's loyalty despite its refusal earlier of his request
for borrowed funds.[14] But against the assertions of loyalty stand reminders

of the city's critical importance to the state, reminders which may have been thought especially appropriate for a king whose dislike of the city had prompted him to disallow any coronation entry at all. The idea of the *camera regis* works both ways: if the king and his court occupy that still point at absolute center, London surrounds them as "the first that receives quickening life and spirit / From the king's grace." The body of which the king is head could not survive without the heart, "the last that dies / In any duty toward good." The king's security depends on London's supporting strength and tutelary role in instructing "all cities through the commonweal." Without the chamber of his sweet security, Middleton implies, the king's order would not—and did not—survive.

Another impulse seems to run throughout the pageants to present the city's greatness and magnificence apart from, if not precisely equal to, the magnificence of Whitehall. Nowhere is this impulse more fully attested to than in Jonson's design and accompanying text for the first coronation arch at Fenchurch. The occasion was one at which the sovereign's presence would seem to matter most of all. Yet the effect of the arch, particularly as represented in Jonson's text, is less to welcome the king from Scotland than to impress him—perhaps in contrast with his native land and capital city—with the power and antiquity of the city he was privileged to rule over. Of course the words running across the front of the arch—"Par domus haec coelo, sed minor est domino"—assured the king that the city was "farre inferior to the master thereof" (l. 22). But even the need for such self-deprecation may suggest how laudatory the rest of the Fenchurch text is about a city which might "(by *Hyperbole*) be said to touch the starres, and reach vp to heauen" (ll. 20–21).

The city's greatness, furthermore, differs substantially from that of kings or masquers. Time, which threatens masquers (because the visible demonstration of their greatness occurs through the dance), verifies the greatness of cities, which exist in and through time. Jonson's numerous classical allusions in the Fenchurch text function not only, as Dekker noted scornfully, "to shew how nimbly we can carve up the whole messe of the Poets,"[15] but also to underscore London's duration as a city and thus its importance as the chief source of Britain's historical continuity with the classical past. As Jonson's allusion to a well-known incident in Tacitus suggests, London was "a busy centre, chiefly through its crowd of merchants and stores" even in A.D. 61 (*Annals* 14. 33).[16] To longevity Jonson adds suggestions of the city's power—both actual and symbolic. If Britain is "a world diuided from the world" (l. 46), London is the nation's epitome, the seat of empire. It is also tempting to find a description of the city's power contained in the motto Jonson attaches to the figure of Wisdom: "Per me reges regnant" (l.

62). If the moralist wants to emphasize a sovereign's need to rule through wisdom, Jonson the native-born city poet might well want to remind the king that he needs to rule through London as well. This suggestion is further reinforced by the figures supporting Theosophia—the "rich, reu-erend, and antique" (l. 70) Genius of the City and the figures flanking him, symbolic representations of the city fathers and the city's military might. "With those armes of councel and strength," Jonson notes, "the *Genius* was able to extinguish the kings enemies, and preserue his citizens" (ll. 94–95).

In such assertions of the city's power lies the essential function of the Fenchurch arch to express not only "the state and magnificence (as proper to a triumphall Arch) but the very site, fabricke, strength, policie, dig-nitie, and affections of the Citie" (ll. 244–46). There is a sense too that London's greatness is self-evident, hardly needing the allegory of the arch. All the allegorical figures and iconographic motifs on the arch's façade were designed to support and lead the eye up to a model of the London skyline, "houses, towres, and steeples, set off in prospectiue" (ll. 3–4). Genius's first words to the king emphasize the freedom of London's re-sponse to his entry, this point of time producing what "the Roman, Sax-on, Dane, and Norman yoke" (l. 275) did not—freely given obedience. Furthermore, Genius goes on to glorify the beauty of the city's welcoming aspect before he even mentions the king directly:

> Now London reare
> Thy forehead high, and on it striue to weare
> Thy choisest gems; teach thy steepe Towres to rise
> Higher with people: set with sparkling eyes
> Thy spacious windowes; and in euery street,
> Let thronging ioy, loue, and amazement meet.   [ll. 276–81]

While James is undeniably at the center of this historical moment, the figure to whom all speeches are directed, the moment itself is defined as the product of the city's long duration in time. It is a duration that has served primarily to produce the city's present magnificence.

The city's history takes on particular significance once we realize the extent to which the civic entertainments identify London's past with that of the nation as a whole. This is particularly noticeable in James's corona-tion entertainments since they did not commemorate the king's actual coronation (which had occurred quietly nearly eight months earlier) but merely his ceremonial ride through London. Even so, the *flamen martialis* which greeted James just before he left the city contrasted the present date of March 15 with Caesar's disastrous Ides of March. And since James's

passage through the city could take place only after the plague epidemic
had fallen off, Jonson introduces the figure Electra who tells her listeners
that she has ceased mourning—both for the fall of Troy and for the sick-
ness in new Troy, London. James's procession through London, freeing
"thy *Chamber,* from the noyse / Of warre and tumult" (ll. 732–33), is the
beginning of a new *pax Augusta.* Strained though such conceits may seem,
Jonson's efforts to bring the Roman past to bear on the present moment are
clearly crucial to London's sense of self-importance in welcoming the new
monarch. As James succeeds Elizabeth, so London succeeds Rome as the
embodiment of the idea of the historical record. And the king should
know it.

Even on smaller occasions the presence of mythological figures in civic
entertainments and the comparison of civic officials to their ancient Roman counterparts are ways of magnifying the importance of the men and
the entertainments. In an entertainment he wrote to celebrate a day set
aside in 1620 for the "generall Training," Middleton had a mounted Pallas
greet the Lord Mayor and his retinue:

> Why here the Ancient Romane Honor dwels,
> A Praetor, Generall; Senators, Colonels;
> Captaines, grave Citizens; so richly inspir'd,
> They can assist in Councell, if requir'd,
> And set Court-Causes in as fayre a Forme,
> As they doe Men, here, without Rage or Storme. [17]
>
> [Entertainment 4. 30–35]

Such mythologizing cannot extend the range of action available to civic
officials as radically as the mythologizing in the masque extends the
powers of the king. But even in a lesser celebration, the classical past
helps to magnify the occasion and thus the city. The social value that
noble birth accords the masquers, the city's history gives to the men
whom civic entertainments are designed to honor. Just as Jonson seeks to
impress James with the antiquity of London's greatness at the Fenchurch
arch, so the pageant writers emphasize again and again in the mayoral
shows and other civic entertainments the continuity of civic traditions and
their place in the historical record. Even on minor occasions, Middleton as
City Chronologer scrupulously records when a celebration has been dis-
continued or if there has been an unusual interval between celebrations.
When Pallas was to meet the group riding out for the General Training,
Middleton had her complain "of nothing but Neglect, / That such a noble
Cities Arm'd Defence / Should be so seldome seene" (Entertainment 4.
39–41). (Unfortunately, Pallas never got to say anything at all, since, as

Middleton somewhat disgustedly observes, the custom's revival was itself deferred.)

More important, Middleton provides the civic entertainments with the same ethical justification used for the lavish entertainments at court, obliging the city to display the Aristotelian liberality that Renaissance political theory customarily required for princes. In a preface to the 1613 *Triumphs of Truth,* which he thought important enough to repeat for the printed texts of *The Triumphs of Integrity* (1623) and *The Triumphs of Health and Prosperity* (1626), Middleton explains:

> Search all chronicles, histories, records, in what language or letter
> soever; let the inquisitive man waste the dear treasures of his time and
> eyesight, he shall conclude his life only in this certainty, that there is
> no subject received into the place of his government with the like state
> and magnificence as is the Lord Mayor of the city of London. This
> being, then, infallible—like the mistress of our triumphs—and not to
> be denied of any, how careful ought those gentlemen to be, to whose
> discretion and judgment the weight and charge of such a business is
> entirely referred and committed by the whole Society, to have all things
> correspondent to that generous and noble freeness of cost and liberality.
> [p. 233]

Many Lord Mayor's Shows involve an explicit recognition of the past and the typological use of historical figures.[18] In Middleton's *Triumphs of Love and Antiquity* (1619), figures personifying example and antiquity praised worthy former mayors from the Company of Skinners. Antiquity insisted upon the importance of the historical record for the proper functioning of the community:

> 'Tis I that keep all the records of fame,
> Mother of Truths, Antiquity my name;
> No year, month, day, or hour, that brings in place
> Good works and noble, for the city's grace,
> But I record, that after-times may see
> What former were, and how they ought to be
> Fruitful and thankful, in fair actions flowing,
> To meet heaven's blessings, to which much is owing.   [p. 323]

The texts of almost every one of Middleton's Lord Mayors Shows include the names, dates, and important accomplishments of past mayors from the company to which the present mayor belonged, "as an example and encouragement to all virtuous and industrious deservers in time to come" (p. 302). Both he and Anthony Munday, his nearest rival in the competition for pageant commissions, seem especially interested in resurrecting historical figures for floats and chariots.[19] Munday used William Walworth, a famous early mayor from the Fishmongers Company, in his 1616 pageant for the company, *Chrysanaleia: The Golden Fishing*. London's Genius, an angel with golden crown and wings, met the resurrected Walworth at his tomb and together they accompanied the mayoral procession through the city. Walworth reminds the assemblage of his great deed as mayor, the suppression of Wat Tyler's insurrection against Richard II, and presents the pageant's Chariot of Triumphal Victory, which

> Some shape of that daies honour doth present,
> By *Heavens protection* of *True Majestie*,
> And beating down *Treason* and *Mutinie*.[20]

Not only does Walworth represent the archetype of all loyal Lord Mayors, as David Bergeron has suggested; his presence at the 1616 installation demonstrates the continuity and vitality of London's own civic history and its crucial role in shaping the history of the nation as a whole.[21]

This insistence on time and on exemplary figures from the past indicates how the pageants could be used to draw connections between a city's traditions and the preservation of civic order. As a yearly celebration, the Lord Mayor's Show recalls the past and augurs the future. Though the person of the magistrate changes yearly, the traditions of the shows themselves and the historical record of "fair actions flowing" which they represent demonstrate that the city's order is essentially self-perpetuating. Unlike the masque, which tries to place its ideal community in a poetic structure outside the world bound by sense and time, the pageant makes the weight of history a central part of its meaning because time is the essential medium for expressing a city's identity and greatness.

Like the masque, then, the pageant seeks to define exemplary figures whom spectators can admire and imitate. Both forms offer the same secular reward—fame—to the people they celebrate. In the masque, however, the masquers need demonstrate neither ability nor qualifications for their roles: they merely have to belong to the courtly society that the masque celebrates. Once they have presented themselves, danced, and inaugurated the revels, they have fulfilled the masque's terms for virtue, for heroic stature. The pageant, on the other hand, insists on the openendedness of its traditions in order to suggest to the Lord Mayor that his significance at the investiture is mostly potential. His fame will depend, like that of the former Lord Mayors commemorated in the shows, on hard work and self-sacrifice. Middleton underscores the difference between the two forms by comparing the self-made citizen with complacent nobility:

And 'tis the noblest splendour upon earth
For man to add a glory to his birth,
All his life's race with honour'd acts commix'd,
Than to be nobly born, and there stand fix'd,
As if 'twere competent virtue for whole life
To be begot a lord: [*Triumphs of Integrity*, p. 387]

The pageants draw on several tropes to indicate the difficulties of the magistrate's year in office. The morality tradition provides a conception of the magistrate as Christian pilgrim, undertaking his duties in part for the promise of salvation. A speech in Middleton's *Triumphs of Health and Prosperity* calls the mayor's year "a time given / To treasure up good actions fit for heaven" (p. 410). The scriptural metaphor of Christ as the bridegroom of the holy city seems to underlie occasional celebrations of the mayor as London's bridegroom. In *Chrysanaleia: The Golden Fishing*, Munday describes London as "Englands Jerusalem" (sig. A4ᵛ) and has Walworth give the new bachelor mayor, John Leman, some marital advice:

> London *(it seemes) did like you best,*
> *(Although you are a Bacheler),*
> *To be her Husband for a yeere;*
> *Love her, delight her. Shee's a Bride,*
> *Never slept by such a Husbands side*
> *But once before. She hath had many*
> *And you may prove as good as any*
> *Have gone before you in this place.*   [sig. C4ʳ]

The mayor's year can also be described as a sort of chivalric test of strength and commitment:

> Great works of grace must be requir'd and done
> Before the honour of this seat be won.
> A whole year's reverend care in righting wrongs,
> And guarding innocence from malicious tongues,
>   [*Triumphs of Honour and Industry*, p. 303]

The Angel of Truth in Middleton's *Triumphs of Truth* describes the year as a series of temptations, making the magistrate's office a test of the soul to perceive illusion and deception:

> Wake on, the victory is not half yet won;
> Thou wilt be still assaulted, thou shalt meet
> With many dangers that in voice seem sweet,
> And ways most pleasant to a worldling's eye;
> My mistress has but one, but that leads high.   [p. 240]

As the buried allusion to the Herculean choice in the verses above suggests, the pageants' emphasis on Christian good works also blends imperceptibly with the classical idea of heroic labors. The Romans, too, describe their most honored citizens as husbands of the city. The 1623 *Triumphs of Integrity,* which Middleton wrote for the Drapers, featured Tamburlaine among "great commanders . . . that were originally sprung from shepherds and humble beginnings" (p. 386). His 1619 *Triumphs of Love and Antiquity* for the Skinners presented Orpheus, who compared a commonwealth to a wilderness needing to be dressed and pruned. And in *The Triumphs of Health and Prosperity,* Middleton used the conventional trope of the sea of state to bring together heroic labor, mercantile adventurousness, and the difficulties of the mayor's office:

> The world's a sea, and every magistrate
> Takes a year's voyage when he takes this state:
> Nor on these seas are there less dangers found
> Than those on which the bold adventurer's bound;
> For rocks, gulfs, quicksands, here is malice, spite,
> Envy, detraction of all noble right.   [pp. 406–7]

This identification of the adventurous commercial spirit with the heroic tradition turns the getting of wealth into a demonstration of heroic accomplishment. Many pageants allude proudly to the far-flung overseas markets of the trading companies by including floating islands with Indian youths among spice trees. In Middleton's *Triumphs of Honour and Industry,* India herself, the Queen of Merchandise, was seated in a pageant car accompanied by Industry and her associate Traffic or Merchandise, who holds a globe in her hand and "knits love and peace amongst all nations" (p. 298). The theme is particularly interesting, of course, because merchandise, the traffic of getting and spending, are unrelentingly singled out in the city comedies as reasons for the absence of "love and peace" within London itself, let alone among all nations. The writer of the "Apologie of the Cittie of London" in Stow's 1603 edition of the *Survey* acknowledges proudly the vast wealth of many London merchants, as a "thing both prayseworthy and profitable," and quotes Cicero in defense of *"Mercatura."* But he also has to defend the city against charges that London had caused the decay of other ports and trade elsewhere in the kingdom.[22]

Criticism of wealth and acquisition has no part in the pageants, for wealth is always presented in terms of its benefit to the commonwealth. The getting of wealth is inseparable from justifications for a growing sense of imperial destiny centered in London. Thus Middleton, one of the severest critics of the acquisitive spirit in his city comedies, celebrates the commercial spirit in the pageants by tying it to a rather medieval notion of Christian service and to his understanding of the needs of the commonwealth. Munday emphasizes the long tradition of public works in *Chrysanaleia,* noting not only that the Fishmongers and Goldsmiths had worked together during one of the Crusades in Jerusalem but also that together they had built the London wall and Moorgate and Cripplegate (sig. A4ᵛ). Middleton tends to transform wealth into bounty, which he describes moreover much as Italian civic humanists had described the manifold blessings of city life. Thus the reverend mother personifying London in *The Triumphs of Truth* makes the development of the individual completely dependent on the benefits of a city, whose careful nurturing of her sons sets "wholesome and religious laws / Before the footsteps of thy youth":

> The duties of a mother I have shown,
> Through all the rites of pure affection,
> In care, in government, in wealth, in honour,
> Brought thee to what thou art, thou'st all from me;
> Then what thou shouldst be I expect from thee.   [p. 237]

Her bounty extends even to those neglectful sons who

> . . . willfully retire
> Themselves from doing grace and service to me,
> When they've got all they can, or hope for, from me.   [p. 238]

With a mercy resembling the divine, London would bless all her sons so that any unkindness reveals "no defect in me" (p. 238). Such civic bountifulness has much in common, of course, with the royal bounty which Jonson images in *The Gypsies Metamorphosed* as "a hand not greiu'd, but when it ceases" (l. 14). The circle of reciprocity which bounty ideally initiates, in eliciting and repaying services, is also echoed in the pageants, which constantly remind the mayor that liberality in office is a measure of greatness. In *The Triumphs of Honour and Industry,* the mayor's honor is his bounty:

> Nothing deads honour more than to behold
> Plenty coop'd up, and bounty faint and cold,
> Which ought to be the free life of the year;
> For bounty 'twas ordain'd to make that clear,
> Which is the light of goodness and of fame,
> And puts by honour from the cloud of shame.   [p. 306]

In part the lines remind us of the hospitality and feasting which was so much a part of the mayor's duties and which required a willingness to spend—with royal alacrity if not with royal sums. But there is a deeper sense underlying the obligatory flattery of all Middleton's civic entertainments of how important generosity of spirit is as a civic ideal. That Middleton never includes generosity of spirit in the citizens portrayed in the comedies may well explain his invoking it here, *laudando praecipere*. The idea of reciprocity is central to urban life, and so the splendor of these shows attests to a fellowship within the sponsoring company that ought to be imitated in the community at large and ought to be exemplified above all in the mayor. In *The Triumphs of Love and Antiquity*, for example, Middleton likens the robes with which the Skinners supply royalty to the Lord Mayors elected from their company. As the robes adorn the king, so the mayor adorns the city. The shows are like robes too, "adorning their adorners with their love" (p. 324). "Be careful, then, great Lord," Antiquity tells the mayor, "to bring forth deeds / To match that honour that from hence proceeds" (p. 324). *The Triumphs of Health and Prosperity* ends on a similar note, telling the mayor that if his year brings noble works "then is thy brotherhood for their love and cost / Requited amply" (p. 410).

The emphasis in these pageants on service and responsibility, on works and the labors of the magistrate's office, is clearly very different from the masque's usual presentation of effortless power and easy social harmony. The ease of the masques gives way to earnestness in the pageants. Yet the pageant writers' purposes are not very different from those of Jonson, for instance, as masque writer: they all attempt to imagine a community of exemplary figures for the communities at large to admire and imitate. While the masques draw, almost exclusively, on legendary and mythological figures, the pageants add historical figures from the city's own past. Their elevation of worthy Lord Mayors, past and present, to heroic stature really serves to glorify the city for whom such labors are undertaken, to make the city's sense of self as satisfying as the court's. Of course the city's virtues are much less abstract than the court's, much more dependent on the service, works, and prosperity of the citizenry. But the pageants' corollary insistence on the city's independent ability to produce, nurture, and finally celebrate its own worthiest citizens reveals the extent to which the pageants ministered to the city's self-esteem by challenging the aristocratic assumptions of the masques that birth, courtly graces, and royal favor matter more than anything else. In the succession of Lord Mayors commemorated every year, the city presents its own community of the elect and reaffirms its own high worth in them. In the pageants, the city could

affirm an order that was essentially self-perpetuating and a greatness that
was the product of its own life in time.

Notes

1. George R. Kernodle, *From Art to Theater: Form and Convention in the Renaissance* (Chicago: University of Chicago Press, 1944), pp. 70–75.

2. See David M. Bergeron, *English Civic Pageantry 1558–1642* (Columbia: University of South Carolina Press, 1971), p. 66.

3. Glynne Wickham, *Early English Stages 1300 to 1600* (New York: Columbia University Press, 1959–), vol. 1, pt. 1, p. 237.

4. See Valerie Pearl, *London and the Outbreak of the Puritan Revolution: City Government and National Politics, 1625–43* (Oxford: Oxford University Press, 1961), pp. 63–71. My information about London population in the period also comes from Pearl (p. 14).

5. Gordon Kipling, "Triumphal Drama: Form in English Civic Pageantry," *Renaissance Drama*, n.s., 8 (1977): 37–38.

6. Quotations from Jonson are to *Ben Jonson*, ed. C. H. Herford, Percy Simpson, and Evelyn Simpson (Oxford: Clarendon Press, 1925–52), which I have cited parenthetically.

7. Kipling, "Triumphal Drama," p. 38.

8. Stephen Orgel, *The Jonsonian Masque* (Cambridge, Mass.: Harvard University Press, 1965), p. 137.

9. Stephen Orgel, "The Poetics of Spectacle," *New Literary History* 2 (1971): 387.

10. I am quoting from Margot Heinemann's discussion of Middleton's city employments in *Puritanism and Theatre: Thomas Middleton and Opposition Drama Under the Early Stuarts* (Cambridge: Cambridge University Press, 1980), p. 127.

11. From "The Magnificent Entertainment" (ll. 921–24); Thomas Dekker, *The Dramatic Works*, ed. Fredson Bowers (Cambridge: Cambridge University Press, 1955), 2:281. But we ought to allow for some exaggeration from Dekker since, as Kipling notes ("Triumphal Drama," p. 38), Dekker also called civic triumphs "the most choice and daintiest fruits that spring from *Peace* and *Abundance*."

12. Quotations from Middleton's civic pageants are to *The Works of Thomas Middleton*, ed. A. H. Bullen, vol. 7 (London: John C. Nimmo, 1886). Since Bullen's edition lacks line numbering, I will cite page references parenthetically.

13. Quoted in John Nichols, *The Progresses, Processions, and Magnificent Festivities of King James the First* (London, 1828), 1:360.

14. See Heinemann, *Puritanism and Theatre*, p. 131.

15. Quoted in *Ben Jonson*, ed. Herford and Simpson, 10:388, l. 69n.

16. Tacitus, *Annals*, ed. John Jackson, Loeb Classical Library (Cambridge,

Mass.: Harvard University Press, 1937). Herford and Simpson do not mention the interesting fact that Stow's Apologist also mentions this passage in Tacitus; see "An Apologie of the Cittie of London," in John Stow, *A Survey of London*, ed. Charles Lethbridge Kingsford (Oxford: Clarendon Press, 1971), 2:201.

17. Thomas Middleton, *Honourable Entertainments*, ed. R. C. Bald (Oxford: Malone Society, 1953). I will quote from Bald's edition of these entertainments throughout.

18. See David M. Bergeron, "Civic Pageants and Historical Drama," *Journal of Medieval and Renaissance Studies* 5 (1975): 89–105.

19. Bergeron, "Civic Pageants and Historical Drama," p. 95.

20. Anthony Munday, *Chrysanaleia: The Golden Fishing, or, Honour of Fishmongers* (London: 1616), STC 18266.

21. Bergeron, "Civic Pageants and Historical Drama," p. 103.

22. See "Apologie of the Cittie of London," p. 211.

Middleton's No Wit, No Help and Civic Pageantry

David M. Bergeron

An issue that occupies much literary criticism and much simple speculation is how and where an artist gets his ideas. Do they spring entirely from imagination? Do they come, as in the example of Stephen Crane's writing *The Red Badge of Courage,* from poring over chronicles of events (newspaper accounts of the Civil War in Crane's case)? Dramatists of the English Renaissance, we know, ransacked myriad sources for their basic plots or episodes within those plots (the likely sources for Shakespeare's plays now fill an impressive eight-volume edition). What, however, is the relationship between the presumed source and the artistic creation? What constitutes a source? These questions, as old-fashioned as they may seem to be, continue to tease our own imaginations. They are implicit in this essay.

In *No Wit, No Help like a Woman's,* a curious and neglected play of 1611, filled with irony, satire, and unmistakable romance, Thomas Middleton presents a wedding masque in Act IV in celebration of the marriage of Lady Goldenfleece (widow of Avarice Goldenfleece) to Mistress Lowwater (disguised as a man). This entertainment, consisting of a mechanical globe from which emerge characters representing the Elements, derives from part of the 1604 royal-entry civic pageant for James I in London. In this instance, the artist, Middleton, borrows from himself—another dimension of where artists get their ideas. Like Shakespeare, who frequently echoes himself, Middleton recalls a scene of the 1604 pageant which he has written. Further, this pageant lingers in Middleton's imagination, evidence of it appearing in some of his Lord Mayor's Shows. An episode first performed on the stage of the streets of London continued to play itself out on the stage of Middleton's mind.

That civic pageants may have influenced the regular drama can be demonstrated in part by reference to the work of Thomas Heywood and Thomas Dekker. Both dramatists recall Queen Elizabeth's 1559 coronation royal entry in London. In a mixture of allegory and realistic historical events, Dekker in *The Whore of Babylon* (1607) looks back to the 1559 pageant in the opening dumb show. The recent commentary on Dekker by Cyrus Hoy helps sort out the strengths and weaknesses of this extraordinary play.[1] The dumb show includes figures of Time and Truth, symbolically costumed. When Titania (the Faerie Queene) enters, "Time *and* Truth *meete her, presenting a Booke to her, which (kissing it) shee receiues, and shewing it to those about her, they drawe out their swordes, (embracing* Truth,) *vowing to defend her and that booke.*"[2] This is an explicit echo of Elizabeth's meeting Time and Truth in the streets of London in Cheapside during her royal entry pageant. Truth presented to Elizabeth the "word of Truth," the English Bible; and Elizabeth "as soone as she had receiued the booke, kyssed it, and with both her handes held vp the same, and so laid it upon her brest, with great thanks to the citie therfore."[3] Heywood also seems to have this pageant episode in mind in the closing scene of his *If You Know Not Me, You Know Nobody,* part 1 (1605). Here the Lord Mayor presents a Bible to Elizabeth, whose final speech praises the value of this English Bible. She comments:

> We thanke you all; but first this Book I kisse:
> Thou art the way to honor; thou to blisse.
> An English Bible![4]

Examining Shakespeare's use of pageantry, Alice Venezky Griffin years ago found many examples of his indebtedness to pageants, seen obviously in something like the coronation processional for Anne Boleyn in *Henry VIII.*[5] I have argued that the restoration of Hermione in the final scene of *The Winter's Tale* may owe a debt to Anthony Munday's Lord Mayor's Show of 1611, *Chruso-thriambos.*[6] If one explores Middleton's drama further, I think one finds a series of interesting connections between *A Chaste Maid in Cheapside* and his 1613 Lord Mayor's Show, *The Triumphs of Truth.*[7] Other examples could be cited. The point is that there is a steady commerce between civic entertainments and the regular drama, that dramatists on occasion looked to pageants for material and techniques. Our compartmentalizing minds have separated drama into several neat categories; practicing dramatists were doubtless less tidy. Middleton seems to be one who moved freely among different dramatic forms.

I

Middleton's first excursion into civic pageantry was his involvement with the 1604 entry of James.[8] This magnificent show, performed in the streets of London on 15 March and financed by the citizens and guilds, is notable for several reasons. It marks the first documentable participation of major dramatists (in this case Jonson, Dekker, and Middleton) in the royal entry pageants; and it is the first such pageant for which there are extant drawings, the marvelous pictures by Stephen Harrison printed in his *Arches of Triumph* (1604). The seven triumphal arches, depicted by Harrison, illustrate how elaborate the pageant was. Dekker wrote most of the show, Jonson part, and Middleton one speech. In addition to the King's Men, who lined the route in the king's livery, two professional actors performed in the pageant: Edward Alleyn and William Bourne[9]— further testimony of the theatrical importance of this event.

Dekker devised the arch at the Conduit in Fleetstreet, but Middleton wrote the principal speech. This arch, referred to as the "New World" device, rivals the others in splendor. Prominent on the upper reaches of the structure is a "Globe of the world, . . . there seene to mooue, being fild with all the degrees, and states that are in the land" (*Dekker* 2:295). The principal figure is Astraea, "sitting aloft, as being newly descended from heauen, gloriously attirde" (p. 295). Dekker lets us know why he does not describe the figure in any detail: "Hauing tolde you that her name was *Iustice,* I hope you will not put mee to describe what properties she held in her hands, sithence euery painted cloath can informe you" (p. 295). Seated beneath Justice is *Arete* (Virtue) and "vnder her *Fortuna:* her foote treading on the Globe, that moude beneath her." Standing in a "darke and obscure place by her selfe" is *Envy,* "vnhandsomely attirde all in blacke, her haire of the same colour, filletted about with snakes." The Four Cardinal Virtues counter this menacing presence, and they are joined by the Four Kingdoms over which James holds sway: England, Scotland, Ireland, and France.

Surrounding the globe are the Four Elements, who "in proper shapes, (artificially and aptly expressing their qualities) vpon the approch of his Maiestie, went round in a proportionable and euen circle" (p. 296). They stood, Dekker says, "as if the Engine had beene held vp on the tops of their fingers." Stephen Harrison adds a detail not in Dekker: "And this Engine [the globe] was turned about by foure persons, representing the foure *Elements.*"[10] Inside the globe are figures representing "all the States of the land, from the Nobleman to the Ploughman" (p. 296). The dramatic action at the arch consists of the speech of Zeal, written by Middleton, and a song that follows.

Between the time of the pageant and Middleton's *No Wit, No Help,* two of Jonson's masques include a globe machine (during the same period none of the street pageants has globe devices). The examples below suggest that in his play Middleton depended on the 1604 civic pageant and not some

Figure 1. New World Arch in Fleetstreet. (From Stephen Harrison,
Arches of Triumph [London, 1604]; reproduced by permission
of the Folger Shakespeare Library.)

other entertainment. In the elaborate *Hymenaei* (1606) Jonson includes Hymen with some kind of globe: *"Here out of a microcosm, or globe, figuring man, with a kind of contentious music, issued forth the first masque, of eight men."*[11] (Alas, there are no Inigo Jones drawings for this masque.) The masquers represent the Four Humours and Four Affections, *"all gloriously attired."* Later in the text Jonson writes that the globe "stood, or rather hung (for no axle was seen to support it), and turning softly, discovered the first masque" (p. 96). Something like a globe is in the *Haddington Masque* (1608), associated here with Vulcan. A cliff parts, revealing *"an illustrious concave filled with an ample and glistering light, in which an artificial sphere was made of silver, . . . that turned perpetually"* (p. 115). From it emerge the masquers, representing the twelve signs of the zodiac.

The closest parallel to the 1604 arch is the device in Anthony Munday's 1615 mayoral pageant, *Metropolis Coronata,* perhaps owing its idea to the royal entry. Though coming after Middleton's play, it gives continuing testimony to the impact of the 1604 pageant. One chariot contains Royal Virtues and the arms of the Drapers; atop the chariot is a globe: "It is supported by the foure Elements, Water, Earth, Ayre, and Fire, as their figures and Emblemes doe aptly declare."[12] Somewhat curiously the chariot runs on seven wheels, representing, Munday assures us, the seven ages of man. Time "as Coach-man to the life of man," guides the whole chariot.

Middleton himself in the 1622 mayoral show, *The Triumphs of Honour and Virtue,* may be borrowing again from the royal entry, thereby demonstrating, I think, the lasting effect of this pageant on the dramatist. One of the devices in 1622 is the Globe of Honour, which suddenly bursts open into eight parts, revealing "eight bright personages most gloriously decked, representing (as it were) the inward man, the intentions of a virtuous and worthy breast."[13] In this speech Honour refers to these attributes as "beatitudes." At the four corners of the device are the Cardinal Virtues, also located on the arch in 1604.

Zeal's speech in the 1604 pageant ranges from interpretation of the arch to praise of and compliment to James. Why Middleton should have written the speech instead of Dekker is unclear. Certainly the speech gains added significance from being delivered by a member of Prince Henry's company (Bourne). Zeal first explains the meaning of the globe, which had presumably moved backward at the death of Elizabeth: "All States / . . . / Mooude opposite to Nature and to Peace" (*Dekker,* p. 297). But the presence of James has changed that situation: "Our Globe is drawne in a right line agen, / And now appeare new faces, and new men." The Elements, noted for being contentious, now move quietly at the peaceful arrival of James: "Earth not deuouring, Fire not defacing, / Water not drowning, and the Ayre not chasing." That the Elements actually turn the globe on the arch, as Harrison indicates, clinches the symbolism of peace and harmony.

If it can be shown—literally on the arch, one presumes—that the world turns smoothly now, then one naturally wants to explore the cause of this change. Zeal, referring to James as the "Mirror of times," gives the king credit, in part because he embodies the Four Virtues: "*Iustice* in causes, *Fortitude* gainst foes, / *Temp'rance* in spleene, and *Prudence* in all those" (p. 298). James's "immortall brightnes and true light" have blinded Envy; in despair Envy flings down her snakes, "Whilst her ranke teeth the glittering poisons chawe" (p. 298). Less graphic but no less significant, the Graces and Hours had removed from Elizabeth's path at Elvetham (1591) the stumbling blocks left by Envy and went before the queen, strewing the cleared path with flowers and singing a sweet song of six parts. Envy must be suppressed in the kingdom if peace is to prevail. James has also succeeded where others have failed, namely by uniting the kingdoms: "By *Brute* diuided, but by you alone, / All are againe vnited and made *One*" (p. 298). Munday pursues this theme in his 1605 Lord Mayor's Show, *The Triumphs of Re-United Britannia*.

At the close of his speech Zeal refers to himself both as a quality and as an actual figure. Zeal is an attribute of the people who

> . . . had harts
> Burning in holy Zeales immaculate fires,
> With quenchles Ardors, and vnstained desires,
> To see what they now see, your powerful Grace.   [p. 298]

Zeal then makes the connection between the quality and his own costume:

> These paynted flames and yellow burning Stripes,
> Vpon this roab, being but as showes and types,
> Of that great Zeale.

Since Dekker does not describe Zeal, Middleton's speech offers the only hint of the costuming of the character. Zeal closes: "So, with reuerberate shoutes our Globe shall ring, / The Musicks close being thus: God saue our king." Acknowledging Middleton's contribution, Dekker writes: "If there be any glorie to be won by writing these lynes, I do freelie bestow it (as his due) on *Thomas Middleton*, in whose braine they were begotten, though they were deliuered heere" (p. 299). Born in 1604, this stunning spectacle continued its life in Middleton's artistic memory. [14]

2

At first glance the earthy, ironic, vengeful goings-on in *No Wit,
No Help* may seem remote from the spectacle, harmony, and praise found
in a triumphal arch located in Fleetstreet in 1604. If the Prologue to the
play is a true reflection of the dramatist's intention, then the play and
pageant are doing radically different things. Recognizing the conflicting
interests and desires of those who come to the theater, Middleton says in
the final line of the Prologue: "We shall both make you sad and tickle
ye."[15] This statement also sketches the dual nature of the play, it being
both romantic and satiric. What happens in the play is that Middleton
uses the civic pageant but changes it, imitating it in part but incongru-
ously, thereby creating a burlesque of the pageant. The wedding masque
in Act IV is therefore an "antimasque" or "antipageant" because Middleton turns his source upside down, as we shall see.

Because the play is not among the best-known Jacobean comedies, I
offer a brief summary of its action. There are two centers of interest,
indeed two plots. One focuses on the Oliver Twilight family; this is the
romantic plot. The other, centering on Lady Goldenfleece and her suitors,
though on its face romantic, is in fact ironic and satiric. About ten years
before the time of the play, Lady Twilight and her six-year-old daughter
had been captured by pirates on the sea and held for ransom. Sir Oliver has
sent his son Philip Twilight and servant Savourwit to ransom them, but
they squander the money on a young woman (Grace) whom Philip marries
and brings home, claiming that she is the long-lost daughter and that the
mother is dead. We are not far into the play before we learn that Lady
Twilight is alive; indeed, she returns to London as early as Act II, and the
family reunites. One problem, though: she recognizes Grace as her
daughter; thus Philip has presumably committed incest. The issue resolves at the end of the play when Lady Goldenfleece reveals that Grace is
not the daughter because she has been swapped for Jane Sunset many years
earlier. Of such stuff romances are sometimes made. Four suitors—
Weatherwise, Pepperton, Overdon, and Sir Gilbert Lambston—pursue
Lady Goldenfleece, but they do not succeed. Instead, she falls in love with
an enemy, Mistress Low-water, disguised as a man. When Mistress Low-
water has achieved her goal, she reveals her identity and compels Lady
Goldenfleece to marry Beveril, the brother of Low-water. The "wit" of the
tale presumably refers to the machinations of Mistress Low-water. A tell-
tale sign that the second plot will not be one of typical romance is that
"Low-water" opposes "Goldenfleece"; immediately one senses that Middleton has turned the romance on its head, as indeed he has.

Several events lead up to the masque. One is the banquet scene, II.i, in which Weatherwise offers a *"banquet, and six of his tenants with the twelve signs* [of the zodiac], *made like banqueting-stuff"* (II.i.89, S.D.). This constitutes part of his appeal to Lady Goldenfleece; Middleton thus establishes early in the play the use of spectacle entertainment. There is much banter among the four suitors; here Mistress Low-water, disguised, enters also and sets in motion her strategy to win the Lady, beginning with exposing Sir Gilbert Lambston for the lecher that he is. Mistress Low-water for the moment successfully dampens the fire of zeal and lust in the suitors. If the four suitors can be seen as Elements, they embody that straining, contending nature, pulling in opposite selfish directions associated with the Elements. Only the unexpected arrival of Mistress Low-water as a suitor serves eventually to unite them.

By II.iii Lady Goldenfleece has made her choice. In full public display before the other suitors, she says: "Then pray be witness all of you; with this kiss / I choose him for my husband" (II.iii.186–87), and she kisses Mistress Low-water. In unison the suitors cry out: "A pox on't" (l. 188). Rejoicing in the new status as "husband," Mistress Low-water plans for entertainment: "I'll spare no cost for th' wedding, some device too, / To show our thankfulness to wit and fortune" (ll. 216–17). Unexpectedly, the one who becomes the deviser of the entertainment will be her brother Beveril, recently returned with Lady Twilight.

Having triumphed over her enemy, Mistress Low-water in an imaginative soliloquy characterizes her success and the failure of others:

> I feel a hand of mercy lift me up
> Out of a world of waters, and now sets me
> Upon a mountain, where the sun plays most,
> To cheer my heart ev'n as it dries my limbs.
> What deeps I see beneath me, in whose falls
> Many a nimble mortal toils,
> And scarce can feed himself! The streams of fortune
> 'Gainst which he tugs in vain, still beat him down
> And will not suffer him, past hand to mouth,
> To lift his arm to his posterity's blessing.   [II.iii.247–56]

In her metaphorical vision Mistress Low-water resembles the figure of Justice high above others on the triumphal arch with the globe and the workings of Fortune beneath. To change the image, she is the Zeal of righteous determination, cheered now by the sun's rays.

Concord reigns among the former suitors as they rally together in III.i to get revenge on Lady Goldenfleece and her new husband. "There's all our hands to a new bargain of friendship," says Weatherwise at the beginning of the scene (III.i.2). Sir Gilbert gives instructions: "Let each man look to his part now, and not feed / Upon one dish all four on's, like plain maltmen" (ll. 52–53). Beveril, as deviser of the wedding entertainment, enters; and we learn in his aside (ll. 181–93) that his fire of lust has been stirred by Lady Goldenfleece, now presumably unattainable. He blames Fortune: "Fortune, too remiss, / I suffer for thy slowness" (ll. 185–86). He reveals to the suitors his plan for the entertainment: " 'Tis only, gentlemen, the four elements / In liveliest forms, earth, water, air, and fire" (ll. 229–30).

The rationale for the Elements Beveril explains:

> . . . that whereas all those four
> Maintain a natural opposition
> And untruc'd war, the one against the other,
> To shame their ancient envies, they should see
> How well in two breasts all these do agree. [ll. 232–36]

What Beveril describes suits the would-be lovers rather precisely; not surprisingly they volunteer for the parts, after getting Beveril to accept the idea that Earth and Water need not be represented by women. Beveril says: "Earth, water, air, and fire, part 'em amongst you" (l. 291). They agree to determine who plays what because, in Sir Gilbert's words,

> . . . we're not factious,
> Or envy one another for best parts,
> Like quarrelling actors that have passionate fits. [ll. 300–302]

But in their asides they determine to disrupt the entertainment: Sir Gilbert: "We'll poison your device" (l. 307); Weatherwise: "We'll make your elements come limping home" (l. 309). They surrender their natural opposition not in response to the joy of the wedding, but rather in determination to turn the spectacle to their own vengeful purposes; together they will make the globe move in an opposite direction.

The Twilight family and the Goldenfleece clan gather for the wedding entertainment in IV.iii. As deviser Beveril offers Lady Goldenfleece an "abstract . . . of what's shown," commending it to her favor (l. 36). When the music sounds, the masque pageant begins. The stage directions are full:

> *Loud music a while. A thing like a globe opens of one side o'th' stage and flashes out Fire, then* Sir Gilbert, *that presents the part, issues forth with yellow hair and beard, intermingled with streaks like wild flames, a three-forked fire in's hand; and, at the same time,* Air [Weatherwise] *comes down hanging by a cloud, with a coat made like an almanac, all the twelve moons*

> *set in it, and the four quarters. . . . And from under the stage, at both ends,*
> *arises Water* [Master Overdon] *and Earth* [Master Pepperton], *two persons;*
> *Water with green flags upon his head standing up instead of hair, and a beard*
> *of the same, with a chain of pearl. Earth with a number of little things like*
> *trees, like a thick grove, upon his head, and a wedge of gold in his hand, his*
> *garment of a clay color.* [l. 41, S.D.]

Middleton has in mind the essential features of the triumphal arch of 1604: globe device and the Elements. He further echoes the pageant by having Sir Gilbert as Fire represent Zeal. Because the former suitors are bent on revenge, Sir Gilbert does not mention his role as Zeal; instead, he becomes the fire of lust—appropriate enough in this play. Beveril prompts him with what were to be the first words: "The flame of zeal—" (l. 41); but he responds: "The wicked fire of lust, / Does now spread heat through water, air, and dust" (ll. 41–42). Recognizing that something is amiss, Beveril offers another whispered phrase: " 'The wheel of time—' " (l. 43); but Sir Gilbert ignores him. The wheel of time recalls both the globe and the presence of Fortune in the 1604 pageant. It is clear to me that Middleton recalls that earlier street pageant and the Fleetstreet arch from which emanated visual and verbal praise of James.

Years later in a masque of 1635, *The Temple of Love,* Inigo Jones and William Davenant include an antimasque of spirits, who are in fact the Elements. Jones's drawings depict these spirits in costumes that are somewhat similar to Middleton's description of the Elements.[16] The description in the text of *The Temple of Love* also makes clear the relationship:

> *. . . the fiery spirits all in flames, and their vizards of a choleric complexion.*
> *The airy spirits with sanguine vizards, their garments and caps all of feathers.*
> *The watery spirits were all over wrought with scales and had fishes' heads and*
> *fins. The earthy spirits had their garments wrought all over with leafless trees*
> *and bushes, with serpents and other little animals here and there about them,*
> *and on their heads barren rocks.* [*Inigo Jones,* 2:602]

Though there are few pictures of the Elements in dramatic presentations, Middleton and Jones rely on a common tradition.

Playfully and ironically Middleton inverts the pageant arch by letting the four suitors destroy Beveril's purpose of praise. They make of the wedding masque an antimasque, rendering Beveril's intention ludicrous. In this way Middleton constructs a type of parody of the pageant arch, reminding one perhaps of that famous episode of the masque presented to James in 1606 at Theobalds in which the various figures, such as the Theological Graces, were stumblingly drunk. The suitors in *No Wit, No Help* of course deliberately set out to wreck the pageant show.

The Elements retain a moral function, but they direct their accusations at the presumed vices of Lady Goldenfleece. As he describes the process of lust and "inconstant heats," Gilbert as Fire drives home the application:

> Rich widows, . . .
> Are now so taken with loose Aretine flames
> Of nimble wantonness and high-fed pride,
> They marry now but the third part of husbands,
> Boys, smooth-fac'd catamites, to fulfill their bed,
> As if a woman should a woman wed. [ll. 64–70]

Several ironies operate here: though Fire has become Lust instead of Zeal, a strong strain of righteous indignation reminiscent of Zeal nevertheless exists; further, the most horrible thing that Fire can imagine, that a woman should marry a woman, is in fact what has happened in the marriage of Lady Goldenfleece to Mistress Low-water. The other Elements in turn attack the Lady. Weatherwise as Air notes the corruption of the air and finds a cause: "Yet some there are that be my chief polluters, / Widows that falsify their faith to suitors" (ll. 85–86). Master Overdon, representing Water, wonders what might happen

> If I sprinkled on the widow's cheeks
> A few cool drops to lay the guilty heat
> That flashes from her conscience to her face. [ll. 115–17]

Pepperton as Earth shifts the focus to the Lady's dead husband: "And as for earth, I'll stop his crane's throat full" (l. 141). At the end of these speeches, Sir Gilbert, still in his role as Fire, says: "And now to vex, 'gainst nature, form, rule, place, / See once four warring elements all embrace" (ll. 147–48). Contrasting with the Elements in the pageant who moved together to produce harmony, the Elements here forego their contentious natures in order to unite for the purpose of insulting Lady Goldenfleece; discord results. The "violence of their wrathfull hands" to which Zeal in Middleton's speech of 1604 refers prevails in the play.

These irascible Elements get their comeuppance in the play, however. Beveril, who had exited earlier, returns with other characters representing the Four Winds, appropriately costumed and dancing to the drum and fife. The Elements *"seem to give back and stand in amaze"* (l. 148, S.D.).[17] At the end of the dance the Winds *"shove off the disguises of the other four"*; the old suitors are thereby "discovered." Lady Goldenfleece dispenses with the Elements:

> Take Fire into the buttery, he has most need on't;
> Give Water some small beer, too good for him;

> Air, you may walk abroad like a fortune teller;
> But take down Earth and make him drink i'th' cellar. [ll. 167–70]

The wheel of Fortune turns against the Elements; for the moment Justice is victorious. Recognizing the suitors' motivation for what it is, Lady Goldenfleece asks: "Was this the plot now your poor envy works out?" (l. 165). Envy that stood "in a dark and obscure place by her selfe" on the triumphal arch is hard at work in the play. In the words of Zeal in 1604, these envious suitors with their "ranke teeth the glittering poisons chawe." They may succeed temporarily in poisoning the entertainment device, as Sir Gilbert promised in III.i, but they are left finally with only their poison.

The last act of *No Wit, No Help* is busy indeed as Mistress Low-water finally reveals her identity and thereby dissolves her marriage to Lady Goldenfleece; the Lady in turn discloses that Jane Sunset and Grace Twilight have been exchanged as infants, thereby making legitimate Philip Twilight's marriage to Grace. The closing act also echoes in several ways the masque entertainment of Act IV and therefore the pageant of 1604. Mistress Low-water, as "husband" to the Lady, refuses to go to bed with her, and eventually arranges events so that the Lady and Beveril are caught together in a compromising situation. At that point Mistress Low-water forcefully assumes the role of Zeal, full of righteous indignation and accusation. (Since there is considerable hypocrisy at work here, perhaps one could call her "Zeal-of-the-land Busy," anticipating Jonson's marvelous character.) She analyzes cause and effect:

> I knew by amorous sparks struck from their eyes,
> The fire would appear shortly in a blaze,
> And now it flames indeed. [V.i.183–85]

She seems to recall Sir Gilbert as Fire in the masque, who discoursed on "the wicked fire of lust." And she orders the couple, somewhat presumptuously, "Out of my house"; "Out of my doors!" (ll. 185, 194). To the Lady she says: "You shall not need oil'd hinges, privy passages, / Watchings, and whisperings; take him boldly to you" (ll. 245–46). The strategy works perfectly as Lady Goldenfleece claims Beveril for her own, suiting Low-water's intentions.

The Lady herself makes the connection to the problem of Envy:

> Let our parting
> Be full as charitable as our meeting was,
> That the pale envious world, glad of the food
> Of others' miseries, civil dissensions,
> And nuptial strifes, may not feed fat with ours. [ll. 203–7]

Is this not comparable to the force of Envy represented on the arch? That is, where there is discord in the kingdom, Envy prevails. Absent that kind of conflict, Envy is left to feed on herself. After Mistress Low-water gains Goldenfleece's treasure—the main point of her revenge—she reveals her identity. She reunites with her brother, Beveril, forgives Lady Gold-enfleece, and in turn is accepted by her. As Sir Gilbert aptly puts it: "Here's unity forever strangely wrought!" (l. 371). As Master Low-water joins this group, one thinks of the Four Elements, formerly at war, now in concord. Embodying at points what Zeal in the 1604 pageant refers to as "holy Zeales immaculate fires, / With quenchles Ardors, and vnstained desires" (2.298), Mistress Low-water has brought about Justice. Fortune has smiled on her as well. The joys of the people, spoken of by Zeal in 1604, are apparent in the play's comic ending. Sir Oliver Twilight's comment might serve as the motto for the end: "Clap hands, and joy go with you" (l. 455).

The presence of Zeal and Envy on the triumphal arch and the references to them in *No Wit, No Help* apparently remained in Middleton's mind as he came to write his first Lord Mayor's Show, *The Triumphs of Truth* (1613).[18] It is a spectacular and costly pageant and clearly Middleton's finest. Envy's primary purpose in the show is to accompany the chief vice of the pageant, Error. In terms more gruesome than those used to describe Envy in 1604, Middleton writes that she is

> eating of a humane heart, mounted on a *Rhenoceros*, attired in Red
> Silke, sutable to the bloudinesse of her manners, her left Pap bare,
> where a Snake fastens, her Armes halfe Naked, holding in her right
> hand a Dart tincted in bloud.[19]

Envy had, of course, been the principal vice in the previous year's mayoral pageant, Dekker's *Troia-Nova Triumphans*.[20]

Zeal functions in the 1613 entertainment mainly as the companion and champion of Truth. In the speech of 1604, Middleton's Zeal had described his robe as having painted flames and yellow burning stripes. The description in 1613 contains this but is more elaborate:

> *Zeale* the Champion of *Truth*, in a Garment of Flame-coloured Silke,
> with a bright haire on his head, from which shoot Fire-
> beames, . . . his Right hand holding a flaming Scourge, intimating
> thereby that as hee is the manifester of *Truth*, he is likewise the
> chastizer of *Ignorance* and *Error*.   [sig. B1ᵛ]

This enriched portrayal may be indebted to Ripa's *Iconologia*, where Zeal appears, having a scourge in the right hand in order to teach and correct the ignorant and castigate error.[21] Zeal drives back Error and his retinue in the pageant and warns them:

> *Bold Furies, backe, or with this scourge of Fire*
> *Whence sparkles out Religious chast-desire*
> *Ile whip you downe to darknesse.*   [sig. B3ᵛ]

Zeal's last action at the close of the pageant is the most dramatic and spectacular. With the permission of Truth, Zeal shoots flames from his head which strike the Chariot of Error, setting "it on Fire, and all the Beasts that are ioynde to it" (sig. D2ᵛ). The fire of Zeal is no longer merely a metaphor.

Middleton himself possessed some zeal for his own original contribution to the 1604 royal entry; if what I have demonstrated is valid, he returned several times to it. What we see in *No Wit, No Help* and subsequent Lord Mayor's Shows is Middleton's actively re-presenting the Fleetstreet arch of 1604, this device that lingered so clearly in his memory. My investigation into Middleton's use of the pageant in *No Wit, No Help* illustrates also a potentially rich area of continued study: the indebtedness of Middleton and other dramatists to civic pageants. Middleton's example demonstrates that the insubstantial pageants did not fade but instead left behind vivid images persisting in the minds of artists. From the example of *No Wit, No Help,* one sees an important issue of artistic creation: the nature and use of sources. What Middleton does with his source, in this case his own earlier pageant drama, illuminates the creative process as he imitates yet parodies, appropriates yet discards. The motto for Middleton, and doubtless for many other writers, is: look into the memory and write.

Notes

1. Cyrus Hoy, *Introduction, Notes, and Commentaries to Texts in "The Dramatic Works of Thomas Dekker"* (Cambridge: Cambridge University Press, 1980), 2:300–310.

2. Thomas Dekker, *The Dramatic Works of Thomas Dekker,* ed. Fredson Bowers (Cambridge: Cambridge University Press, 1955), 2:500. All quotations from Dekker will be from this edition.

3. *The Quenes Maiesties Passage Through the Citie of London,* ed. James M. Osborn (New Haven, Conn.: Yale University Press, 1960), pp. 48–49.

4. Thomas Heywood, *The Dramatic Works of Thomas Heywood,* ed. R. H. Shepherd (1874; rpt. ed., New York: Russell and Russell, 1964), 1:246.

5. Alice S. Venezky [Griffin], *Pageantry on the Shakespearean Stage* (New York: Twayne, 1951).

6. David M. Bergeron, "The Restoration of Hermione in *The Winter's Tale,*" in *Shakespeare's Romances Reconsidered,* ed. Carol Kay and Henry Jacobs (Lincoln: University of Nebraska Press, 1978), pp. 125–33.

7. See my essay "Middleton's Moral Landscape: *A Chaste Maid in Cheapside* and *The Triumphs of Truth,*" in *"Accompanying the Players": Essays Celebrating Thomas Middleton, 1580–1980,* ed. Kenneth Friedenreich (New York: AMS Press, 1983), pp. 133–46.

8. For fuller discussion of his pageant career, see my *English Civic Pageantry 1558–1642* (Columbia: University of South Carolina Press, 1971), pp. 179–200. Also see R. C. Bald, "Middleton's Civic Employments," *Modern Philology* 31 (1933): 65–78.

9. For more details about the pageant see my discussion in *English Civic Pageantry,* pp. 71–89. Also see my "Actors in English Civic Pageants," *Renaissance Papers* 1972 (1973): 17–28. For recent discussion of an eye-witness account of the pageant, see my "Gilbert Dugdale and the Royal Entry of James I (1604)," *Journal of Medieval and Renaissance Studies* 13 (1983): 111–25.

10. Stephen Harrison, *Arches of Triumph* (London, 1604), sig. H1.

11. *Ben Jonson: The Complete Masques,* ed. Stephen Orgel (New Haven, Conn.: Yale University Press, 1969), p. 79. All quotations are from Orgel's edition.

12. Anthony Munday, *Metropolis Coronata* (London, 1615), sig. B4.

13. Thomas Middleton, *The Works of Thomas Middleton,* ed. A. H. Bullen (Boston: Houghton, Mifflin, 1886), 7:365.

14. Though it is not fashionable these days to say so, I think that Shakespeare in Prospero's speech recalls the 1604 civic pageant when he refers to "The cloud-capped tow'rs, the gorgeous palaces, / The solemn temples, the great globe itself, / Yea, all which it inherit" (IV.i.152–54). *The Complete Pelican Shakespeare,* ed. Alfred Harbage (New York: Penguin, 1969).

15. Thomas Middleton, *No Wit, No Help like a Woman's,* ed. Lowell E. Johnson (Lincoln: University of Nebraska Press, 1976). All quotations are from this Regents Renaissance Drama edition.

16. See the drawings in Stephen Orgel and Roy Strong, *Inigo Jones: The Theatre of the Stuart Court* (Berkeley and Los Angeles: University of California Press, 1973), 2:618–21. The quotation from the masque is from this edition.

17. In *A Handbook of Renaissance Meteorology* (Durham, N.C.: Duke University Press, 1960) S. K. Heninger, Jr., points out the hierarchy of the Elements: Fire, Air, Water, and Earth, based on Renaissance texts, which are modeled on the Aristotelian arrangement (p. 37). One notes that Middleton follows this order when the masquers present themselves. In III.i, Beveril enumerates the Elements in ascending order: "the four elements / In liveliest forms, earth, water, air, and fire" (ll. 229–30); he follows the same order in l. 291. Middleton carefully preserves the traditional hierarchical order of the Elements. Heninger also explores the connection of the Elements and the Winds (esp. pp. 110–14). Middleton here also follows a convention of Renaissance thought. Heninger writes: "The char-

acter of each cardinal wind [there were four] was fundamentally defined by an identification with both an Element and its corresponding humor: Boreas with Earth and black bile, Auster with Air and blood, Eurus with Fire and yellow bile, and Favonius with Water and phlegm" (pp. 110–12).

18. For discussion of this pageant, see my *English Civic Pageantry*, pp. 179–86.

19. Thomas Middleton, *The Triumphs of Truth* (London, 1613), sig. B2. All quotations for this pageant are from this text.

20. See my *English Civic Pageantry*, pp. 163–70.

21. Cesare Ripa, *Iconologia*, facsimile ed. of the 1603 text, introd. Erna Mandowsky (New York: Georg Olms, 1970), p. 522.

Part Two

Richard II's "Sumptuous Pageants" and the Idea of the Civic Triumph

Gordon Kipling

Long before Shakespeare described him as a king of "tradition, form, and ceremonious duty" (III.ii.173), Richard II was famous for his love of pageantry. Froissart, for example, tells the story of Richard's so envying the "splendid feasts and entertainment" with which the French celebrated Queen Isabella's state entry into Paris that he immediately ordered a grand tournament to rival and surpass the "magnificence and pompe" of the Parisian festival.[1] And when the city of London sought a means to regain its liberties—Richard had taken them away in a dispute over a loan—it could think of no more effective way to dramatize its repentance than to stage a pageant: "The citizens . . . did not onelie prepare themselues to meet him, and to present him with gifts in most liberall manner; but also to adorne, decke, and trim their citie with sumptuous pageants, rich hangings, and other gorgeous furniture, in all points like as is vsed at anie coronation."[2]

Indeed, the very association of "sumptuous pageants" with coronation processions, which Holinshed plainly thinks of as traditional in this passage, was an innovation of Richard's reign. By the same token, the origin and first flowering of the great mystery cycles—both at London and in the provinces—has always been associated with Richard's reign. While the king himself was thus patronizing the great London cycle, the Clerkenwell "play of the Passion of our Lord and the Creation of the World," York, Beverley, and Coventry were experiencing the first recorded performances of their respective cycles.[3] Whether we look to the tournament, the royal entry, or the pageant play, in short, Richard's reign witnessed an extraordinary efflorescence of civic pageantry and courtly spectacle.

In our attempts to account for this phenomenon, the civic triumph has always played a particularly prominent role. Perhaps the most extensively documented of all these forms of "sumptuous pageants," civic triumphs graced no less than three of the grand occasions of Richard's reign: his own coronation (1377), that of his first queen, Anne of Bohemia (1382), and his reconciliation with the city of London (1392). Not only does Richard's coronation triumph mark the earliest recorded appearance of actors and pageantry at a royal entry anywhere in Europe, but the three triumphs accorded Richard's reign also exceed in number those staged in London for any other reign, not excepting Henry VIII with his six wives.[4] To such earlier scholars as E. K. Chambers and Robert Withington, on the one hand, all this dramatic activity in general suggested the workings of a Darwinian providence and the civic triumph served as their Galapagos thrush. In the pageants of the royal entry appeared the obvious evolutionary descendant of earlier species: the miracle play, trade symbolism, the tournament, and the court of love.[5] Glynne Wickham, on the other hand—noting that the same guilds staged both the mystery cycles and civic triumphs and observing that the first records of both forms coincide exactly—uses the well-documented history of the royal entry to reconstruct the sparsely documented origins of the mystery cycles. Hence, as the civic triumph moves from its first short, mimetic performance on a single pageant stage in 1377 to more elaborate playlets, complete with Latin speeches, in 1392, to still more elaborate civic triumphs with vernacular speeches at the beginning of the fifteenth century, so we can reconstruct the largely undocumented, but presumably parallel, development of the mystery cycles from brief, mimetic performances with Latin speeches to elaborate vernacular cycles.[6]

However appealing, both theories present important difficulties. On the one hand, the civic triumph can hardly have evolved from the miracle play if both forms appeared at exactly the same time. On the other hand, the civic triumph can hardly have paralleled the development of the mystery cycles from brief, mimetic performances to more elaborate vernacular plays if, as now seems the case, actors in civic triumphs did not deliver speeches at all until 1445, and if these speeches never amounted to more than brief monologues in the entire history of the form.[7] The more we examine the records, the more the civic triumph seems always to have resisted full dramatic development while the mystery cycles seem to have experienced an early and determined dramatic elaboration.

Above all, the two forms of pageantry seem to aim at such disparate purposes that it is hard to see why they should be related at all. The mystery cycles, to be sure, have always seemed to aspire to high purpose:

the reenactment of the history of a shared Christian faith. The civic triumph, however, has always seemed to reflect a trivial one: as George Kernodle puts it, these shows consist merely of "general ornament and flattery," one means among many by which medieval citizens might honor or cajole their prince.[8] In this respect, the show's origin in the reign of Richard II has doubly reinforced this impression. Given Richard's reputation for empty pomp and ceremonial posturing, it has been easy to see these shows as the reflection of the vanity of Shakespeare's "skipping king." But we cannot dispose of the question of purpose so easily. Londoners had many ways of honoring and cajoling their princes, after all. If this method proved particularly successful, why did they resort to it so infrequently? Kings often entered their cities in style, but with the exception of Richard alone, London never received any king with pageantry more than once in his reign.[9] If, on the contrary, such shows fulfilled no useful purpose, why were they almost inevitably repeated with each new reign? And why did they become ever more elaborate, more expensive, more popular? Clearly, only when we understand better the purposes that led to the origin of the civic triumph will we be in a position to understand better the dramatic impulse that produced not only the royal entry, but also the mystery plays and all those other forms of "sumptuous pageants" that so characterized the Tudor era.

Richard II's reconciliation triumph (1392) neatly illustrates the limitations of our current thinking and suggests new approaches that may help explain the artistry and purposes of these shows. The earliest English royal entry to employ multiple pageants and to leave detailed descriptive records, Richard II's reconciliation triumph serves particularly well for this purpose.[10] It uses many of the pageants, symbols, and ceremonies that characterize these shows throughout northern Europe for the next 150 years. In addition, Richard Maydiston's lengthy commentary can help us explain the meaning and purpose of the show from the viewpoint of a contemporary witness. Finally, because it stands among the first of these shows, not only in England but in all northern Europe, it can perhaps suggest reasons for the civic triumph not only as an English, but also as a European, institution.

Having been deprived of its ancient rights and liberties, suffered the deposition and imprisonment of its mayor and sheriffs, and seen the courts removed to York—all because it had denied the king a thousand-pound loan that he deemed his by feudal right—London dramatized its capitulation by means of the most extensive civic triumph yet attempted in England.[11] The city stationed at least four pageants along the route of the king's procession.[12] Carefully coordinated in theme, the pageants each depicted a celestial place populated by angels and saints. The first of the series, for example, stood atop the Great Conduit in Cheapside and consisted of a choir of singers costumed to look like one of the heavenly orders of angels. [13] The conduit miraculously ran wine instead of water, and the angels both sang and scattered pieces of gold. The second pageant, the most technically ambitious of the series, took the form of a high, castlelike tower hung on ropes above the street. From the tower a youth and a maiden, dressed as angels, descended to the street "enclosed in clouds . . . floating down in the air." The youth offered a golden chalice of wine to Richard while the maiden delivered a pair of golden crowns to the king and queen. They then miraculously reascended to their celestial tower. At the next station, a pageant throne fixed to the Little Conduit and surrounded by three circles of angels of both sexes, symbolized three more angelic orders in attendance before the throne of the Almighty. God himself, played by a youth dressed in snow-white robes, sat above these heavenly hierarchies, a light beaming like the sun shining upon him. The three circles of angels sang and played musical instruments so sweetly, according to Maydiston, that the watchers were ravished with the beauty of it. Finally, a pageant set above Temple Bar depicted John the Baptist preaching in a wilderness teeming with a great variety of wild beasts and an equally large catalogue of trees. The beasts ran about, fighting, biting, leaping "as savage beasts do in the desolate forest." Saint John stood in the midst, dramatically pointing: *Agnus et Ecce Dei.* An angel descended from the high roof above this pageant to the street, bringing two golden altarpieces with images of the Crucifixion upon them so that the king and queen might contemplate Christ's mercy and his forbearance toward his enemies.

Modern commentary has so far approached the meaning and purpose of these extraordinary pageants only through an antiquarian perspective of trade symbolism and of "influences" from elsewhere. [14] Chambers, for instance, thinks that the pageant of John the Baptist may reflect "the regular contemporary drama" as such a scene "pretty obviously came from the miracle-plays." [15] Withington, on the other hand, noting that a Grocer was mayor in 1392, thinks that trade symbolism must account for the trees and animals of the same pageant, and he further suggests that the second pageant, the celestial tower hung on ropes above the street, "may show a chivalric influence" because such castles "came from the 'Court of Love' literature, possibly by way of the tournament." [16] George Unwin similarly detects the Skinners' hands in the Saint John pageant because of the presence of wild beasts. [17] Wickham does grant the show a "firm didactic intention," but otherwise he is content to follow Withington and

Unwin, differing in detail but not in substance. He would thus assign "the choice of St. John as the governing figure" in the last pageant to the Merchant Taylors because "Richard had himself become an honorary member of that company in 1385 and in 1392 had granted them their second charter recognizing St. John the Baptist as their patron saint."[18] On the whole, discussion of these pageants remains where Withington's summation left it in 1918: "By 1392 we have a pageant which shows the influence of the miracle-play; which combines elements of trade-symbolism and tournament, and which includes appropriate speeches."[19]

From the viewpoint of the show's meaning and purpose, however, such hypotheses fail to account for the pageants. Take John the Baptist as a trade symbol, for example. London trade-symbol pageants almost always take the form of portable structures carried in procession. The Fishmongers' set of four golden sturgeons and three silver salmons, which they carried in procession to celebrate Edward I's victory at Falkirk (1298), illustrates this type, and several sixteenth-century mayors marched to their inaugurations behind portable pageants symbolic of their guilds.[20] Conceivably, guilds might also gather about a stationary pageant symbolic of their trade to witness a king's royal entry. In either case, the pageant serves as an identifying totem, a mascot, for the guild. But in 1392, as Maydiston points out, the guilds marched in the royal procession past stationary pageants. They identified themselves not with pageantry but with splendidly distinctive liveries.[21] The Saint John pageant, therefore, could not serve as a trade symbol in the usual sense, and the exceptional senses that one might imagine all seem frivolous: An advertisement for groceries? A boast of the glory of Merchant Taylors? In the end, this hypothesis fails because it confuses guild participation with symbolic meaning. We may rightly suspect, in other words, that the Skinners supplied pelts from which to fashion Saint John's wild beasts without concluding that the pageant symbolized the Skinners' trade.[22]

If the trade-symbol hypothesis seems barren, the various "influence" hypotheses seem at first more promising. By explaining the suspended tower pageant with its ingenious machinery of ascending and descending angels as an example of miracle-play or Court-of-Love influence, we avoid the question of meaning altogether. We can claim, in effect, that such shows "represented" nothing more than the desire of the city to receive its prince with splendor—with "general ornament and flattery"—and that any pageant subject would serve as well as any other provided it made a suitably magnificent show. But if the subject matter was irrelevant, why do we find such an impressive coordination of pageant subjects in the series, each pageant reflecting a celestial theme? Above all, the thematic consistency of these pageants, as we shall see, belies the suggestion that they are the haphazard products of a trade symbol here, a warmed-over miracle play there, and a tournament castle farther on. Rather, such consistency suggests the presence of a governing scheme, however simple or complex.

The city designed its pageantry, indeed, according to a thoughtful and consistent scheme traditional in its iconography and familiar throughout Christian Europe. The four pageants are not merely "celestial" or "heavenly," but seek to identify London as a type of New Jerusalem. Long before European cities began decorating their streets with pageantry, they imagined themselves transformed into another Zion, a celestial Jerusalem, whenever a king made his ceremonial entry.[23] A contemporary London chronicler, for example, uses this traditional metaphor in describing the reception of Edward II and Queen Isabella in 1308: "Then was London seen ornamented with jewels like New Jerusalem."[24] Not surprisingly, Maydiston finds himself relying upon this traditional image in describing how colorful tapestries hung along the parade route turned the city into "new heaven."[25]

Given the traditional nature of this metaphor, it was perhaps inevitable that the first known civic triumph should attempt to see Richard's entry into London for his coronation as a prefiguration of his soul's future entry into the Celestial Jerusalem. When, as a boy of eleven, he entered London for the first time as king, Richard thus found the Great Conduit transfigured as the City of Heaven. Angels stood atop the four towers scattering gold leaves in his path and golden florins upon his person. A sign of the transformed city, wine spouted miraculously from the heavenly castle where water customarily had run from the earthly conduit. Angels offer him cups of the wine, an act portentous of the Eucharist. Atop the dome between the four celestial towers, a mechanical golden angel bows down to the king, offering him a heavenly crown.[26] So successful was this first attempt, indeed, that a second, similar castle greeted the coronation triumph of Anne of Bohemia (1382), and thereafter the heavenly castle became the single most popular pageant structure in the repertoire of the civic triumph—so much so that we find one of Henry VII's Household Ordinances (1494) routinely calling for "a sight with angelles singing" to be erected upon each of the city conduits "when a queen should next be received into London."[27]

In seeking once again to transform this traditional metaphor into visual imagery for the 1392 civic triumph, London based its pageants specifically upon Saint John's Apocalyptic description of the New Jerusalem: "And I John saw the holy city, the new Jerusalem, coming down out of heaven from God, prepared as a bride adorned for her husband. And I heard a great voice from the throne saying: Behold, the tabernacle of God with men, and he will dwell with them. And they shall be his people; and God himself with them shall be their God."[28] In this vein, a band of musical angels first appear atop the Great Conduit to welcome Richard to the holy city. The king next encounters the high tower of New Jerusalem itself. Hung upon ropes above the streets and populated by angels, the heavenly castle comes "down out of heaven" just as Saint John had seen the holy city in his dream. Having beheld the "tabernacle of God," Richard next arrives before the Almighty's throne itself, as the Evangelist's vision predicts. There God sits in glory, amidst his court of angels, having come to "dwell with men."

The descriptive imagery, formal speeches, and dramatic action associated with the pageants further emphasize and define this Apocalyptic metaphor. Both Maydiston and the city's "custos," for example, repeatedly refer to Richard as a "bridegroom" (*sponsus*) and to London, traditionally known as "the King's Chamber," as Richard's "bridal chamber" (*thalamus*). "Let not the bridegroom," begs the custos in a typical example, "hate the bridal chamber he has always loved."[29] This application of the imagery of Canticles to *sponsus* Richard and *sponsa* London appropriately reflects Saint John's own description of the holy city as "a bride adorned for her husband." So in like manner Richard himself is made to echo the Apocalyptic speech that God makes from the throne of the holy city: the citizens of London, he promises, "will now be my people and I shall henceforth be king to them."[30] When angels descend from the tower of New Jerusalem to bring golden crowns to Richard and Anne, the custos is quick to point out that these are but the material types of the crowns of glory worn by the faithful in the holy city: "May He that gives you the diadems of the terrestrial kingdom grant you also the eternal heavenly kingdom."[31] The city is transformed: angels and spirits appear among the earthly citizens; they cense the procession, spread the streets with flowers, sing psalms, and fill the air with musical harmonies. Even as angels become citizens, so citizens become angelic; the guilds marshal themselves so splendidly that "whoever should witness these squadrons . . . would not doubt that he was seeing the forms of an angelic order."[32] Wine runs in the conduits where water formerly ran. Like Saint John, Richard sees "new heaven and a new earth. For the first heaven and the first earth was gone" (Apocalypse 21:1).

If London progressively takes the form of the New Jerusalem, Richard even more emphatically stands revealed as a type of Christ—the Anointed One, Heavenly Spouse, Savior, and Lord. Angels descend to crown him;

water turns to wine at his approach; for him is reserved the golden Eucharistic chalice sent down from heaven. As savior, Richard redeems and pardons—first a banished murderer who throws himself before the king's horse as the procession is about to enter the city,[33] later the city itself as the mayor and sheriffs stand before his judgment throne repenting their offenses. Indeed, the pageantry does not merely compare Richard to Christ. Rather, it stages Richard's epiphany as a type of Christ. All the pageants make this point generally whenever angels descend to welcome the Beloved of God, but the last pageant at Temple Bar takes Richard's epiphany as its particular theme. In this final pageant, John the Baptist preaching in the wilderness recognizes the Savior in Richard and proclaims his epiphany to all: Behold the Lamb of God. Further, the city pairs this manifestation of Richard's Christlikeness with a reminder of Christ's forbearance and humility. An angel descends from heaven to bring Richard a pair of golden altarpieces. The image of the Crucifixion depicted on them expresses the city's hope that Richard will "be mindful of Christ's death," that he will "be sparing of the ignorant even as that Heavenly King though unavenged was always forbearing to his enemies."[34] Having once rejected its *sponsus,* the city now longs for the return of the Lamb to the holy city, but it prays for a coming in humility and forbearance rather than a coming in majesty and judgment.

As these dramatic metaphors suggest, these pageants lie on the very frontier between drama and ritual. Considered as drama, they establish a complex relationship between actors "on stage," Richard himself, and the citizens who gather round to watch. As "divertissements" or street decoration, they may indeed serve to entertain and impress the king. At this level, perhaps, Richard serves only as the most important of all the watchers who come to be entertained by the show or instructed by the custos's explanatory speeches. But the pageants also include the king in a mimetic action defined by the actors and scenery: Richard enters the New Jerusalem and experiences an epiphany. From this point of view, Richard is made to play the protagonist's role in a drama witnessed by the citizens.[35] But the role he plays borders on ritual in that the mimetic action he performs in the drama visibly symbolizes an invisible "spiritual" action performed in reality. Like Christ at the Second Coming, Richard comes to his kingdom for the second time. He had already been received at his first coming by citizens dressed as angels, and his epiphany had then been declared by a golden angel who bowed down from heaven to offer him his crown. But his people have broken faith with their lord. How now will he come to them again? With mercy, or with a terrible last judgment? Thanks to the pageantry, he plays forgiving bridegroom of an errant but penitent spouse, and he takes his now-faithful city to himself again. They shall henceforth be his people, he shall be their king, and he will dwell with them forever.

In characterizing Richard's coming to his kingdom as a type of Christ's coming to the New Jerusalem, this civic triumph takes its pageant subjects from the liturgy of Advent, a season specifically set aside by the church both to celebrate Christ's first coming in mercy and humility and to prepare for his Second Coming in majesty and judgment.[36] The idea of Advent unites the descent of the New Jerusalem of the first three pageants with John the Baptist's preaching in the last. The city's pageants in fact manipulate the two aspects of the Advent idea to insure mercy for themselves rather than judgment. In its first three pageants, the city grants Richard his celestial advent in majesty and glory as he comes to judge his errant people. But in the last pageant, Richard encounters John the Baptist, the "forerunner of Christ" and the king's "special patron saint."[37] This is no mere trade pageant. Founded upon the very scriptural passage which the Sarum missal prescribes for the fourth Sunday of Advent (John 1:19ff.), it depicts Saint John as "the voice of one crying in the wilderness, 'make straight the way of the Lord.'" Standing in the wilderness of the Old Law, he points to the Lamb of God who comes to save the world.[38] Further, he presents Richard with an image of the Crucifixion, Christ's consummate example of the New Law of self-sacrifice and love. The city substitutes, in short, the Advent of Redemption for the Advent of Judgment. This tactic, in fact, follows the outline of the Sarum Advent liturgy precisely in that the Gospel readings of the second Sunday in Advent are devoted to the Second Coming, while those of the third and fourth Sundays center upon John the Baptist's preaching. Apparently the strategy proved politically successful as well as liturgically accurate—in Maydiston's highly idealized account at least—for the monkish poet tells us that this image of the first Advent extinguished the righteous anger characteristic of the second: "If there was aught of anger in the King, it was immediately extinguished to nothing with the contemplation of this exhibit."[39]

Although the devisers of Richard's civic triumph proved themselves extraordinarily skillful in their use of these themes, their decision to turn to the Advent liturgy of the church for inspiration would not have struck contemporaries as remarkable in the least. As a general rule, the liturgy of Christ's Advent, which extended from the first week of Advent to the last Sunday in Epiphany,[40] provided the civic triumph with its most prominent idea. Throughout the observance of the Advent season, the liturgy insisted in linking the coming and manifestation of Christ with the ceremonial receptions of princes. This linkage partly derives from the coincidence that the technical terms for princely receptions—*adventus, parousia,* and *epiphany*—became the names of liturgical concepts as well. Readers of the Vulgate found, for example, the Second Coming described in precisely the same language usually reserved for the receptions of Roman emperors: *Adventus Filii hominis* refers in the Vulgate to the Second Coming; *Adventus Augusti Judaeae* reads the inscription of a typical medallion struck to commemorate the reception of a Roman Emperor.[41] Although the *adventus* procession resembled the triumph in some respects, the *adventus* (*parousia* and *epiphany* were synonymous terms[42]) reception was not a reward for military victory. Rather, the *adventus* marked the arrival of a Roman emperor to one of his subjects' cities, where he was received with due enthusiasm and ceremonially accepted as sovereign lord. As Sabine MacCormack points out, "such rulers were generally regarded as in some sense divine, and were welcomed as saviours, benefactors and lords." Consequently, "when the emperor arrived, he could be welcomed as a god; this added religious overtones to the *adventus* ceremony, or made it a religious event in itself."[43] In describing Christ's Palm Sunday Entry into Jerusalem as just such a ceremonial reception, the Gospels are being literally accurate. Since the greetings, shouts of welcome, and palm branches all form part of the usual ritual of receiving Hellenistic rulers and Roman emperors as deities, they are doubly appropriate for the *adventus* of Christ, which marks the public recognition—the *epiphany*—of the Savior's divinity. So closely linked were these concepts, in fact, that medieval artists conventionally borrowed, as Gertrud Schiller puts it, "the Roman image of the imperial *adventus*" for "the pictorial schema of the Entry into Jerusalem."[44]

But in deliberately associating Christ's Advent—whether his approaching Nativity or his Second Coming—with the ceremonial of princely receptions, the liturgy developed this linkage of ideas in a different direction: the ceremonial of royal reception became the church's most characteristic metaphor for Advent. From the earliest times, the Roman liturgy prescribed Matthew's account of the Palm Sunday *adventus* as an Advent lesson. At first sight, this reading seems badly misplaced since it belongs more obviously to the Passiontide sequence. Because the liturgy deliberately forces the association of the *adventus* ceremony and the celebration of Advent, however, the lesson makes excellent sense in context. The liturgy, in short, envisions the coming of Christ to the world in terms of the coming of a king to a city. The cry used by the Children of Israel to receive Jesus into Jerusalem on Palm Sunday—*Benedictus qui venit in nomine domini*—now serves to mark Jesus' Advent, his coming into the world. To support this idea, the liturgy further specifies a number of readings, introits, antiphons, and offertory hymns for Advent to suggest further the same idea of royal *adventus*. The *Tollite Portas*, for example, which imagines the King of Glory entering a city, does double service as a gradual psalm and an offertory hymn ("Lift up your gates, O ye princes: and be ye lifted up, O eternal gates, and the King of Glory shall enter in," Psalm 23).[45] So Luke's account of the Second Coming, described as a celestial *adventus* (21:25–33), serves as the Gospel for the second Sunday. An offertory hymn likewise calls upon the people of the holy city to rejoice at the reception of their Savior: *Exsulta satis, filia Sion praedica, filia Jerusalem: ecce Rex tuus venit tibi sanctus et salvator* ("Rejoice greatly, O daughter of Sion, Shout for Joy, O daughter of Jerusalem; behold thy King will come to thee, the holy and Saviour," Zacharias 9:9). By the late Middle Ages, the liturgy had so far succeeded in imposing this metaphor that we find a popular theologian like Bromyard advising his readers to prepare themselves for Advent in the same manner that a city prepares itself for a royal *adventus*: "For with the coming of the king the streets are cleaned and whatever should offend his sight is carried away; the homes are decorated and hung with tapestries and hangings; the citizens are dressed up. Therefore put away sins from the street of the mind: let the house of the mind be adorned and decorated with virtues; and let hangings be hung upon the backs of the poor."[46]

This liturgical metaphor exerted a powerful influence over late medieval conceptions of the civic triumph. Above all, it insured that the idea of Advent, rather than the example of Christ's Palm Sunday *adventus*, would determine the ceremonial for the receptions of medieval princes. Since the Entry into Jerusalem placed, as it were, the seal of Christ's own approval upon the classical ceremonial, we might reasonably expect Christian Europe to model its princely receptions upon biblical example. Indeed, Ernst Kantorowicz, in a brilliant study unaccountably neglected by historians of the stage, argues just this point: "the Entry into Jerusalem on Palm Sunday was the prototype after which the receptions of mediaeval princes were modelled."[47] The weight of evidence, however, suggests otherwise. In fact, the fathers of the church—and medieval liturgists after them—persistently represented the Entry into Jerusalem as but an earthly prefiguration of Christ's ascension, which they see as a celestial *adventus:*

> as comparing things spiritual with spiritual, . . . if you long with your every desire to see that day, when Christ the Lord shall be received in the heavenly Jerusalem, the Head with all the members, bearing the triumphs of His victory, not now amidst the applause of popular crowds, but angelic powers, the people of both covenants crying aloud

on every side, "Blessed is He that cometh in the Name of the Lord;" if,
I say, in the procession you have considered wither you must hasten,
learn in the Passion the way by which you must go.[48]

Consequently, the streets of the city which the medieval prince enters are
more often decorated to resemble "the New Jerusalem"—as the London
streets seemed to do for Edward II—than antique Jerusalem. Richard II's
reconciliation triumph thus illustrates this typical medieval pattern: rec-
ollections of the First Coming (John the Baptist) and the Second Coming
(the descent of the New Jerusalem) predominate over momentary recollec-
tions of Passiontide (the Crucifixion altarpieces). According to one designer and theorist of such shows, "the very form of these receptions" appeared
not in the Palm Sunday lesson itself but rather in Psalm 67, where "the
glory of the entry of Jesus Christ into heaven" was described as if it were
"the entry of a sovereign into one of the principal cities of his realm." By
contrast, the Palm Sunday *adventus* seemed but an example of this type, an
example, moreover, which Christ deliberately modified in order to fulfill
Advent prophecies. Jesus thus entered Jerusalem "in order to accomplish
what the prophets had predicted concerning His coming to the world,"
and his entry into Jerusalem upon a donkey "conformed to the state of
humiliation that he had chosen for His first Advent."[49]

The idea of Advent suited the civic triumph so universally because it
defined exactly the nature of the occasion which these shows were designed to celebrate. The king might enter a city in state at any time; civic
triumphs, however, were usually reserved for one particular type of royal
entry. In essence, they were inaugural shows. In capital cities they took
place immediately before or after the coronation itself. In other major
cities the shows took place upon the prince's first official appearance there
as sovereign, even if his arrival might be delayed for a considerable time.
As such, civic triumphs marked the king's first advent; they celebrated his
coming to his kingdom. They continued into medieval times the custom
of the imperial *adventus*. Newly consecrated with the holy balm, the
prince comes to his city manifest for the first time as the Lord's anointed, a
savior to his people. Reflecting this symbolism, civic triumphs may appropriately emphasize Epiphany imagery. But the sovereign also comes
wearing his crown and bearing the orb and scepter. Like the risen Christ,
he comes also in majesty and glory. If the occasion especially warrants it,
therefore, the pageantry may instead emphasize the imagery of the Second
Coming. Whichever strategy they adopted, however, these shows rarely
ignored their inaugural function. Second civic triumphs remained com-
paratively rare; third ones were almost unheard of.[50]

When second advents, like that of Richard II's reconciliation triumph, do occur, they often do so under circumstances that emphasize the primarily inaugural function of the show. In Richard's eyes, London's refusal of a loan had constituted a breach of the city's feudal loyalty. Consequently, the city resorted to a civic triumph "in all points like as is vsed at anie coronation" to emphasize the restoration of that feudal tie. Appropriately, the city's pageantry makes careful use of the familiar hymn "Urbs beata Hierusalem," which serves in most medieval missals to celebrate the dedication of churches,[51] to suggest the rededication of London to its king. Both the pageantry and the hymn thus envision the Advent of Christ to the New Jerusalem in precisely the same way:

> Urbs beata Hierusalem, dicta pacis visio,
> Quae construitur in caelis vivis ex lapidibus,
> Et angelis coornata ut sponsata comite!
>
> Nova veniens e caelo, nuptiali thalamo
> Praeparata ut sponsata, copulatur Domino.
> Plateae et muri eius ex auro purissimo;
>
> Portae nitent margaritis, adytis patentibus
> Et virtute meritorum illuc introducitur
> Omnis, qui pro Christi nomine hic in mundo premitur.
>
> Tunsionibus, pressuris expoliti lapides
> Suis coaptantur locis per manum artificis,
> Disponuntur permansuri sacris aedificiis.
>
> Angularis fundamentum lapis Christus missus est,
> Qui compage parietis in utroque nectitur,
> Quem Sion sancta suscepit, in quo credens permanet.
>
> Omnis illa Deo sacra et dilecta civitas
> Plena modulis in laude et canore iubilo
> Trinum Deum unicumque cum favore praedicat.
>
> Hoc in templo, summe Deus, exoratus adveni
> Et clementi bonitate precum vota suscipe,
> Largam benedictionem hic infunde iugiter.
>
> Hic promereantur omnes petita adquirere
> Et adepta possidere cum sanctis perenniter,
> Paradisum introire translati in requiem.

Just as in the pageantry, Christ enters the New Jerusalem (*hoc in templo
. . . exoratus adveni*) which descends for that purpose from heaven (*nova
veniens e caelo*). Angels singing from the conduits of London find their
counterparts in the singers of the perpetual melodies and eternal hymns
which pour from "urbs beata Hierusalem" to extol "God the Three-in-
One" (*trinum Deum unicumque*). As in the civic triumph, the people entreat
the "highest Lord" to come into the city (*hoc in templo, summe Deus, exoratus
adveni*) where they sing "glad hymns to him eternally in exultant jubila-
tion." Further, the hymn describes the city as a "bridal chamber" (*thal-
amo*), just as Maydiston and the custos do, and it likewise develops fully
the *sponsus* and *sponsa* relationship between Christ and his people. Finally
the hymn closes with the request made also by the people of London that
the king might take his people to himself, that they might enter paradise
with his saints forever. This close paralleling of processional hymn and
processional pageantry emphasizes the inaugural function of the civic triumph, even though it is Richard's second such ceremony. By means of the
imagery borrowed from a hymn prescribed for the dedications of churches,
the triumph celebrates the rededication of the holy city London to its
Christ-King Richard.

In recognizing Richard's Christlikeness, the citizens of London are responding in a perfectly conventional manner to the so-called "theology of
kingship," according to which the king was conceived of as possessing two
bodies: a divine and immortal one in his person as the embodiment of the
state, and a mortal and personal one in his private capacity. In receiving
their king as a type of Christ, they pay homage to the king as the head of a
political *corpus mysticum* of which they are all members.[52] The ceremonial
of the king's coronation—especially his ritual anointment which made
him the anointed of God, a *christus* of the church—had prepared him well
to play such a role.[53] The king's first, formal entry into a city thus constitutes the first manifestation of the king as the anointed one to his people. In this, the medieval civic triumph continued, to some extent, the
ceremonial of the Roman *adventus,* according to which the emperor was
received as a god. When Richard II thus pauses before the final pageant of
his reconciliation triumph, he indisputably experiences an epiphany—he
becomes manifest as Christlike—before the pointing finger of John the
Baptist: *Behold the Lamb of God.* Indeed, this dramatized epiphany cuts
two ways. In describing Richard as the king whom "God appointed . . . to be His own king," the custos, on behalf of the citizens, ac-
claims this epiphany. In so doing, the acceptance of this epiphany seals the
reconciliation of the city to its king. As the appearance of Richard before
this pageant is *like* the Advent of Christ, so their reception of their politi-

cal lord is *like* the reception of their Savior. Their fealty to their king is a
political image of their devotion to their Lord.

By the same token, the king, through his willing acceptance of the
Christlike role that the civic triumph thrusts upon him, must *imitate*
Christ the King. In part, the king's willingness to play his Christlike role
in the civic triumph serves the purposes of conventional piety. Kings, like
other Christians of the late Middle Ages, sought union with Christ
through imitating the Savior. In particular, one of the most influential
mystics of Richard's age, Heinrich Suso (1300–1365), championed the
imitatio Christi as a spiritual exercise leading to union with Christ.
Through "imitation of My forgiveness of My crucifiers," Christ tells Suso
in a vision, "then truly art thou crucified with thy Beloved." To which
Suso responds, "My soul implores Thee to accomplish the perfect imagery
of Thy miserable Passion on my body and soul."[54] But more to the point,
the city often relies upon the king's pious willingness to imitate Christ.
Thus in staging Richard's epiphany before John the Baptist, London took
its opportunity to remind the king of the cross and the crown of thorns.
An angel descended from the upper reaches of the pageant to present
Richard with tablets illustrating the Crucifixion—a gift which "a faithful
people have presented to a faithful king," according to the custos. In
offering this symbol of the city's renewed faith, the angel explicitly asks
Richard to imitate Christ and does so in words strikingly reminiscent of
Heinrich Suso: "They [the citizens] ask that the King, though moved by
anger, might contemplate these tablets and that he might wish to be
mindful of Christ's death. Let him be sparing of the ignorant even as the
Heavenly King, though unavenged, was always forbearing to His enemies."

His anger "immediately extinguished to nothing with the contemplation of this exhibit," the king extends his hand to receive these "sacred
gifts." Turning to speak to his subjects, he is moved—at least in the
highly idealized description of Maydiston—to imitate Christ's forgiveness
and forbearance as the citizens hoped he would: "Peace to this city and to
my citizens. In the sight of Christ, His own noble mother, and John the
Baptist who is my special patron saint, and also the saints whose figures I
now see, I freely forgive all the crimes of my people."[55]

We may well—and rightly—suspect that both king and citizens are
merely playing predetermined roles to dramatize political decisions already made. But the play, after all, *is* the thing. In this dramatized exchange of faith between king and subjects, capped by Richard's suspense-
ful and decisive *imitatio Christi,* we discover the very essence of the
medieval civic triumph. Just as late medieval Christians, as members of

the Body of Christ, declared their devotion to their Lord in a Corpus Christi procession, so the same men received their newly crowned king as feudal lord—as he whom "God appointed . . . to be His own king"— through civic triumphs in a kind of *Corpus Rei Publicae* celebration, so to speak. The pageants may, indeed, flatter and cajole the prince, but their primary purpose lay in the celebration of the communal political bond which united the sovereign and his people. If, as medieval political thinking would have it, the king came to his throne as a political Christ—as an anointed one—the pageantry of the civic triumph staged his pious imitation of Christ's Advent and his subjects' joyful acclamation of his coming. The best of these shows, of course, stage an ideal; they avoid merely personal adulation by acknowledging the Christlike role of kingship. They celebrate the Christlikeness of the king by way of celebrating the ideal of Christian polity towards which king and people must together aspire. In short, they celebrate a political ideal more than they glorify a particular royal personality. So important was that ideal to the citizens of London in the late Middle Ages that they conceived and established the civic triumph as its emblematic expression, its palpable manifestation. By playing their ideal roles among these "sumptuous pageants," they might better achieve them in real life. Richard's coronation, so far as we know, marked the first English attempt to celebrate the advent of the king. The second and even more sumptuous performance of that drama, "in all points like as is vsed at anie coronation," both represented an admission of failure to achieve an ideal so bravely proclaimed, and declared a renewed commitment to achieve it. In this way, the history of the drama in Richard II's reign tells us a great deal about our attraction to political ideals and our difficulties in achieving them.

Notes

1. Jean Froissart, *Chronicles,* trans. Thomas Johnes (London, 1839), 2:398–405, 477–81. See also John Silvester Davies, ed., *An English Chronicle,* Camden Society, no. 64 (London, 1856), p. 6, for an English report.

2. Raphael Holinshed, *Chronicles of England, Scotland, and Ireland* (London, 1807), 2:819.

3. For the Clerkenwell plays, see Alan H. Nelson, *The Medieval English Stage* (Chicago: University of Chicago Press, 1974), pp. 170–73. For the coincident dating of the provincial Corpus Christi cycles with Richard's reign, see Glynne Wickham, *Early English Stages 1300 to 1660* (New York: Columbia University Press, 1959–), 1:123–24.

4. Henry's own coronation procession was apparently not a civic triumph in the sense that term is used here; it did not have dramatic pageantry. Consequently, Henry's long reign surprisingly was graced by only two of these shows: one for the arrival of the Emperor Charles V in 1522 and one for the coronation of Anne Boleyn in 1533. On these see Robert Withington, *English Pageantry: An Historical Outline* (1918–20; rpt. ed., New York: Benjamin Blom, 1963), 1:174–79, 180–84, and Sydney Anglo, *Spectacle, Pageantry, and Early Tudor Policy* (Oxford: Clarendon Press, 1969), pp. 170–206, 243–61.

5. E. K. Chambers, *The Mediaeval Stage* (London: Oxford University Press, 1903), 2:149–78; Withington, *English Pageantry*, 1:131. For the Darwinian presumptions inherent in these earlier literary histories, see O. B. Hardison, Jr., *Christian Rite and Christian Drama in the Middle Ages* (Baltimore: Johns Hopkins University Press, 1965), pp. 20–28.

6. Wickham, *Early English Stages*, 1:123–24.

7. The first script for a civic triumph in England dates from 1445, the year of Margaret of Anjou's coronation. Before that time, actors did not declaim lines from pageant stages. Rather, brief "scriptures" attached to the pageant communicated the sense of the show, or an expositor traveling with the royal cortege explained the show directly to the king in a kind of running commentary. For a discussion of these points, together with a restoration and edition of the 1445 script, see Gordon Kipling, "The London Pageants for Margaret of Anjou: A Medieval Script Restored," *Medieval English Theatre* 4 (1982): 5–27. Wickham is apparently mistaken in thinking that "mimed direct address" by pageant actors characterized the English civic triumph as early as 1392 (*Early English Stages*, 1:348).

8. George R. Kernodle, *From Art to Theatre: Form and Convention in the Renaissance* (Chicago: University of Chicago Press, 1944), p. 68.

9. Of course, more than one civic triumph might occur during the course of a given reign if, for example, a queen were to celebrate a separate triumph from her spouse or if a distinguished foreign monarch were thought worthy of a triumph during a visit.

10. Richard Maydiston, "Concordia: Facta Inter Regem Riccardum II et Civitatem Londonie" has been edited by Thomas Wright for the Rolls Series (London, 1859–61), 1:282–300, and edited and translated by Charles R. Smith (Ph.D. diss., Princeton University, 1972). Maydiston's text may be supplemented in a few important details by Helen Suggett, "A Letter Describing Richard II's Reconciliation with the City of London, 1392," *English Historical Review* 62 (1947): 209–11. The most useful discussions of the triumph itself appear in Maydiston, "Concordia," ed. and trans. Smith, pp. 42–112, and Wickham, *Early English Stages*, 1:64–70. Except where I occasionally differ in shades of meaning, I follow Smith's translation in my quotations from Maydiston.

11. For the political background to this extraordinary entry, see Caroline M. Barron, "The Quarrel of Richard II with London 1392–7," in *The Reign of Richard II*, ed. F. R. H. Du Boulay and Caroline M. Barron (London: University of London, Athlone Press, 1971), pp. 173–201. Wickham (*Early English Stages,*

1:64) thinks that the pageantry reflects Richard's, rather than London's, capitulation in this quarrel, a judgment hard to reconcile with the enormous fine the city was forced to pay, the imprisonment its officers were forced to suffer, or (as we shall see) the imagery of the civic pageantry. On the whole I am persuaded by Barron's less romantic view of the affair.

12. There may in fact have been as many as six pageants. Maydiston describes only four in detail, but he also refers in passing to: "in Lud quoque porta / Consimilis cultus stat similisque nitor; / Ad fluvii pontem nimium bene culta refulgent / Agmina spirituum" (ll. 353–56).

13. "Celicus ordo," l. 273.

14. Smith's introduction to his edition of Maydiston marks a welcome departure from this general trend.

15. Chambers, *The Mediaeval Stage,* 2:173.

16. Withington, *English Pageantry,* 1:129–31.

17. George Unwin, *The Guilds and Companies of London,* 4th ed. (London, 1863), p. 271.

18. Wickham, *Early English Stages,* 1:368.

19. Withington, *English Pageantry,* 1:131.

20. Ibid., pp. 124–25.

21. "Hos sequitur phalerata cohors cuiuslibet artis— / Secta docet sortem quemque tenere suam" (ll. 79–80). Cf. accounts of the Goldsmiths' liveries in 1382 (William Herbert, *The History of the Twelve Great Livery Companies of London* [London, 1837], 2:217–18).

22. Maydiston, "Concordia," ed. and trans. Smith, p. 93.

23. Ernst H. Kantorowicz, "The 'King's Advent' and the Enigmatic Panels in the Doors of Santa Sabina," *Art Bulletin* 26 (1944): 209–11. See also the same author's *Laudes Regiae* (Berkeley: University of California Press, 1946), p. 71: "Every city on earth preparing itself for the liturgical reception of one anointed, becomes a 'Jerusalem' and the comer a likeness of Christ."

24. "Tandem Londoniam venerunt, cui copiosa civium turba obviabant, et per regales vicos tapetos aureos dependebant, et tunc visa est Londonia quasi nova Jerusalem monilibus ornata" (William Stubbs, ed., *Chronicles of Edward I and II,* Rolls Series, no. 1 [London, 1882], p. 152).

25. Maydiston, "Concordia," l. 62.

26. Edward Maunde Thompson, ed., *Chronicon Angliae,* Rolls Series, no. 64 (London, 1874), p. 155, a better text than that given in Wickham, *Early English Stages,* 1:55, from Walsingham.

27. Francis Grose and Thomas Astle, eds., *The Antiquarian Repertory,* new ed. (London, 1807), 1:303.

28. Apocalypse 21:2–3. All scriptural quotations are taken from the Douay translation.

29. "Non oderit thalamum sponsus quem semper amavit" (l. 147). Cf. ll. 11, 21, 24, 42, 66, and 209, among others. See Maydiston, "Concordia," ed. and trans. Smith, pp. 145–47, for a discussion of this point.

30. "Plebs mea nunc erit hec, rex et ero sibi nunc" (l. 220). Cf. "Et ipse populus eius erunt et ipse Deus cum eis erit eorum Deus" (Apocalypsis 21:3 [Vulgate]). Maydiston, "Concordia," ed. and trans. Smith, p. 148.

31. "Qui dat terreni vobis dyademata regni, / Regna perhennia celestia donet item" (ll. 301–2).

32. "Cerneret has turmas quisquis . . . non dubitaret / Cernere se formas ordinis angelici" (ll. 97–98).

33. Ll. 185–92.

34. Maydiston, "Concordia," ed. and trans. Smith, p. 211.

35. Gordon Kipling, "Triumphal Drama: Form in English Civic Pageantry," *Renaissance Drama*, n.s., 8 (1977): 41–45.

36. For this commonplace, see among other sources Theodore Erbe, ed., *Mirk's Festial*, Early English Text Society, extra series, 96 (London: Oxford University Press, 1905), pp. 1–5; Th. Graesse, ed., *Legenda Aurea* (Leipzig, 1846), pp. 3–4; Rupert of Dietz, *De Divinis Officis*, 3.1 (*Patrologia Latina* 170:55–56).

37. For Saint John as "forerunner," see Kantorowicz, "King's Advent," p. 218. For Saint John as Richard's "special patron saint," see Maydiston, "Concordia," l. 426 ("Baptisteque Iohannis michi precipui") and pp. 95–96 of Smith's edition.

38. Maydiston, "Concordia," ed. and trans. Smith, pp. 98–99.

39. "Huius ad intuitum, si quid sibi manserat ire, / Extitit extinctum protinus usque nichil" (ll. 379–80); Maydiston, "Concordia," ed. and trans. Smith, p. 207.

40. Although Advent, properly speaking, extends only from the Sunday nearest Saint Andrew's Day (November 30) until Christmas Eve, the themes of the festival continue throughout the entire Christmas section of the liturgical year, which consists of Advent, Christmastide, and Epiphany. *Advent* throughout will be used in this wider sense to refer to the celebration of the Coming and Manifestation of Christ. As we shall see, the words *adventus* and ἐπιφάνεια from which we get the names of the liturgical seasons, are themselves synonyms for royal processions.

41. See, for example, the Vulgate heading for Luke 21:25–37 (which is also the reading prescribed for the second Sunday in Advent). Also the parallel readings, Mark 13:24–37 and Matthew 24:29–35. For *adventus* coinage, struck from the reign of Trajan onward, see Jocelyn M. C. Toynbee, *The Hadrianic School* (Cambridge: Cambridge University Press, 1934) and Kantorowicz, "King's Advent," pp. 213–14.

42. Kantorowicz, "King's Advent," pp. 210–11; Sabine MacCormack, "Change and Continuity in Late Antiquity: The Ceremony of *Adventus*," *Historia* 21 (1972): 724–25.

43. MacCormack, "Change and Continuity," pp. 721–22.

44. Gertrud Schiller, *Iconography of Christian Art*, trans. Janet Seligman (London: Lund Humphries, 1972), 2:19.

45. For liturgical commentary on the use of the *Tollite Portas*, see Guillelmus Durandus, *Rationale*, VI.iii.5.

46. John Bromyard, "Summa Praedicantium," A.13.33, trans. Charles R. Smith (Ph.D. diss., Princeton University, 1972), p. 146.

47. Kantorowicz, "King's Advent," p. 211, and *Laudes Regiae,* pp. 71–72: "Every liturgical reception of the *adventus* of a monarch reflects, or even stages, the Christian archetype of the performance: that is, the Lord's entry into Jerusalem, which was depicted time and again after the model of an imperial *adventus.*"

48. Saint Bernard, "In Dominica Palmarum Sermo I," *Patrologia Latina* 183:255: "si tota concupiscentia videre desideras diem illam, quando suscipietur in coelesti Jerusalem Christus Dominus, caput cum omnibus membris, portans triumphum victoriae, applaudentibus jam non popularibus turmis, sed virtutibus angelicis, clamantibus undique populis utriusque testamenti, Benedictus qui venit in nomine domini." Cf. Durandus, *Rationale,* I.iii.14: "Palmers, they who come from Jerusalem, bear palms in their hands in token that they have been the soldiers of that King Who was gloriously received in the earthly Jerusalem with palms: and Who afterwards, having in the same city subdued the devil in battle, entered the palace of heaven in triumph with His angels, where the just shall flourish like a palm-tree, and shall shine like stars." I quote from the translation by John Mason Neale and Benjamin Webb: *The Symbolism of Churches and Church Ornaments* (Leeds, 1843), p. 64.

49. Claude François Menestrier, "Des entrées solennelles et réceptions des princes dans les villes," in J. M. C. Leber, *Collection des meilleurs dissertations, notices et traités particuliers relatifs a l'histoire de France,* vol. 13 (Paris, 1838), pp. 121–23.

50. Conceived of in this way as inaugural shows, civic triumphs even assumed a certain legal status in some parts of Europe. In the Netherlands and in France, the shows customarily served as the ceremonial means of sealing the feudal contract between ruler and subject. Their explicit inaugural functions here teach us a great deal about how the shows were regarded throughout Europe. Successive dukes of Brabant from 1356, for example, were required to confirm a charter of rights known as the *Joyeuse entrée* before they could be received as lawful sovereigns. As the Burgundian dukes gradually extended their dominion throughout the Low Countries, this custom spread as well. See Bruce D. Lyon, "Fact and Fiction in English and Belgian Constitutional Law," *Medievalia et Humanistica* 10 (1956): 82–101. The Low Countries civic receptions, also known as *joyeux entrées,* thus served as the ceremonial acknowledgments that the charter had been agreed and the prince had legally entered his reign. Since French kings usually entered Paris only after being crowned at Rheims, they could not be prohibited from entering the city until they had sworn to uphold a charter of rights. Instead, a French king celebrated his *adventus* first, but at the end of it he would find the Cathedral of Notre Dame barred to him until he swore a solemn oath promising to uphold the rights and privileges of the Three Estates: Clergy, Nobles, and Commons. See for example, the coronation triumphs of Charles VII and Louis XII in Bernard Guenée and Françoise Lehoux, *Les Entrées royales françaises de 1328 à 1515* (Paris: Centre National de la Recherche Scientifique, 1968), pp. 116, 134. In both these cases, the pageantry of the civic triumph served as the counterpart to the prince's oath. He swore a formal oath to be his subjects' good lord, and

the pageantry dramatizes his subjects' acceptance of their sovereign and their joy at his advent.

51. Anton L. Mayer, "Renaissance, Humanismus, und Liturgie," *Jahrbuch für Liturgiewissenschaft* 14 (1938): 123–71; Clemens Blume, *Thesauri Hymnologici Hymnarium*, Analecta Hymnica Medii Ævi, no. 51 (1908; rpt. ed., New York: Johnson Reprint, 1961), pp. 110–12. J. M. Neale's translation of this hymn, "Blessed city, heavenly Salem," is familiar from its appearances in successive editions of *Hymns Ancient and Modern* since 1851.

52. Ernst Kantorowicz, *The King's Two Bodies* (Princeton, N.J.: Princeton University Press, 1957).

53. Kantorowicz, *Laudes Regiae,* pp. 80–82.

54. Heinrich Suso, *Little Book of Eternal Wisdom,* trans. C. H. McKenna (London: Angelus, 1910), pp. 91–92. See also Suso's *The Life of the Servant,* trans. James M. Clark (London: James Clarke, 1952).

55. Maydiston, "Concordia," ed. and trans. Smith, p. 211: "Orat ut inspiciat has rex, cum tangitur ira, / Mortis et ut Christi mox velit esse memor. / Parcat et ignaris veluti rex celicus ille / Hostibus indulgens semper inultus erat" (ll. 413–16). "Intuitu Christi, matrisque sue generose, / Baptisteque Iohannis michi precipui, / Necnon sanctorum quorum modo cerno figuras, / Sponte remitto me crimina cuncta plebis" (ll. 425–28). The angel does not actually speak; rather, the custos delivers the speech on the angel's behalf.

The Interlude of the Beggar and the King in Richard II

James Black

Everyone is by now perfectly familiar with the point of view that regards *Richard II* as an exposé of the sham of kingship. Criticism has come, with its little pin, to pierce through the hollow crown or burst the bubble of "Ceremony." And we also are familiar with the idea that a metaphor of playacting is developed throughout this tragedy to expound the lesson that it is futile for anyone to embrace this sham of kingship too seriously. In *Richard II* Richard does not "play the king" as efficiently as Bolingbroke does; nor indeed can anyone—even Bolingbroke—quite satisfactorily bridge the chasm that yawns between the "realities" of political power and the "appearances" of majesty itself. At the end of his reign, in 2 *Henry IV* (IV.v.198–99) Bolingbroke will admit that "all [his] reign has been but as a scene Acting [the] argument" of half-deserved kingship. G. A. Bonnard, Leonard F. Dean, and Anne Righter[1] have prompted us to regard *Richard II* as a play about *playing,* whose action frequently is *acting,* with first Richard and then Bolingbroke as producers of the scenes in which they appear—all this despite Peter Ure's well-taken caution that in fact it is neither Richard nor Bolingbroke but Shakespeare who sets these scenes before us.[2]

If a theme of *Richard II* is playacting, what kind of play or scene is being enacted in the passages which follow just after Richard's deposition and parting from his queen? These are the passages (V.ii; V.iii) in which Aumerle's plot is discovered, proclaimed to the new king, and pardoned. Analyzing these scenes in his article "Aumerle's Conspiracy," Sheldon P. Zitner asserted that they are "fully intended farce, sometimes roaring, sometimes savage, but farce with such salt and savour as to distress the taste for pageant, pathos, and elevated death the play otherwise appeals to and satisfies. . . . In the Aumerle scenes Shakespeare has inserted a satyr play into the last act of his tragedy."[3] "Distress the taste" hints at a vitiation of the more serious scenes by this farcical element, and Zitner's conclusion is explicit: the Aumerle conspiracy scenes "mock [*Richard II*'s] elevation and seriousness; they riddle its style. They destroy the fine trajectory of emotion that ends in the intensity of Richard's murder in Pomfret Castle and the eloquent guilt of Bolingbroke in the last scene. They strike at almost everything that moves us in the tragedy. [Yet they indicate] Shakespeare's complexity and toughness of mind."[4]

Zitner's conclusion of farce is predicated mainly upon the action the scenes clearly seem to call for: Aumerle with his plot indenture foolishly hanging from his clothing; York struggling with his riding boots; the seriatim arrivals at Bolingbroke's presence chamber and the hammering on the doors by the old duke and duchess; the exaggerated kneeling. There seems no doubt that Shakespeare meant these scenes to be comic. The question is, Did he mean them to be comic in a way that mocked the rest of the play and tended to drag *that* playacting down to their level?

Bolingbroke is made to comment upon the comic turn. Taking up the words of Aumerle's mother, "A beggar begs that never begg'd before," he says, "Our scene is alt'red from a serious thing, And now chang'd to 'The Beggar and the King'" (V.iii.77–78). It is the first time in the play—in his trilogy—that he speaks in "theatrical" terms. When he last speaks so—saying that all his reign has been but as a scene—he will use the same word, "scene," that he uses here in *Richard II*. And this should make us ask whether, though Bolingbroke is capable of irony and of the rather stiff witticism, he is exactly the kind of character we would associate with full-blooded farce. I think that the farce of these scenes may be in flow, but it is a flow which, like the flow of argument in the trial scene which Bolingbroke conducted in IV.i (Aumerle is one of the disputants there), beats without injury against Bolingbroke's adamant. Perhaps his word "scene" refers not just to *this* scene in which he is an embarrassed participant, but the wider scene which embraces the events in which he already has played. Those events are to him "a serious thing" indeed; they may be meant to be serious to us as well, and the "farce" may be supposed to counterpoint that seriousness.

The "serious thing" that the beggar and the king matter follows is the deposition scene of Richard and that scene's aftermath: Richard's parting from Isabel and York's report of Bolingbroke's and Richard's entry (about which I will say more later on) into London. In V.i Richard and his queen in parting play out a duet of grief. The scene has a distinct parallel in Romeo's and Juliet's first meeting, which takes place at a masquelike domestic revel (*Romeo and Juliet* I.v). Just what did Shakespeare in the 1590s conceive a masque to be? Enid Welsford discusses *A Midsummer Night's*

Dream as "a masque-like" play while affirming that "the suggestion that [the *Dream*] should be regarded as [a masque] has little to recommend it."⁵ In *The Merchant of Venice* Shylock describes a masque as a kind of street revel, a saturnalia with fife and drum and a "shallow foppery" indulged in by "Christian fools with varnish'd faces" (II.v.28–36). The rout of young men approaching the Capulet house in *Romeo and Juliet* initially has something of this flavor, but Capulet's old-accustomed feast, which is called a masque by Romeo and in quarto and folio stage directions,⁶ has all the ordered dignity befitting the festivity of "earth-treading stars that make dark heaven light" (I.ii.25)—a spectacular display of wealth and courtliness, masked revelers and stately dancers. The most common Elizabethan form of masque was simply a formal dance by the masquers alone.⁷

The patterned speech and patterned movement of Romeo's and Juliet's meeting fuse in the complete and partial sonnets (I.v.95–111) which they join in speaking. Their lyrical speech is appropriate to a masque though also (and more importantly) to the tragedy denoted by their brief spell of perfect harmony's being broken into by the feud's hatred and danger. In *Richard II* the deposed king and queen, surrounded by enemies, also "let lips do what hands do" (*Romeo and Juliet* I.v.103) as they develop and speak a sonnetlike conceit while they touch, kiss and part:

> *Richard.* Come, come, in wooing sorrow let's be brief,
>   Since, wedding it, there is such length in grief:
>   One kiss shall stop our mouths, and dumbly part;
>   Thus give I mine, and thus take I thy heart.
> *Queen.* Give me mine own again; 'twere no good part
>   To take on me to keep and kill my heart.
>   So, now I have mine own again, be gone.   [V.i.93–98]

This little ceremonial at the parting of Richard and his queen also emphasizes—as masques could do⁸—a theme of seasonal change:

> Part us, Northumberland: I towards the north,
> Where shivering cold and sickness pines the clime;
> My wife to France, from whence set forth in pomp,
> She came adorned hither like sweet May,
> Sent back like Hallowmass or short'st of day.   [V.i.76–80]

What we appear to have in these scenes from *Romeo and Juliet* and *Richard II,* then, are examples of what Welsford refers to as "the masque influence":

The masque influence made itself felt, not only by causing interruptions in the action, but by permeating the form and spirit of tragedy in a way that is easier to feel than to define. In the Elizabethan age masquerading was so much in the air that insensibly, inevitably, it coloured the imagination of playwright and play-goer, and infected the epical imitative play with something of the symbolic movement of the masque.[9]

In fact, *Richard II* is strongly "infected . . . with . . . the symbolic movement of the masque." The masque influence is especially present in the high ceremonial of Richard's deposition—the "inverted rite" as Walter Pater called it, a "long, agonizing ceremony, reflectively drawn out, with an extraordinary refinement of intelligence and variety of piteous appeal, but also with a felicity of poetic invention."[10] No such ceremonial is indicated in Holinshed's account of Richard's overthrow, which confines itself to Richard's capitulation at Flint Castle and his committal to the Tower, with detailed transcriptions of the major articles and instruments of deposition. Far more striking in Holinshed is the description of "the manner and order of the king's [that is, Richard's] coronation," which runs to nearly two thousand words (by way of comparison, Edward II's and Edward III's coronations are not described at all by Holinshed; Edward I's is recounted in about two hundred words). Richard's crowning, as Gervase Mathew notes, was a new, elaborate ceremonial for an English king.[11] In Holinshed it is an astonishing event, with the anointing ritual amounting to an assault on the senses:

> When the people with a lowd voice had answered that they would obeie him, the archbishop vsing certeine praiers, blessed the king; which ended, the archbishop came vnto him, and tearing his garments from the highest part to the lowest, stripped him to his shirt. Then was brought by earles, a certeine couerture of cloth of gold, vnder the which he remained, whilest he was annointed.
>
> The archbishop (as we haue said), hauing stripped him first annointed his hands, then his head, brest, shoulders, and ioints of his armes with the sacred oile, saieng certeine praiers, and in the meane time did the queere sing the antheme, beginning, Vnxerunt regem Salomonem, &c. And the archbishop added another praier, Deus Dei filius, &c. Which ended, he and the other bishops soong the hymne, Veni creator spiritus, the king kneeling in a long vesture, & the archbishop with his suffraganes about him. When the hymne was ended, he was lift vp by the archbishop, and clad first with the coate of saint Edward, and after with his mantell, a stoale being cast about his necke, the archbishop in the meane time saieng certeine praiers ap-

pointed for the purpose. After this, the archbishop and bishops deliuered to him the sword, saieng, Accipe gladium, &c.[12]

Mathew conjectures that the ceremony may well have influenced Richard
for the rest of his life, and Pater shrewdly conceives that the chronicle
accounts of this terrific ritual influenced the creation of a Shakespearean
tragic hero who emphatically reiterates his dream of sacredness:[13]

> Not all the water in the rough rude sea
> Can wash the balm off from an anointed king.

The coronation account is unmatchable by anything that the Elizabethan theater could have displayed in terms of pageantry. (It is easy to
imagine a playwright's wistfulness on reading this section of Holinshed,
and it is impossible to conceive of the play without the deposition events,
which were omitted from the printed quartos 1–3, quite likely because of
the political climate in 1597–98. As Peter Ure suggests, the deposition is
likely to have been performed on the stage even though it was considered
too risky for print.[14]) The high point of *Richard II* is at any rate the
deposition moment which, as mentioned, Holinshed tends to surround
with a thicket of documentation. Shakespeare not only clears away the
verbiage here; he also has the idea of extending the play's rhetorical device
(noticed by Miriam Joseph[15]) of negative or privative terms—"undeaf,"
"unhappied," "uncurse," "unkiss." Richard becomes "unkinged," and in
becoming so goes through a form of uncoronating, a ceremony of decoronation. The abdication scene of IV.i is rather like a coronation ritual
filmed and then run backwards, not with the speed and jerkiness usually
associated with a film so run, but with elaborate stateliness. For Richard's
music at the close of his reign is spoken to accompany a pattern of movement as well: the proferring of the crown (IV.i.181), the "buckets in the
well" tableau; the visible process ("in common view," l. 155) of giving
away the crown, then the scepter, washing away the balm, and proclaiming the successor: "God save King Henry, unking'd Richard says" (l. 220).

The poetic invention seen by Pater comes so predominantly from one
character that it is very easy to conceive of Richard's deposition scene as
written for solo voice and figure. But Bolingbroke's cryptic and reluctant
contributions actually make him as much a foil and partner for Richard as
the queen will be in the next scene. In fact, the queen there is at first as
reluctant (see V.i.26–34) to join Richard's recital of grief as Bolingbroke
is to particpate in Richard's deposition ritual. Bolingbroke's contribution
to the decoronating is notably wary, stilted, and even clumsy. Richard, all
too skilled in this patterned self-destruction, has to place his rival's hand
for the tableau with the crown:

> Give me the crown. Here, cousin, seize the crown.
> Here cousin,
> On this side my hand, and on that side thine.   [IV.i.181–83]

Thus Bolingbroke's first touch of the crown is a compelled one—and how he must involuntarily start to comply with the order, "Here, cousin, seize the crown," and then draw back! He makes as sure of being forced as Richard does of forcing him, and in *Henry IV Part Two* will say, "I and greatness were compelled to kiss" (III.i.74). But once his hand is on the crown he is a close, thralled participant in Richard's tragic rite, suffering the agonies of Richard's apparent indecision:

> *Bolingbroke.* Are you contented to resign the crown?
> *Richard.* Ay, no; no, ay; for I must nothing be.
>   Therefore no "no," for I resign to thee.   [IV.i.200–203]

Daniel's *Civil Wars* has it that " 'Tis said with his owne hands he gave the crowne / To Lancaster" (II, st. 119), and it is tempting to speculate that in the decoronation Richard adds to the silent Bolingbroke each appurtenance of kingship which he removes from himself. Finally, there is the business with the mirror, and at last the shattering of the glass leaves Richard face to face not with himself but with Bolingbroke, beggar and king:

> *Richard.* I'll beg one boon,
>   And then be gone, and trouble you no more.
>   Shall I obtain it?
> *Bolingbroke.* Name it, fair cousin.
> *Richard.* Fair cousin! I am greater than a king;
>   For when I was a king, my flatterers
>   Were then but subjects; being now a subject,
>   I have a king here to my flatterer.
>   Being so great, I have no need to beg.
> *Bolingbroke.* Yet ask.
> *Richard.* And shall I have?
> *Bolingbroke.* You shall.
> *Richard.* Then give me leave to go.   [IV.i.302–12]

Editors have tended to look outside *Richard II* for some ballad prototype of Bolingbroke's "The Beggar and the King," but there really is no need to do so. Richard says of himself:

> Sometimes am I king,
> Then treasons make me wish myself a beggar,
> And so I am. Then crushing penury

Persuades me I was better when a king;
Then am I king'd again. . . . [V.v.32–36]

"The Beggar and the King" could be the title of this deposition episode as well as of the Aumerle scenes which follow. The deposition episode's seriousness and harmonies, matched by those of the immediately following duet with the queen, are soon contrasted with the disorganized blundering of the Aumerle incident in V.ii. For example, Richard's unwillingness to read for Northumberland the articles of his wrongdoings (IV.i.222–69) seems to be reversed in York's eager perusal and proclamation of Aumerle's incriminating bond; we may wonder whether York's struggle with his boots is not a kind of comic dressing which counterpoints Richard's dismantling of himself; and the duke's robust tearing away from his duchess—"Make way, unruly woman!" (l. 110)—together with the general violent dispersal of wife, husband, and son to ride pell-mell to King Henry must surely glance at the long-drawn-out parting of the preceding scene.

To return to the question which I posed at the outset, What kind of play or scene is being enacted in these passages which follow just after, and both echo and contrast so sharply with, the scenes of Richard's deposition and parting from his queen? If it could be argued that Richard's "passion" (to use Peter Ure's term[16]) is a masque, then the Aumerle episode might be classified as a kind of antimasque. But although, as I have suggested, music and gesture are lovingly drawn out in IV.i and IV.ii, these masquelike scenes are not a masque. At any rate, losers like Shakespeare's Richard II traditionally do not figure in masques, which are for winners. As Stephen Orgel points out (by an irony, citing a Christmas 1377 entertainment in which Prince Richard actually participated), "The sovereign wins, the masque says, because it is his nature to win; and this concept of the nature of the monarch is, in one form or another, at the root of every court masque."[17]

The most helpful proposal on this question of classification comes in the play itself from the abbot of Westminster, to whom the spectacle of Richard's decoronation is "a woeful pageant" (IV.i.251). The abbot is right, of course: Richard has been a pageant king, a king of shows and a king in show. At Flint Castle, for instance, he *looks* marvellous:

See, see, King Richard doth himself appear,
As doth the blushing discontented sun
From out the fiery portal of the East,
When he perceives the envious clouds are bent
To dim his glory and to stain the track

Of his bright passage to the occident.
   Yet looks he like a king. Behold, his eye,
As bright as is the eagle's, lightens forth
Controlling majesty.   [III.iii.62–70]

Yet the spectacle, like that mounted on any pageant wagon, is pasteboard-thin. At this particular moment it is propped up by Aumerle, who stands behind this cut-out of a king almost as it were with paste, scissors, wire, and string, repairing the flimsy and battered image between speeches. Aumerle will do anything for Richard (though he is the very same duke of York who will die so magnificently at Agincourt, fighting for Bolingbroke's son). His loyalty to Richard makes him, to use the metaphor of the king's career as theater, construct the appearance of Richard at Flint, possibly script it ("Good my lord, let's fight with gentle words," l. 131), certainly prompt it ("Northumberland comes back from Bolingbroke," l. 142), then weep with frustration (l. 160) at Richard's unpredictable conceits of despair.

The pasteboard cut-out at Flint, the mockery-king of snow (IV.i.260), the hollow crown—all of these tend to suggest a crude kind of theatrical pageantry. The entry into London is a pageant show of king and beggar. To Bolingbroke:

  . . . all tongues cried "God save thee, Bolingbroke!"
You would have thought the very windows spake,

. . . .

  . . . and that all the walls
With painted imagery had said at once
"Jesu preserve thee! Welcome Bolingbroke!"

While of Richard

  No man cried "God save him!"
No joyful tongue gave him his welcome home,
But dust was thrown upon his sacred head.   [V.ii.11–17, 28–30]

Could Shakespeare, when he has the decoronation events described (by a churchman) as "a woeful pageant," possibly be glancing at the theater of Richard's time and the theater of Passion plays—the pageant mysteries? Seeing Richard fancy his deposition as a passion wherein he is mocked, stripped, and delivered by Pilates and Judases to his "sour cross" (compare IV.i.167–71, 239–42), we remember that what usually comes next in the mystery cycles is the "Harrowing of Hell" interlude, that passage of thunderous knocking at the gate, devil-portering, and high excitement. Shakespeare will look more directly at the harrowing of hell in *Macbeth;*

here in *Richard II* we at most can say only that he has it in the corner of his eye. Some of the sounds are there: *"The Duke of York knocks at the door and crieth"* (Qq. V.iii.275, S.D.), and undoubtedly his duchess thunders on the same door to Bolingbroke's presence-chamber when she arrives after her husband. And there is a muted Resurrection note at the end when, after Aumerle has been pardoned, his mother says, "Come, my old son, I pray God make thee new," wherein she seems to echo the Book of Common Prayer's "Grant that the Old Adam in this child may be so buried, that the new man may be raised up in him." (Aumerle gets more interesting the more we look at him: errant Aumerle is not just a preview of errant Hal, but in his final acceptance by Bolingbroke and rejection of the Old Adam he adumbrates Hal's reformation as well.)

"The Beggar and the King" does not go very far at all along the way to being a harrowing of hell: the chief correspondence with the mystery incident is in its placing directly after the passion scenes. Yet the fact that we are able to speculate or muse upon possibilities—upon the possibility that "The Beggar and the King" is an interlude in a woeful pageant, seems to suggest that the business which Shakespeare is about is *not* that of undercutting or mocking the seriousness of the play, but rather intensifying that seriousness by contrast or counterpoint. For if the "beggar and king" relationship is something to smile about in the Aumerle scenes then we may be meant to take it all the more seriously in the Richard scenes; the passion in the mysteries is intensified, not lessened, by the comic interlude in hell.

And so I believe that "The Beggar and the King" episode with its farcical element is designed to make us consider and value the stately ceremonials of kingship and grief that precede it. For even when these ceremonials of kingship are performed "backwards" and then burlesqued they still are very grand. The pageant may be pasteboard-thin and the patterns of the ceremony of monarchy ultimately shattered—indeed, Shakespeare requires us to consider all the hollowness and mockery. Authority, he is saying, is little and brief, and can decline to farce. The figures that move in the rays of *Richard II*'s setting sun are motes; yet they are beautiful, and worth the elegy of music at the close.

Notes

1. G. A. Bonnard, "The Actor in *Richard II*," *Shakespeare Jahrbuch* 87 (1952): 87–101; Leonard F. Dean, *"Richard II:* The State and the Image of the The-

atre,"*PMLA* 67 (1952); 211–18; Anne Righter, *Shakespeare and the Idea of the Play* (Harmondsworth: Penguin Books, 1967), chap. 5.

2. Peter Ure, Introduction to *King Richard II,* New Arden Edition (London: Methuen, 1961), p. lxxix. All references to *Richard II* in this essay cite this text.

3. Sheldon P. Zitner, "Aumerle's Conspiracy," *Studies in English Literature* 14 (Spring 1974): 240.

4. Ibid., p. 257.

5. Enid Welsford, *The Court Masque: A Study in the Relationship Between Poetry and Revels* (1927; rpt. ed., New York: Russell and Russell, 1962), p. 324.

6. *Romeo and Juliet* I.iv.48; I.iv.1, S.D.; I.v.16, S.D.

7. John C. Meagher, *Method and Meaning in Jonson's Masques* (Notre Dame, Ind.: University of Notre Dame Press, 1966), p. 7.

8. Welsford, *The Court Masque,* p. 3.

9. Ibid., p. 294.

10. Walter Pater, "Shakespeare's English Kings," in *Appreciations* (London: Macmillan, 1927), p. 198.

11. Gervase Mathew, *The Court of Richard II* (London: John Murray, 1968), p. 15.

12. Raphael Holinshed, *Holinshed's Chronicles* (New York: AMS Press, 1965), 2:713.

13. Mathew, *The Court of Richard II,* p. 11; Pater, "Shakespeare's English Kings," pp. 196–97.

14. Introduction to New Arden Edition, pp. xiii–xiv. But for a contrary view, see David M. Bergeron, "The Deposition Scene in *Richard II*," *Renaissance Papers 1974* (1975), pp. 31–37.

15. Sister Miriam Joseph, *Shakespeare's Use of the Arts of Language* (New York: Columbia University Press, 1949), p. 140.

16. See Ure, Introduction to the New Arden Edition, pp. xiii–xiv.

17. Stephen Orgel, *The Jonsonian Masque* (Cambridge, Mass.: Harvard University Press, 1965), p. 19.

"Ciphers to This Great Accompt": Civic Pageantry in the Second Tetralogy

Barbara D. Palmer

A single definition of pageantry in Shakespeare's plays is elusive at worst and probably unprofitably reductive at best, but the diversity of forms that scholars have called pageantry does make discussion confusing. As Robert Withington observed in his pioneering study, "We have in *pageant* a term which is extremely elastic,"[1] stretching to include tableaux vivants; emblematic representation; acrobats, waits, and minstrels; tournaments and jousts; royal, civic, and ecclesiastical ceremonies; masques, interludes, and allegories; dancing, from morris to bear; and any procession slightly more orderly than Wat Tyler's. Its general characteristics, however, can be agreed upon. An event or action of living picture calculated to be seen, the form of display is as important to its effect as the content. It is public rather than private, orderly and planned rather than chaotic and spontaneous. Above all, pageantry is spectacle with a public purpose: to entertain, to impress, to appease, to reassure, to reaffirm a belief or commitment, sacred or secular.

One difficulty in analyzing pageantry stems from disagreement about whether what is shown is more definitive than how it is shown and, further, the relation of pageantry to or within the drama of the public theater. Essentially, the question is whether pageantry within drama is active or static, whether its function is to advance the themes, pace, and structure or to suspend them while perhaps adding stature, scope, and color. The most extreme expression of static pageantry invites us to see Shakespeare's audience as that fictive tribe of unlettered apprentices, dissolute young gentlemen, and distracting orange-wenches, tolerating the soliloquies for the hope of the swordfights, not hearing the pentameter because gawking at the procession.[2]

Such a naïve view of pageantry, on- or off-stage, underestimates its political dimension. Whether pageantry at court, pageantry by or for the commons, or pageantry in the drama, these displays all share a political purpose beyond their obvious function as entertaining spectacle. That political purpose of course varies with the occasion, and this study in no way seeks to link court with commons with theater pageantry: the concern here is simply to assert and examine a political bias to pageantry, not to trace connections from historical monarch to civic display to dramatic character.

This point of view, the assertion that all pageantry is inherently political, also may seem naïve because it rests on very basic and often overlooked human factors. In general, people seldom spend time, effort, and money unless either they have to or else they get something of value in return, a generalization particularly apt to the intermittently parsimonious Tudors and consistently parsimonious middle-class Elizabethans. For these tremendously expensive displays to continue, as they did year after year, both royalty and commons must have received satisfaction, one aspect of which was visible advertising: a city's prestige or loyalty, a guild's products or skills, a king's power.[3]

Content aside, the mere fact of such presentations was a political statement, whether the impressive display of a victorious king's person or the purposeful Harmony of Heaven pageant contrived for Henry VII's first visit to the city of York. Part of rising nationalism, class identity, civic pride, and conscious governance, pageantry can be viewed as a reflection of social and political phenomena rather than as disengaged entertainment.[4] The medieval and Renaissance dramatic records, which give detailed accounts of civic pageantry, support such a political interpretation of spectacle. That interpretation, in turn, encourages a reexamination of the verbal and visual ways in which Shakespeare presents pageantry in the four plays from *Richard II* to *Henry V*, plays often cited as devoid of pageantic spectacle.

These four plays are particularly interesting because they picture a world in change: the fall of a divine-right king, the rise of a citizen king, the washing off of balm, the very process of exchanging kingly robes for an almsman's gown, a progress from the flower of all chivalry to the mirror of all Christian kings. Because the concept of governance changes in these plays, one might expect Shakespeare's treatment of pageantry, the display of governance, to change as well, and so it does. Instead of innocent, timeless ritual or popular entertainment alone, pageantry in these plays can be defined as the calculated public display of the king's person and the commons' response to such a display, what Richard II calls "respect, /

Tradition, form, and ceremonious duty" or what Henry V characterizes as "general ceremony . . . place, degree and form, / Creating awe and fear in other men."[5] Rather than static spectacle, pageantry or ceremony is a gauge of the king's power, a metaphor for the way in which and the success with which he governs.

In the "citizen king" plays, one might expect an abundance of civic pageantry, the kings' public appearances to the commons. Here kingship ostensibly is based on the goodwill of the commons, and here are kings who lose or gain their thrones by their relation to and manipulation of the people they govern. Instead, however, of presenting civic pageantry on stage in these plays, Shakespeare seems to rely on his audience's knowledge of such pageantry, reinforcing that knowledge with numerous textual references to the commons and their displays of power. To argue thus, that civic pageantry is a thematic force albeit not a visual one in these plays, is no more farfetched than to argue that the Elizabethan audience's familiarity with Renaissance psychology, rhetoric, or fashion informs other plays.

That Shakespeare does not choose to display civic pageantry on stage in these plays is not surprising: the content and forms of such displays were essentially unvaried over the years, his audience brought their collaborative imaginations and memories with them, and his thematic perspective in these plays is looking down from the throne rather than up from the street. As David Bergeron points out, however, "Something as innocent as a civic pageant can be a two-edged sword in serving nationalistic purposes,"[6] and Shakespeare's kings are not the only force wielding the weapon of pageantry. The English town, whether Coventry or York or Bristol, was not a pawn in a feudal system but a powerful, wealthy, corporate body seeking to define and exert its individual identity. One of the public means of displaying this identity was civic pageantry, particularly the pageantry devised for a king's entrance to the city. Although apparently naïve in content and form, such civic display "often carried meanings far beyond anything which its surface tedium might suggest."[7] As various scholars have noted, the content of civic pageantry at kings' entries seldom was overtly political.[8] The event itself, however, was political, an open statement of a city's power, wealth, ingenuity, technology, culture, and identity.

Representative examples of these entries can help modern readers to share the vision of civic pageantry possessed by Shakespeare's audience as well as to understand the support or threat that the commons held for the king.[9] Full texts of welcoming speeches, physical necessaries for shows, exact procession routes, yardage and colors of livery, banquet menus, and costs—always costs—are recorded, visit after visit. The sheer repetition of detail substantiates the generalization that Shakespeare's audience was familiar with these forms: civic pageantry was dictated by tradition and then varied as political and economic circumstances demanded. One finds frequent reference to how it was done at the last king's visit, often a decade or more earlier; in York, at least, these forms were so securely in memory and in record that an "etc." sometimes suffices. "Certain blanks are filled with new names, as the years pass; but the formulae remain pretty nearly the same. . . . Kings, queens, archbishops, and mayors may come and go; but the companies and the citizens are always there to greet their successors."[10]

The four major divisions of a king's visit that can be examined for political and propaganda nuance from the records are the initial meeting site and company, the mayor and civic officials' meeting site and pageantry, the preparation of city and citizens along the procession route, and the welcoming ceremonies themselves. In general, numbers and distance count: how far from the city the initial authority rides out to meet the king's party, whether the mayor goes outside the city walls,[11] how many city streets are included in the procession route and consequently have to be refurbished, and the number of citizens on horse and foot at various stations carry significance to both king and commons. Thus in the York records, Richard III's visit in 1483 reflects the unease occasioned by the Wars of the Roses, and Henry VII's first visit to the city in 1486 stands in striking—and, at this distance, amusing—contrast.[12]

The competitive nature of civic displays deserves further study, as the accounts from the remainder of this 1486 progress suggest.[13] Hereford seems to have received Henry rather shabbily only a mile outside town and laid on a Saint George pageant, Gloucester's officials rode out three miles but produced no pageant or speech, and Bristol's three-mile meeting and pageantry are comparable to York's. Certainly the cities compared notes, most likely for both prestige and for cost reduction, as the York record of Princess Margaret's 1503 visit attests: "Item that my lord of the common costez schall send an Officer vnto Colyweston to knawe howe the Qwene of Scottes hase ben receyued at Northamton & othir placez & if she kepe hir gestes appoynted."[14]

These brief examples, among many others, are representative of the pageantry employed for a king's visit to a civic community. Aside from the detailed production knowledge one gains from the records—for example, civic officials usually are scarlet-gowned, sheriffs' ceremonial white rods are four and a half feet long, streets are indeed strewn with rushes and herbs, bells are rung and trumpets blown—one also gains a sense of pageantry's being used to political profit. The citizens are absolutely clear on why they are going to all this bother and expense: to have their particular city in a king's "tendre and graciouse remembraunce."[15] The king is equally clear on his purpose: "I will haue no Coach, for the people are desirous to see a King, and so they shall, for they shall aswell see his body as his face,"[16] a calculated statement that James I did make and which Shakespeare's Richard II, Henry IV, or Henry V could have made.

Of the history plays, *Richard II* is the most formally patterned, and certainly of the four considered here it displays the most conventional pageantry: court entrances, the elaborate mock tournament, the deposition, tableaux vivants, in addition to the diction and imagery of pageantry. The abundance of chivalric language, the rhetoric of courtesy, points to the central conception of pageantry in this play: words without action, form without content, a substitute for proper governance instead of an orderly display of it. Heavily centered in personal adornment and the signs of office, pageantry here is a self-indulgent display directed to nobles and court while utterly disregarding the commons.

Part of Shakespeare's treatment of pageantry in *Richard II* is simply to show it as empty, an aspect that becomes visible in the aborted tournament.[17] The preparation for Mowbray's and Bolingbroke's physical confrontation is replete with visual and verbal pageantry. According to Holinshed, "There was a great scaffold erected within the castell of Windsor for the King to sit with the lords and prelates of his realme,"[18] and the gages, trumpets, formal entrance, combatants' chairs, and "such officers / Appointed to direct these fair designs" are an eyeful. The language of chivalry supports the visual effect of "this princely presence" as language and spectacle become an inflated substitute for action in the alternation of speeches and the extenuated repetition of formulas. Further characterization of such pageantry ironically is foreshadowed in Richard's diction as he stops the combat with words that describe a rebellion rather than a formal tournament ("wake our peace," "boist'rous untun'd drums," "fright fair peace," "trumpets' dreadful bray," "grating shock of wrathful iron arms"), describe rebellion so accurately, in fact, that Shakespeare will use many of them again in Henry IV's opening speech.

A second aspect of pageantry in this play is what one only can call negative or reversed pageantry: the formal stripping of "respect, / Tradition, form, and ceremonious duty," the undecking of "the pompous body of a king." This "woeful pageant" Richard himself anticipates before the actual deposition as he verbally exchanges jewels for beads, scepter for palmer's staff, and so on. Both of these types of pageantry, empty abortive ceremony and negative, reverse ceremony, are seen by the audience of

Richard II. A third type of pageantry, however, is wholly verbal rather than visual: accounts of Bolingbroke's entrances to the towns and his own diction in this play. Whereas Richard's visual spectacle is much like his kingship, "seen, but with such eyes / As sick and blunted with community," Bolingbroke's pageantry often is heard but not seen.

One can be tempted to portray Richard as a chivalric, poetic king in this play and Bolingbroke as an unrefined usurper, a simplistic contrast that Bolingbroke's language belies. His diction and rhetorical structure in the prebanishment scenes convey the liberal temper and imagination assigned to Hotspur later: "And even as I was then is Percy now" describes more than the act of rebellion itself. Characterized as "bold . . . Boist'rous . . . high-stomach'd . . . full of ire / In rage, deaf as the sea, hasty as fire," Bolingbroke's fury elicits Richard's "How high a pitch his resolution soars!," a line remarkably echoed in Northumberland's and Worcester's asides on Hotspur's outburst in *1 Henry IV*, I.i. Likewise, the imagery of Bolingbroke's "Shall I seem crestfallen in my father's sight? / Or with pale beggar-fear impeach my height" is paralleled in Hotspur's "To pluck bright honour from the pale-fac'd moon."

But highflown as Bolingbroke starts out in language and behavior, the reality of banishment quickly tempers his nature, his view of pageantry, and his expression. The change is rung in his response to Gaunt's plea for him to use his imagination: "O, who can hold a fire in his hand / By thinking on the frosty Caucasus?" (*Richard II,* I.iii.294–95). From here until his death in *2 Henry IV,* Bolingbroke's imagination and use of ceremony consistently will be yoked to political expediency. Although his language retains the elegance of courtesy, his visual pageantry is of war, a juxtaposition of martial threat with courtly parlance heard distinctly on his drum-and-colors entrance to Berkeley Castle:

> If not, I'll use the advantage of my power,
> And lay the summer's dust with showers of blood
> Rain'd from the wounds of slaughtered Englishmen—
> The which, how far off from the mind of Bolingbroke
> It is, such crimson tempest should bedrench
> The fresh green lap of fair King Richard's land,
> My stooping duty tenderly shall show.   [*Richard II,* III.iii.42–48]

The visual images of the two protagonists are as clearly juxtaposed: Henry's "glittering arms" and "barbed steeds" below, Richard's "so fair a show" above. Richard "yet looks . . . like a king"; Henry is well on his way to being one.

Perhaps Northumberland best summarizes the effect of hollow pageantry in his hopes for Bolingbroke:

> If then we shall shake off our slavish yoke,
> Imp out our drooping country's broken wing,
> Redeem from broking pawn the blemish'd crown,
> Wipe off the dust that hides our sceptre's gilt,
> And make high majesty look like itself,
> Away with me in post to Ravenspurgh.   [*Richard II*, II.i.291–96]

Although using the terms of pageantry, Northumberland implicitly is referring to the necessary content of kingship: sound finances, allegiance of commons and nobles, and good management, a thoroughly Tudor view of governance. Richard's pageantry and domestic extravagance have cost an enormous amount of money, money drained from both nobles and from "wavering commons," whose "love lies in their purses." Bolingbroke will not miscalculate so grossly, and his concept of pageantry as a tool of governance, a weighing of the show's value against its cost, prevades the two *Henry IV* plays.

It frequently has been asserted that the *Henry IV* plays are devoid of pageantry, with various reasons, from Falstaff's consuming stage presence to Henry's guilt to possible shifts in the Chamberlain's Men's fortunes speculated as the cause. In fact, these plays are not devoid of pageantry: they simply do not show the kind of court spectacle found in *Richard II* because Henry's court is not Richard's. Had it been, this canker Bolingbroke, "this vile politician," would not have seized the throne from that sweet, lovely rose, Richard. In these plays, as in *Richard II*, Shakespeare structures the pageantry to the dramatic or thematic explication of a king instead of using spectacle solely for its own sake. [19]

As noted above, Henry's opening speech on civil war echoes Richard's phrases on the Bolingbroke-Mowbray dispute, but the first account of civil war hardly is chivalrous. Instead of seeing a mock tournament, we hear of Welshwomen mutilating bodies, discharges of artillery, "civil butchery" indeed. The image of governance which Henry sets in his first speech, however, is not Richard's glistering show: the end of this king is that his subjects

> Shall now, in mutual well-beseeming ranks,
> March all one way, and be no more oppos'd
> Against acquaintance, kindred, and allies,   [*1 Henry IV*, I.i.14–16]

a military image of order which almost characterizes the pageantry, visual and verbal, in *1* and *2 Henry IV*. [20]

Before establishing a new image of pageantry, however, Shakespeare first blackens both the language and spectacle of the pageantry seen in *Richard II* by here turning it into mock pageantry. Most clearly this debunking occurs in the tavern play, where Falstaff's state is a joint stool, his golden scepter a leaden dagger, and his precious rich crown a cushioned bald crown. Through this parody of pageantry both the mock symbols of kingship and the real are brought into question, inviting us to look to the further reality of power behind the symbols. Richard looked like a king but failed to rule like one; Falstaff does not remotely look a king except perhaps of Misrule or Vice; Hal does not behave like a king but tells us in his first soliloquy that he knows how to be one; Douglas cannot tell who the king is because all men on the field of battle can dress like a king. The message to look through the hollow crown, through the appearance or symbol of kingship, to the power beyond is clear.

As courtly ceremony and the signs of office are questioned in this play, so too is inflated courtly language mocked, although both Henry and Hal are capable of being articulate in the extreme when it serves their purposes. Fulsome language—"holiday and lady terms," "bold unjointed chat"—is mocked in Hotspur's scathing account of the perfumed courtier, while Falstaff's lying, bandying words of honor, courage, and kingship point to a further schism between word and deed. In *Richard II,* language was presented as an alternative, albeit an ineffectual and temporary one, to action. In this play, however, both language and spectacle are directed toward war, whether the action of the mock war centered in the tavern activities or the very visible war at the end of the play. Falstaff by his words and his very presence provides the contrast of mock war to real: his cowardice, the self-inflicted nosebleeds and hacked swords from the robbery, his numerous references to the heir apparent, honor, and "instinct" all build to point to Hal's payment of "the debt [he] never promised," his real courage in his father's field of battle and later in his own.

Two juxtaposed descriptions bring the image of real war and mock war into inescapable contrast, the first Vernon's account to Hotspur of Henry's troops and the second Falstaff's account of his own "toasts-and-butter." Vernon's description of Hal and his comrades is a pageantic description, complete with costumes and *deux ex machina,* while Falstaff's mock soldiers are "the cankers of a calm world and a long peace, ten times more dishonourable-ragged than an old fazed ancient," a straggling assortment of villains and cowards whom he paints wandering by the hedges to steal linen.

In contrast to these stragglers is the repeated orderly appearance of Henry, his sons, and his armed nobles, marching all one way "in mutual well-beseeming ranks," the image with which the play began and with which it ends. The king himself characterizes the change in pageantry as he charges that the rebels "made us doff our easy robes of peace / To crush our old limbs in ungentle steel," and instead of the "gay apparel" of Richard's court, we here see the armor, plumes, and bloody swords of Henry's. This pageantry may not be the courtly ceremony of *Richard II,* but to deny it as pageantry at all is nit-picking. In the armed, orderly war councils, in the trumpets, colors, and plumes, and in the abundance of chivalric language, Shakespeare here has created an image of display linked with force, display with a purpose, not an inappropriate image for his "vile politician." Instead of the interminable hurling of gages in *Richard II,* the pageantry of *1 Henry IV* repeatedly shows the pulling on of gages.

If pageantry is, as has been asserted above, a metaphor for the way in which and the success with which a king governs, then *2 Henry IV* is almost a long discussion of ceremony rather than the thing itself, a summing up of how to turn "past evils to advantages." This extensive reference to ceremony and its function pulls together the strands of display woven in the preceding two plays. In *Richard II* the symbols of office were seen as adornment, the decking of the pompous body of a king. In *1 Henry IV* these symbols were first parodied and then exchanged for war weeds. In *2 Henry IV* the crown and other appointments are firmly associated with duty, worry, and care: the omnipresent crown in this play comes to symbolize the orderly and responsible passing of power.

On-stage pageantry, however, is minimal, restricted to the initial appearance of "Rumour, painted full of tongues," Henry V's first entrance as king,[21] and the final rejection-of-Falstaff procession. This sparcity of ceremony does not necessarily suggest that the court scenes are informal: quite the contrary, with the consistent presence of princes, counsellors, and Henry IV's elaborately balanced rhetoric. But the visual images in this play are not of court or civic pageantry: instead, one retains scenes of tavern, country, and town streets, populated by bawds, whores, diseased soldiers, and garrulous old men. Even the scenes of the armed rebels bring no visual fruit as no actual combat occurs in the play: it essentially is a play of talk rather than of action. It is a play that debates at length whether order or chaos will rule the kingdom, a tenuous condition best expressed by Henry IV in terms suggestive of pageantry when he fears that Hal will pluck down his officers, break his decrees, and "mock at form."

That Henry IV need not fear that his "poor kingdom . . . wilt be a wilderness again" is seen clearly in Henry V's post coronation procession. Here, where ceremony and drama are linked, Shakespeare employs elaborate pageantry: rushes are strewn, trumpets sound, a full procession follows the king's entrance, all exit, shouts and trumpets sound again, and the king and his train reenter. One might ask, as various scholars have done, why Shakespeare does not show the coronation itself, since he obviously had sufficient resources for the elaborate procession. A possible answer lies in his propensity to yoke pageantry to theme in these plays, to avoid empty spectacle unless it substantiates the portrayal of kingship.

The audience does not see Hal's coronation; neither, apparently, does Falstaff, nor does he see Hal's initial processional entrance, which prepares the audience for the inevitable confrontation between the majestically arrayed, anointed king and his "stain'd with travel" former companions. Falstaff's interruption of the procession thus is both visually and verbally inappropriate, a point which the audience grasps somewhat earlier than Falstaff.[22]

The primary thematic issues of this play are the death of Henry IV, the state of the kingdom, and the capability of his successor, not the coronation itself. From his heir-apparent garters on, the true prince's being crowned was not in doubt; the only question Shakespeare raises is what kind of king he will prove. The final focus on the rejection rather than on the coronation answers the question, and thus once again pageantry is chosen to illustrate governance, the dramatic incident over the static display.

Henry V, a play curiously flat in many respects, is extraordinarily subtle and complex in its treatment of pageantry. We have been assured by Henry IV that the crown "shall descend with better quiet, / Better opinion, better confirmation" to Hal, and we have been assured by Hal that he will maintain it "with more than a common pain / 'Gainst all the world": we thus might expect to see the courtly pageantry of *Richard II* restored to symbolize Henry V's right to the throne. Shakespeare instead, however, collects the various aspects of pageantry presented in the preceding three plays and uses them all; in terms of the fullest definition of pageantry, *Henry V* does indeed reflect "the mirror of all Christian kings."

In its formal opening and formal close, verbal pageantry frames the play. The Prologue sets a picture of pageantry but then confesses the inadequacy of representation, asking that we use our imaginations to piece out the imperfections of the theater. We have served as "ciphers to this great accompt" before: Bolingbroke's civic entrances, Vernon's description of Hal, and Hal's coronation, among many other verbal accounts of or references to pageantry, ceremony, or chivalry. The Chorus's four speeches that open the acts further invite imaginative collaboration as they verbally present the pageantry of the English army's preparations, their departure "with silken streamers," the night vigil that asks us to mind "true things by what their mock'ries be," and the full description of a victorious king's entrance to London, "which cannot in their huge and proper life / Be here presented."[23] In the Chorus's close as Epilogue, both content and structure are formal and ceremonious, the content again reminding us that the "full course of their glory" cannot be portrayed in stage pageantry, the structure a sonnet.

These verbal descriptions of pageantry not shown on stage serve several functions, namely, bridging time, space, and cast limitations, but the one most relevant here is the indirect enhancement of the throne. By extending the glory, the scope of power through words, Shakespeare is able to focus on the king as man, "his ceremonies laid by," and retain some of the complex character of Hal developed in the preceding two plays. Only at two points are we shown Henry V in active pageantry: I.ii, a formal entrance to the presence chamber, and V.ii, the full court entrance of both French and English. The first scene is contrived carefully to build up a sense of history, tradition, justice, and chivalric nostalgia (vis-à-vis the Black Prince): in many respects, this scene serves as Hal's coronation ceremony, the visible proof of an anointed king sanctioned by church and state. The challenge Henry issues to the Dauphin clearly suggests that he understands the function of arrogant display:

> But tell the Dauphin I will keep my state,
> Be like a king and show my sail of greatness
> When I do rouse me in my throne of France:
> For that I have laid by my majesty
> And plodded like a man for working-days,
> But I will rise there with so full a glory
> That I will dazzle all the eyes of France,
> Yea, strike the Dauphin blind to look on us.   [*Henry V,* I.ii.273–80]

The Constable's summary to the French of the occasion attests to the stage display's pageantry: "With what great state he heard their embassy, / How well supplied with noble counsellors." The court entrance of French and English in V.ii also allows Shakespeare to shift to the character of Hal in the following wooing scene without loss of face to the character of Henry V and England. After the splendor of that entrance, the number of actors, the formality of language, Hal can rather charmingly protest to Katharine his being "such a plain king that thou wouldst think I had sold my farm to buy my crown" without disturbing the political balance and nationalistic fervor of the play as a whole.

In the middle three acts, however, no formal pageantry is ascribed to the king; instead, Henry is presented repeatedly in images of war, but they are images stripped of glamour and orderly form. Not here does one find the "glittering arms" or "barbed steeds" of *Richard II* or *1 Henry IV*; rather, the stress is on a reverse pageantry, an insistence on the English poverty of appointment. The grime and tatter accumulate—"poor soldiers," "yond poor and starved band," "island carrions," "ragged curtains," "poor jades"—until Henry directly links the absence of martial pageantry with the thematic point:

> It earns me not if men my garments wear;
> Such outward things dwell not in my desires:
>
> . . . .
> We are but warriors for the working-day;
> Our gayness and our gilt are all besmirch'd
> With rainy marching in the painful field;
>
> . . . .
> And time hath worn us into slovenry.
>
> [*Henry V*, IV.iii.26–27, 109–11, 114]

If martial pageantry is so determinedly stripped from the English soldiers, it is used to dress the French, who display the empty spectacle of *Richard II*. Their Act III entrances are alternated with homely scenes of English soldiers, the Dauphin's incessant hot-tempered boasting of his armor and horse sounds vaguely like a less-commendable Hotspur, and the image one receives is of a decorative French court waiting for a war to happen, a static vision of inactivity. The Dauphin's remorseful conclusion, that "Reproach and everlasting shame / Sit mocking in our plumes," again suggests that Shakespeare has harnessed pageantic appointments to political theme.

These various uses of pageantry suggest that the show of kingship cannot replace the substance of kingship, but when the substance of power and governance is present, ceremony effectively can display and enhance it. Such a summary of royal spectacle, however, does not begin to address the full scope of pageantry in this tetralogy, for it omits the vital role of the commons in destroying or forming these kings. In the Henry plays, particularly, Shakespeare gives no view of a naïve kingship unaware of the uses of pageantry, and the dramatic records, conversely, give no view of a naïve citizenry unaware of the city's importance to the throne. We see instead two forces, king and commons, charily using pageantry to manipulate each other, a tool intrinsic to the changing concept of governance that these plays embody. Reinforced repeatedly is the commons' response to king and king's consciousness of commons, starting with Bolingbroke's climb to the throne in *Richard II*. Whereas Richard has "quite lost their hearts" and "the commons they are cold," Bolingbroke "did seem to dive into their hearts / With humble and familiar courtesy": no fewer than six accounts in the play cite Henry's calculated attention to the commons,[24] and Holinshed confirms this attention as well.[25]

His son, the madcap prince of Wales, learns his lesson well but modifies it to include knowledge of the commons, an amplification of pageantry into governance. From his early statement to Falstaff that "wisdom cries out in the streets and no man regards it" to the image in his first-act soliloquy of "bright metal on a sullen ground," which will "show more goodly and attract more eyes / Than that which hath no foil to set it off," Hal both knows and uses the commons with pageantry as propaganda. Although he asserts that "the king is but a man, as I am: . . . his cere-monies laid by, in his nakedness he appears but a man," he seldom is foolish enough to lay by those ceremonies, as the Chorus clearly shows in his imagined account of Henry V's victorious entrance to London.

At no point in the plays, however, does Shakespeare suggest that either Bolingbroke or Hal actually feels love and respect for the commons. Rich-ard's initial characterization of the populace as "slaves . . . poor crafts-men" and Bagot's contempt for "the wavering commons . . . the hateful commons" are not amended by Bolingbroke: at no place in the text does he utter a positive word about the citizens of the country he has just usurped. In *1 Henry IV,* his concept of the commons as a tool to be manip-ulated emerges in his account to Hal of how he got the throne, and in his final accusation of the rebels his description of the commons is more scathing than Bagot's: "fickle changelings," "poor discontents," "moody beggars." For all his direct contact with "the very base-string of humility," Hal has no more love for them than his father had, nor does he ever find cause to alter the Archbishop's view of "the fond many," "the beastly feeder," "the common dog."

The view of the commons is not flattering in these plays: they clearly are a force to be manipulated by the throne, and Shakespeare's kings waste no words of admiration or affection about them. But as the nature of governance shifts through these plays, so too does the means of control-ling the commons. From Richard's fatal mistakes of ignoring them, piling them "with grievous taxes," attempting to subdue by force the "rough rug-headed kerns" of his Irish kingdom, and casting them aside as "waver-ing," we see Henry IV's calculated moves to gain their goodwill through pageantry and the selective display of his royal person. If the commons indeed are "wavering," and little in these plays suggests that they are otherwise, both Bolingbroke and his son draw the wavering toward their throne rather than in opposition to it.

As the dramatic records show, however, "the still-discordant wav'ring multitude" could be as adept in its use of pageantry as the crown. Its "general ceremony" is not that of kings but on that account no less significant as a political force behind these plays. Shakespeare's kings have their "tide of pomp," the

> balm, the sceptre, and the ball,
> The sword, the mace, and crown imperial,
> The intertissued robe of gold and pearl,
> The farced title running 'fore the king,
> The throne he sits on . . . ,   *[Henry V,* IV.i.257–61]

and the commons too has its tide of pomp: the costumes, signs of office, processions, welcoming ceremonies, calculated exhibits of their persons and cities. Both forces, king and commons, share a motivation and purpose: "Creating awe and fear in other men" through the judicious use of pageantry.

Shakespeare's dramatic treatment of pageantry is equally judicious in these four plays. Not spectacle alone, not mere entertainment, not empty static ritual, pageantry is a symbol of kingship. When backed with power, economic, political, or martial, the display of kingship becomes a vital means of keeping the throne. When not backed with power, however, the empty display of kingship is shown to be a means of losing the throne. The hollow crown, the symbol of pageantry, ceremony, and governance in these plays, thus takes its definition from the power, purpose, and wisdom of the king himself. To note this glistering stage property's shift from egocentric adornment on Richard's head to uneasy burden on Henry IV's to parodic misrule on Falstaff's to near-divine approbation on Henry V's is also to note Shakespeare's fluid treatment of ceremony as a political tool.

Notes

1. Robert Withington, *English Pageantry: An Historical Outline* (1918–20; rpt. ed., New York: Benjamin Blom, 1963), 1:xix. Other helpful studies include David M. Bergeron, *English Civic Pageantry 1558–1642* (Columbia: University of South Carolina Press, 1971); Alice S. Venezky [Griffin], *Pageantry on the Shakespearean Stage* (New York: Twayne, 1951); Stephen Orgel, *The Illusion of Power: Political Theater in the English Renaissance* (Berkeley and Los Angeles: University of California Press, 1975); Glynne Wickham, *Early English Stages 1300 to 1660* (New York: Columbia University Press, 1959–); and, of especial use to the approach taken here, Sydney Anglo, *Spectacle, Pageantry, and Early Tudor Policy* (Oxford: Clarendon Press, 1969).

2. In part Venezky presents this view—"the promise of a glittering parade

drew many to the playhouse" (p. 27)—but she also adds that "even playwrights of the popular stage might forego the splendor of a royal entry in favor of a more dramatic effect" (p. 41).

3. Long noted as has been the frequent correspondence of medieval guild to the business of properties of the cycle play assigned to it: Shipwrights, Fishmongers, or Drawers to the Noah pageant; Tanners clothing God in a white leather robe for their Creation pageant; Goldsmiths or Merchants responsible for the elaborately garbed Magi; or Vintners for the Miracle at Cana. Whether parodic (the Shipwright Noah's ineptitude in ark building or the Vintners' starting with water) or practical assignments, the guild's abilities and products nevertheless were advertised.

4. Also reflecting Tudor sociopolitical phenomena was the popularity of English chronicles, which stressed such pageantic splendor. See Louis B. Wright, *Middle-Class Culture in Elizabethan England* (Chapel Hill: University of North Carolina Press, 1935), pp. 297–338.

5. *King Richard II,* ed. Peter Ure, 5th ed. (London: Methuen, 1961), III.ii. 172–73; and *King Henry V,* ed. J. H. Walter (London: Methuen, 1954), IV.i.243–44. Other Arden editions cited in the text are *The First Part of King Henry IV,* ed. A. R. Humphreys, 6th ed. (London: Methuen, 1960); and *The Second Part of King Henry IV,* ed. A. R. Humphreys (London: Methuen, 1966).

6. Bergeron, *English Civic Pageantry,* p. 25.

7. Anglo, *Spectacle, Pageantry, and Early Tudor Policy,* p. 3.

8. See Bergeron (*English Civic Pageantry*), Venezky (*Pageantry on the Shakespearean Stage*), and Anglo (*Spectacle, Pageantry, and Early Tudor Policy*), although all three cite instances that were sufficiently political to approach treason.

9. Gordon Kipling's essay in this volume centers on one of the more remarkably political entries, Richard II's 1392 return from York, where he had moved his court "for grete malice of the cite of London" when its citizens refused him a loan. See Withington, *English Pageantry,* pp. 129–30.

10. Ibid., p. 180. The volumes of dramatic records currently being edited by the Records of Early English Drama, University of Toronto Press, are a source for continuous rather than selective civic pageantry and, consequently, for the continuous political subtext that motivates that pageantry.

11. "Typically, it was their walls that the men of London and Canterbury, of Oxford, Colchester and Shrewsbury, chose to depict on their seals. In contemporary art, it was the wall of a city which identified it." Colin Platt, *The English Medieval Town* (London: Granada, 1979), p. 50.

12. The archbishop, civic officials, and Sir Henry Hudson, who devised the pageants, conspired to represent York as poor, loyal, and exhausted, in order that Henry might "the rather be movid to think that the said maier Aldermen Sheriffes and other inhabitances heyr be gladdid and loifull of the same his commyng of other kinges yer souerain lord." Alexandra F. Johnston and Margaret Rogerson, eds., *York Records* (Toronto: University of Toronto Press, 1979), 1:138.

13. See Withington, *English Pageantry,* pp. 159–60, and Anglo, *Spectacle, Pageantry, and Early Tudor Policy,* pp. 28–36.

14. Johnston and Rogerson, *York Records,* 1:193.

15. Ibid., 1:193.

16. Ibid., 1:515.

17. See Wickham, *Early English Stages,* 1:13–50, where he notes that "the performance, for such it may be called, at first no more than a crude mock battle, was gradually transformed into an elegant entertainment which conformed to an etiquette as elaborate as its staging."

18. Geoffrey Bullough, ed., *Narrative and Dramatic Sources of Shakespeare* (London: Routledge and Kegan Paul, 1957–75), 3:389.

19. For further discussion of this point, see Gerard H. Cox's essay in this collection.

20. Froissart's account of Henry IV's 1399 coronation in fact describes an almost military show of power in the king's procession of six thousand horses; likewise, his entry to London earlier that year displayed pomp and power but no pageantry as entertainment. Withington comments that "perhaps the troublous times account for the absence of pageantic features at this royal-entry" (*English Pageantry,* p. 132).

21. There seems no reason not to read Henry V's entrance lines in V.ii.44 as literal description: "This new and gorgeous garment, majesty, / Sits not so easy on me as you think."

22. Alice Venezky cites only a single procession "returning from the coronation ceremonies at Westminster"; rather, there are two entry processions, separated by Falstaff and his followers' arrival and longish discussion. "Shouts within. The trumpets sound," which ends the discussion and signals the second entry, seems to suggest that the coronation has occurred in the interval, thus strengthening Venezky's estimate of "this effective technique of placing an irregular incident within a framework of formality" (*Pageantry on the Shakespearean Stage,* p. 29).

23. Considering that Henry was greeted, at various stations, by mayor, aldermen, twenty thousand citizens, a giant, lion, antelope, singing angels and patriarchs, twelve singing apostles, twelve kneeling "kings," and fourteen bishops, the Chorus's judgment probably is wise. See Withington, *English Pageantry,* pp. 132–36.

24. The six accounts are by Richard (*Richard II,* I.iv.23–36), York (V.ii.7–21), Henry IV (*1 Henry IV,* III.ii.39–84), Hotspur (IV.iii.66–88), Scroop (*2 Henry IV,* I.iii.88–108), and Westmorland (IV.i.131–39).

25. Holinshed notes the "woonder it was to see what a number of people ran after him in everie towne and street where he came, before he tooke the sea, lamenting and bewailing his departure" and, on Bolingbroke's return, how he "shewed himselfe now in this place, and now in that, to see what countenance was made by the people, whether they meant enviouslie to resist him, or freendlie to receive him." Bullough, ed., *Narrative and Dramatic Sources,* 3:394, 397.

"Like a Prince Indeed": Hal's Triumph of Honor in 1 Henry IV

Gerard H. Cox

If there is one topic to which most of the criticism of 1 *Henry IV* points, it is the problematic nature of Prince Hal. Hal is an *animal amphibium*: he lives in the divided worlds of tavern and court; and, to use Falstaff's phrase about the otterlike hostess in a more general sense, no one on stage knows where to have him until the play is over. And even then, we may feel, Hal's actions raise disquieting possibilities that run counter to the satisfaction we tend to expect from the ending of a play—and certainly from a play in which Hal's own "satisfaction" is given so much prominence.

The metaphor of redemption is both central and pervasive. Promising at the close of his soliloquy, "I'll so offend, to make offence a skill, / Redeeming time when men think least I will," Hal dutifully vows to the king that he will call Hotspur to "so strict account" that Percy shall "render every glory up."[1] And, of course, that is what seems to be happening when Hal kills Hotspur. As the dying Hotspur proclaims,

> O Harry, thou hast robb'd me of my youth!
> I better brook the loss of brittle life
> Than those proud titles thou hast won of me.   [V.iv.76–78]

This is "a conquest for a [true] prince to boast of," to reapply the king's declaration about Hotspur in I.i. By triumphing over Hotspur, Hal has redeemed the time.

But, almost perversely, Shakespeare contrives to offset this process of redemption by having Hal kill Hotspur unseen by any on stage save perhaps Falstaff, who of course comically proceeds to claim the honor rightly due Hal. It is disquieting that Falstaff is not exposed as a fraud, and it is even more disquieting that Hal promises to gild Falstaff's lie. In similar fashion, if the king roundly declares after Hal has rescued him from Douglas, "Thou hast redeem'd thy lost opinion" (V.iv.47), no more is made of this recognition in *Part 1*, and, presumably for metadramatic reasons, the king has conveniently forgotten this redemption by the opening of *Part 2*.

These troublesome features are made even more problematic by the theatrical nature of Hal's characterization. Hal's role has a markedly stagy quality to it, a stagy quality that resists any simple resolution and that, judging from critical opinion, runs counter to our own sensibilities. Hal often seems too much his father's son, too much the calculating opportunist who in *Part 1* cynically chooses the best moment to reform and in *Part 2* cuts off his old companions without a qualm.

Before we pass judgment too readily, however, we need to be sure we have assessed the evidence correctly—and in the instance of *1 Henry IV* I believe that we have overlooked a significant element in Prince Hal's characterization: the symbolic use of emblems, shows, and pageantry associated with chivalry in the Renaissance. Once we become aware of these conventions, it is obvious that Hal's challenge to Hotspur and their subsequent combat provide yet another instance of parallel staging in *1 Henry IV*. This parallel staging presents Hal "as a prince indeed," first through his ability to play his part worthily and then through his ability to perform in action what he has vowed to do. Hal triumphs over Hotspur, yet, at the very moment when one would expect Hal's victory to be celebrated as a triumph—what Florio defined as "a solemne pompe or showe at the returne of a captaine for some victory gotten"[2]—Shakespeare has Falstaff take the credit. Hal's victory over Hotspur provides a theatrical equivalent of "bright metal on a sullen ground," and given his tarnished reputation it does "show more goodly, and attract more eyes / Than that which hath no foil to set it off" (I.ii.209–10). But these eyes, of course, are only our own, for Shakespeare has worked one final, ingenious inversion: he has invoked the conventions of chivalric pageantry only to let us see how inadequate they are to define Prince Hal.

Prince Hal attracts the most attention from those on stage when, shortly before the Battle of Shrewsbury, he suddenly breaks into the acrimonious charges and countercharges of the king and Worcester to challenge the absent Hotspur to single combat:

> In both your armies there is many a soul
> Shall pay full dearly for this encounter

If once they join in trial. Tell your nephew,
The Prince of Wales doth join with all the world
In praise of Henry Percy: by my hopes,
This present enterprise set off his head,
I do not think a braver gentleman,
More active-valiant or more valiant-young,
More daring or more bold, is now alive
To grace this latter age with noble deeds.
For my part, I may speak it to my shame,
I have a truant been to chivalry,
And so I hear he doth account me too;
Yet this before my father's majesty—
I am content that he shall take the odds
Of his great name and estimation,
And will, to save the blood on either side,
Try fortune with him in a single fight.   [V.i.83–100]

Several points about this speech deserve attention. In the first place, it is relatively long, so its recital effectively disrupts the gathering momentum of the play. Second, it seems almost completely beside the point, as indeed the king's brusque dismissal indicates:

And, Prince of Wales, so dare we venture thee,
Albeit, considerations infinite
Do make against it.

One can readily supply some of these considerations, if not "considerations infinite": on the odds, as Hal admits, he is likely to lose; more important, that's not the way battles are fought. Still another consideration would concern historical accuracy: Shakespeare—and presumably some of his audience—knew that there had been a Battle of Shrewsbury, and although he could take dramatic liberties with its action—Hotspur died in the battle, but there is no evidence that Hal killed him—its occurrence was virtually a given. Hal's challenge thus seems to have no bearing on the situation; considered in the abstract, it seems about as purposeless an episode as one could imagine.

What, then, we may ask, is this speech doing here? In my view, the challenge serves as a pageant for Hal in which he can demonstrate to all on stage that he has reformed. Dover Wilson termed *Henry IV, Part 1* "Hal's Return to Chivalry" and *Part 2* Hal's "Atonement with Justice."[3] Although Wilson never indicated precisely *when* Hal returns to chivalry, this challenge would seem to afford the occasion. Certainly the language of the speech rings changes on the themes of Hal's earlier declarations. "I have a truant been to chivalry" recalls Hal's "playing holidays" in his soliloquy about his eventual reformation, and "Yet this before my father's majesty" recalls Hal's vows to his father to redeem his shames on Percy's head. Finally, "by my hopes" recalls first his soliloquy ("By how much better than my word I am, / By so much shall I falsify men's hopes") and, second, the king's statement to him at court:

> The hope and expectation of thy time
> Is ruin'd, and the soul of every man
> Prophetically do forethink thy fall.   [III.ii.36–38]

Paradoxically, however, Hal falsifies these hopes through a dramatic double negative: rather than demonstrating that he has been misjudged by appearances that are false because they do not reveal his true nature, or that within which passes show, Hal reconstrues how he appears to others by giving the challenge—which is itself only a show, an action that a man might (and does) play. Vernon's account of the challenge to Hotspur makes this reconstruction explicit through a prophecy that neatly inverts the one pronounced by the king in III.ii:

> There did he pause: but let me tell the world—
> If he outlive the envy of this day,
> England did never owe so sweet a hope
> So much misconstru'd in his wantonness.   [V.ii.65–68]

If Hal reconstrues his public image by delivering a princely challenge to Hotspur, the occasion of his Return to Chivalry raises once more that troublesome question of how we are supposed to react to this heir apparent. Perhaps the best guide to the effect Shakespeare wanted is provided by the recapitulation Vernon makes to Hotspur, for his comments furnish the actor playing Hal with a set of embedded stage directions:

> And, which became him like a prince indeed,
> He made a blushing cital of himself,
> And chid his truant youth with such a grace
> As if he master'd there a double spirit
> Of teaching and of learning instantly.   [V.ii.60–64]

If we press the question, *What* "became him like a prince indeed"? we can only answer, "How Hal *gives* his challenge," for, as we have seen, the challenge as a call to single combat is not remotely germane to what is going on: determining who will wear the crown of England. But that was indeed part of the point of such challenges, for they afforded the opportunity for a ruler to "act" like a prince or a king. By understanding the function of these chivalric shows, we can better evaluate not only how Hal performs his challenge but how he acts in his victory over Hotspur.

Although no source is known for Hal's challenge to Hotspur, his speech conforms to chivalric convention. The historical Henry V apparently did make a challenge to the Dauphin that is comparable to Hal's challenge to Hotspur. According to the influential "Translator of Livius," Henry sent heralds to the Dauphin before the siege of Caen to declare that "if the Dolphine woulde assure him to fight against him, body against body, without the ayde of both ther peoples, then whether of them obtayned the victorie shoulde for euer inioy the land and people of Fraunce."[4]

This single combat did not occur, for the simple reason that the Dauphin declined the challenge. The ostensible motive given by the chronicler was cowardice, the Dauphin "fearinge to submit himselfe to so great a perill." It seems more likely, however, that the Dauphin refused the challenge from Henry V for the same reason that the king of France refused the challenge of Edward III in 1340 (who in turn refused a subsequent challenge from the king of France) and for the same reason that Henry IV refused the challenge of Louis d'Orléans, brother of Charles VI, in 1402: these challenges were understood to be a matter of form, a chivalric pageant, not an actual alternative to real warfare. In the later Middle Ages, Johan Huizinga has pointed out, preparations for single combat between kings and princes "were made with great solemnity and in great detail, the express motive always being '*pour éviter effusion de sang chrestien et la destruction du peuple.*'" But however pompously announced, Huizinga continues, the battle royal never came off: "It had long been an international comedy, a piece of empty ceremonial between royal houses."[5]

If we return to the text of Hal's challenge, it is obvious that Shakespeare—with no precedent in his known sources—has made Hal's motive be the one traditional for such combats. As Hal states at the outset,

> In both your armies there is many a soul
> Shall pay full dearly for this encounter
> If once they join in trial.

At the close, in order "to save the blood on either side," Hal declares he will try fortune with Hotspur in a single fight.

That the challenge is not in earnest is also consonant with chivalric convention. As we have seen, the king's impatient response underscores the impracticality of such combat: "considerations infinite / Do make against it." Even Hotspur's response to Vernon's news of the challenge has the quality of a condition contrary to fact:

> O, would the quarrel lay upon our heads
> And that no man might draw short breath today
> But I and Harry Monmouth!   [V.ii.47–49]

Although there is clearly no possibility of single combat substituting for the encounter of the two armies, this episode equally clearly cannot be dismissed as another example of what Huizinga termed "a piece of empty ceremonial." On the contrary, Hal's challenge is fraught with significance, for it functions like a pageant to represent Hal's Return to Chivalry. Just as the tournament gave visible form to the ideals associated with the revival of chivalry in the Tudor period, so Hal's challenge displays him as the ideal prince of chivalric honor to others on stage and in the audience.[6]

Vernon speaks for those on stage, and it is indicative that his account to Hotspur is less concerned with the fact of Hal's challenge than with its merits as a performance. If the Hostess can exclaim about Falstaff's roleplaying as king, "O Jesu, he doth it as like one of these harlotry players as ever I see!" (II.iv.390–91), Vernon relates that Hal's words and actions "became him like a prince indeed." Here is a higher conception of acting, for an act "becomes" a prince much as manners "make" the man.

Watching Prince Hal give his challenge, a discerning Renaissance audience would presumably agree with Montaigne, *"The sharpest and most difficile profession of the world, is (in mine opinion) worthily to act and play the King."*[7] As Stephen Orgel has recognized, the image of the prince was paramount in the Renaissance, and that image was naturally construed in the theatrical terms of an actor beheld by an audience: " 'We princes, I tell you,' said Queen Elizabeth, 'are set on stages, in the sight and view of all the world duly observed.' "[8] The admonitions of James I to his son in *Basilicon Doron* expand on this notion in a way that glosses virtually all of Shakespeare's tetralogy: "It is a true olde saying, That a King is as one set on a stage, whose smallest actions and gestures, all the people gazinglie do beholde: and therefore . . . the people, who seeth but the outward part, will euer iudge of the substance, by the circumstances: and according to the outwarde appearance, if his behaviour be light and dissolute, will conceiue prae-occupied conceits of the Kings inward intention: whiche . . . will breede contempt, the mother of rebellion and disorder."[9] Hal's behavior has been dissolute, and disorder and rebellion are precisely the conditions that predominate in *1 Henry IV*. By giving the challenge to single combat, however, Hal reverses the way others see his "outward part."

Does any inward change precede and direct this altered appearance? A question not to be asked, any more than we can ask at what point Bolingbroke decides to seize the crown in *Richard II*. Indeed, in *1 Henry IV* Shakespeare seems to delight in making us judge of the substance by the circumstances—witness the "issue" of the joke on Francis, for example. Even after this practical joke is over, its point is still sufficiently obscure that Poins (who is after all one of its two participants) must ask what it all means: "What cunning match have you made with this jest of the drawer: come, what's the issue?" (II.iv.87–89). Another dramatist might well make Hal's reply, "I am now of all humours that have showed themselves humours since the old days of goodman Adam to the pupil age of this present twelve o'clock at midnight" (II.iv.90–93), be the climax to a straightforward, Pauline conversion: it is midnight, the dividing point between the time of the old Adam and the new, and if the moment still belongs to the "pupil age," that period in which one is a minor at school, these "playing holidays" are about to give way to a new day and a new Prince Hal. The point is, of course, that such a redemptive scheme does not square with the action of the play. Far from turning over a new leaf, Hal thinks about playing the role of Hotspur and then, after Falstaff enters, first "reproves" Falstaff's cowardice at Gad's Hill and then improvises the "King and Prince" play-within-a-play.

Now it has been argued, and well argued, that the Francis episode is a mirror scene that reflects Hal's own conflicting obligations: that is, Francis stands for Hal, as indeed the name substitution in "Tom, Dick, and . . . Francis" suggests. [10] According to this interpretation, Hal puts Francis in the position he himself occupies, conscious of the demands made on him by the court and by the tavern, postponing serving the one in favor of the other. This is an attractive interpretation, but it suffers from an important limitation: it fails to account for Hal's explicitly associating Francis not with himself but with Hotspur.

Rather than taking the Francis episode as a mirror scene reflecting Hal's obligations, we might consider it as a kind of perspective glass, analogous to the pictorial device that from one angle shows one view and from another angle yet another. What the two have in common is their focus on honor.

It may be useful here to recall how the king will rebuke Hal at court this coming morning. The king is concerned to establish a comparison between Richard and Hal. Richard, Henry declares,

> carded his state,
> Mingled his royalty with cap'ring fools,
> Had his great name profaned with their scorns,
> And gave his countenance against his name
> To laugh at gibing boys, and stand the push
> Of every beardless vain comparative.   [III.ii.62–67]

That is to say, Richard indulged in indiscriminate social mingling ("carded his state"), submitted to impudence ("standing the push") and thus profaned his royal dignity. At the close of his speech, the king makes the comparison explicit:

> And in that very line, Harry, standest thou,
> For thou hast lost thy princely privilege
> With vile participation. [III.ii.85–88]

Far more is at issue here than the political liabilities of acting like one unfortunate individual, Richard, and unless we are aware of this larger meaning we cannot fully appreciate how Hal acts with Francis. In contrast to the democratic assumption that a ruler should have a common touch, Renaissance treatises on kingship emphasize the opposite: a prince must avoid contamination by the lower classes. In chapter 21, "How a Prince Ought to Govern to Gain Reputation," Machiavelli grants that a prince ought to encourage those employed in trade and agriculture and even meet with them from time to time to give them examples of his benevolence and munificence. "At all times, and on all occasions, however," Machiavelli warns, "he should take care to maintain the dignity of his position which should never suffer diminution for any reason."[11]

If it is not surprising to find Henry IV largely agreeing with Machiavelli, it may be surprising to find that their concern is also shared by Erasmus. In *The Education of a Christian Prince,* Erasmus inveighs against the stupidity of judging the merits of a prince on the basis of such a shameful accomplishment as drinking with gusto.[12] The true prince ought to be removed from the sullied opinions and worthless activities of the common folk, Erasmus declares, and consequently the "one thing which he should consider base, vile, and unbecoming to him" is to be like them (p. 150).

Although Hal has become "so good a proficient in one quarter of an hour" that he "can drink with any tinker in his own language," Hal appears to consider this use of his time to be "base, vile, and unbecoming to him," for he remarks to Poins, "I have sounded the very base-string of humility" (II.iv.5–6).

Hal's motivation for his ensuing practical joke on Francis may be supplied by a passage on honor in the *Nicomachean Ethics,* a work that may well be the eventual source for the characterization of Hal as a mean between the two extremes of Falstaff and Hotspur.[13] Aristotle observes that, in contrast to the vain man (a "proud Jack like Falstaff"), the rightfully proud man will utterly despise honor awarded on trifling grounds by ordinary people, the reason being that he knows himself worthy of great honors awarded by great men. As Hal tells Poins about his drinking bout in which he was awarded the title of "the king of courtesy," his tone is bitter and sarcastic: "I tell thee, Ned, thou hast lost much honour that thou wert not with me in this action" (II.iv.19–21). As Fredson Bowers has noticed, Hal's use of "action" to mean a battle or encounters parodies Hotspur's "so honourable an action" in the preceding scene (II.iii.33–34).[14] The assurance of "three or four loggerheads" that he "shall command all the good lads in Eastcheap" when he is king of England appears to have galled Hal's pride, his rightful sense of self-worth. Playing the joke on Francis could thus be one means of assuaging his contempt for such epithets as "a Corinthian, a lad of mettle, a good boy (by the Lord, so they call me!)" awarded by persons of no higher status than "a leash of drawers" (II.iv.7–13).

If this interpretation is valid, it is possible that Shakespeare meant the joke on Francis to illustrate a version of comic catharsis—and I use "illustrate" as a cautionary reminder that we as audience do not know *why* Hal plays this practical joke. By laughing at Francis's predictably automatic responses, Hal could be said to purge himself of this "base" association and thereby restore himself to a better mood. At the close of the joke, Falstaff is finally at hand, and Hal rhetorically asks Poins, "Shall we be merry?" "As merry as crickets, my lad," Poins responds, and then asks, "But hark ye, what cunning match have ye made with this jest of the drawer: come, what's the issue?" The baffling answer Hal makes can record the result of his comic catharsis. Hal's temperament is now in balance, and he has come into harmony with the time: "I am now of all humours that have showed themselves humours since the old days of goodman Adam to the pupil age of this present twelve o'clock at midnight" (II.iv.90–93).

Hal's next line emphasizes the time: "What's o'clock, Francis?" Shakespeare, never loath to exploit a formula ruthlessly, gives Francis one last "Anon, anon, sir" and takes him off. With his exit, the perspective shifts, for Hal associates the predictable response of Francis with Hotspur:

> His industry is up-stairs and down-stairs, his eloquence the parcel of a reckoning. I am not yet of Percy's mind, the Hotspur of the north, he that kills me some six or seven dozen of Scots at a breakfast, washes his hands, and says to his wife, "Fie upon this quiet life, I want work." "O my sweet Harry," says she, "how many has thou killed today?" "Give my roan horse a drench," says he, and answers, "Some fourteen," an hour after; "a trifle, a trifle." I prithee call in Falstaff; I'll play Percy, and that damned brawn shall play Dame Mortimer his wife. [II.iv.97–108]

This is a devastatingly accurate parody of Hotspur, not only in respect to his greater concern for his horse than for his wife, but in respect to his quantitative conception of honor.[15] The "parcel of a reckoning" is, after all, exactly what Hal takes from Hotspur at Shrewsbury, for Hotspur cares more about the loss of his proud titles than of his life. Hal is "not yet of Percy's mind," nor will he ever be so single-minded, but his explicit parody of Hotspur's characteristic behavior is the first suggestion that Hal can play whatever part he likes with a masterful "double spirit of teaching and of learning instantly."

Rather than taking the Francis episode as a mirror scene reflecting Hal's conflicts, therefore, I prefer to take it as a perspective glass reflecting two views of honor. Hal first plays a joke on Francis to redeem his honor from contamination by the common man; he then displays the ease with which he can imitate Hotspur, the "theme of honour's tongue." In both instances, however, we as audience are not given privileged information about Hal's intentions. Like the people regarding the ruler that King James describes in *Basilicon Doron,* we see only the outward part of Hal, and hence we can only judge of his inward intention by the circumstances.

An even more extreme example of having to judge by the circumstances is provided by an episode in IV.i, an episode that focuses on Hal's outward parts from so great a distance that Hal takes on emblematic attributes in our imagination. After Hotspur contemptuously asks the whereabouts of the "nimble-footed madcap Prince of Wales," Vernon replies in terms that create a world of figures as well as the form of what Hotspur—and we—should attend:

> All furnish'd, all in arms;
> All plum'd like estridges that with the wind
> Bated, like eagles having lately bath'd,
> Glittering in golden coats like images,
> As full of spirit as the month of May,
> And gorgeous as the sun at midsummer;
> Wanton as youthful goats, wild as young bulls.
> I saw young Harry with his beaver on,
> His cushes on his thighs, gallantly arm'd,
> Rise from the ground like feather'd Mercury,
> And vaulted with such ease into his seat
> As if an angel dropp'd down from the clouds
> To turn and wind a fiery Pegasus,
> And witch the world with noble horsemanship.   [IV.i.97–110]

As James Black has perceived, "What cannot be shown on Shakespeare's stage—the horses and the accoutrements—is turned into heraldry and heraldic terms for the audience's mental eye, into 'arms' and 'golden coats,' and 'images' of heraldic beasts unreeled in a verbal pageant: estridges, eagles, youthful goats, young bulls."[16]

This verbal pageant climaxes with Prince Hal's feat of horsemanship, one that melds various kinds of action: "rise from the ground," "vaulted," "dropp'd from the clouds / To turn and wind a fiery Pegasus." Such "noble horsemanship" points to the derivation of "chivalry" from the Old French *chevalerie* and from the Latin *caballarius*. So great is the evocative power of "witch the world with noble horsemanship" that it is a distinct comedown to look at, rather than to imagine, a rendering of this notion like the one Peacham dedicated in 1612 to Henry, prince of Wales (see figure 1). Here, in the most literal way, is the hope and expectation of this prince's time: "Thus, thus young HENRY . . . Ought'st thou in armes before thy people shine." Through Vernon's speech, Hal and his followers, "plumed" and "glittering in golden coats like images," are meant to shine before us in imaginative splendor.

The most extreme example of how we are forced to judge of Hal's inward intentions by outward circumstances follows hard upon his combat with Hotspur. Considered together, Hal's challenge and their actual combat illustrate yet another example of parallel staging in this play. Just as Falstaff's cowardice is proved at Gad's Hill and "reproved" at the Boar's Head, and just as Hal practices an answer in the play-within-a-play and then actually does answer his father's charges at court that same morning, so Hal's challenge to Hotspur is paralleled by their actual combat. Contrary to history, therefore, chivalric ritual becomes dramatic reality.

The larger action of the battle first serves as a foil to set off Hal's performance. By refusing to withdraw even when wounded, Hal proves his courage; by rescuing the king from Douglas, Hal proves that he is a true son to his father. Once Hal has "redeem'd [his] lost opinion," as the king exclaims, he meets Hotspur in a battle royal.

The parallels to the earlier challenge are unmistakable. The dialogue centers on Hal's identity, and once again it is construed in visual terms. Hotspur sees Hal as a private individual whom he can overawe, but, as in the challenge, Hal asserts his public, royal position—and now he does so not modestly but with a pride at least equal to Hotspur's:

> *Hotspur.* If I mistake not, thou art Harry Monmouth.
> *Prince.* Thou speak'st as if I would deny my name.
> *Hotspur.* My name is Harry Percy.
> *Prince.* Why then I see
>   A very valiant rebel of the name.
>   I am the Prince of Wales, and think not, Percy,
>   To share with me in glory any more. [V.iv.58–63]

True to his vows to the king, Hal reaffirms his determination to redeem his shame on Percy's head: "all the budding honours on thy crest / I'll crop

Hopefull, ʜᴇɴʀɪᴇ Prince of ᴠᴠᴀʟᴇꜱ, &c.

Βρεῆαννίκε τῇ χαρτί.

ʜᴇɴʀɪᴄᴠꜱ Walliæ Princeps.

Par Achillis, Puer vne vinces.

T HVS, thus young ʜᴇɴʀʏ, like Macedo's ſonne,
  Ought'ſt thou in armes before thy people ſhine.
A prodigie for foes to gaze vpon,
But ſtill a glorious Load-ſtarre vnto thine :
  Or ſecond ᴘʜᴏᴇᴇᴠꜱ whoſe all piercing ray,
  Shall cheare our heartes, and chaſe our feares away.

Figure 1. "To the most renowned, and hopefull, Henrie Prince of Wales."
(From Henry Peacham, *Minerva Britanna* [1612].)

to make a garland for my head." That the issue is in earnest rather than play is emphasized by Falstaff's encouragement to Hal as they fight: "Well said, Hal! To it, Hal! Nay, you shall find no boy's play here, I can tell you." "Boy's play" recalls Hal's "playing holidays," but it might also refer to Renaissance tournaments. These tournaments were associated with youthful pastimes—and by convention were always won by the prince. [17]

Be that as it may, their combat leads to Hotspur's death, and that in turn to a visual pageant of honor, complete with symbolic staging. The true prince stands over the fallen Hotspur and the shamming Falstaff, the respective embodiments of presumptuous pride and of pusillanimity; and, depending on whether Blunt, dressed in the king's suit, is still in view, Hal can also stand over an ostensibly royal "Counterfeit Countenance," a morality figure familiar from Skelton's *Magnyfycence* and the cardinal virtue tradition, that is disturbingly parallel to that other "counterfeit," Falstaff. [18]

Westmoreland's earlier praise for Hotspur's victory now accurately describes Hal's: "In faith, / It is a conquest for a prince to boast of" (I.i.75–76). In contrast to Hotspur, who dies regretting the loss of his proud titles, Hal apparently no longer is motivated by a quantitative conception of honor. Instead of cropping "all the budding honours" on the crest of Hotspur's helmet, Hal covers Hotspur's mangled face with his own favors.

If these favors are the plumes of his helmet, then Hal's action extends the symbolism of this pageant of honor. A. R. Humphreys notes in the new Arden edition that Hal's favors are less likely to be scarves or gloves than a torse of silk or the plumes from his helmet. Given that plumes were generally associated with the chivalric revival in the Renaissance as well as specifically associated with the prince of Wales, it seems reasonable to suppose that these favors are less likely to be a silken torse than ostrich plumes. For example, notice how prominently plumes figure in Nicholas Hilliard's full-length portrait of Sir Anthony Mildmay, circa 1596 (figure 2). [19] More specifically, three plumes were—and of course still are—the emblem of the prince of Wales, and Vernon has already called attention to Prince Hal and his followers "all plum'd like estridges" (IV.i.98). [20]

If Hal covers Hotspur's mangled face with his plumes, then his "show of zeal" (V.iv.94) takes on symbolic significance. In contrast to Hal's giving the challenge to single combat before an audience on stage that could appraise how his performance "became him like a prince indeed," no one on stage (unless Falstaff is keeping one eye open as he shams death) sees either how Hal kills Hotspur or how he performs his "show of zeal." After his resurrection, Falstaff can make a joke about this freedom ("Nothing confutes me but eyes, and nobody sees me") and abuse it to give Hotspur a

Figure 2. "Sir Anthony Mildmay" by Nicholas Hilliard, circa 1596. (Reproduced by permission of the Cleveland Museum of Art, purchase from the J. H. Wade Fund.)

wound in what he euphemistically calls the thigh, a disturbing replication of the "beastly shameless transformation" practiced by the Welsh on the corpses of those who followed Mortimer, "such misuse" as "may not be / Without much shame retold or spoken of" (I.i.43–46). But this misuse Falstaff enacts before us.

As opposed to Falstaff, however, Hal acts as if it did not matter whether anyone saw him or not. In so doing, Hal undercuts the conventional Elizabethan conception of power as deriving from carefully stage-managed appearances. Furthermore, assuming that he shrouds the face of Hotspur with his plumes, Hal becomes the diametrical opposite of "plume-pluck'd Richard," for he transforms his role into reality: he stands as an emblem of the knight *sine pluma* (see figure 3). As Peacham's clumsy verse declares, this synecdochic "warlick Helme . . . No featherie creast, or dressing doth desire, / Which at the Tilts, the vulgar most admire." Peacham gives a number of explanations, each of which has the unfortunate result of making the preceding less persuasive, but for our purposes the first is the most helpful: "For best desert, still liveth out of view, / Or soone by Envie, is commaunded downe."

Recounting how Hal had delivered his challenge, Vernon ended with a prophecy:

> There did he pause: but let me tell the world—
> If he outlive the envy of this day,
> England did never owe so sweet a hope
> So much misconstru'd in his wantonness.   [V.ii.65–68]

Hal has "outlived the envy of this day," at least in the literal sense that he is still alive, but he has not escaped scot-free. As we are told in Falstaff's catechism, honor will not live with the living. "Why? Detraction will not suffer it" (V.i.139–40). Not content with castrating Hotspur's corpse, Falstaff brazenly claims the reward of nobility dative by royal action: "There is Percy! If your father will do me any honor, so; if not, let him kill the next Percy himself. I look to be either earl or duke, I can assure you" (V.iv.138–40). Standing there with his plumeless helmet beside Prince John, Hal represents Peacham's Best Dessert; unrecognized by the nobility and by the vulgar, he is comically commanded down by Envy:

> *Prince.* Why, Percy I kill'd myself, and saw thee dead.
> *Falstaff.* Didst thou? Lord, Lord, how this world is given to lying!
> [V.i.143–45]

Needless to say, of course, we the audience know better. Precisely by making use of an outward "show" of giving his favors to Hotspur, Shake-

THIS warlick Helme, that naked doth appeare,
  Not gold-enchaſed, or with Gemmes beſet,
Yet doth the markes, of many a battaile beare,
With dintes of bullets, there imprinted yet,
  No featherie creaſt, or dreaſſing doth deſire,
  Which at the Tilts, the vulgar moſt admire.

For beſt deſert, ſtill liveth out of view,
Or ſoone by Envie, is commaunded downe,
*· Nor can her heauen-bred ſpirit lowly ſue,
Though t'were to gaine, a kingdome, and a crowne:
  Beſide it tells vs, that the valiant heart,
  Can liue content, though wanteth his deſert.

* — Emitur ſola
virtute poteſtas,
Claudian:

Figure 3. The knight *sine pluma*. (From Henry Peacham, *Minerva Britanna* [1612].)

speare emphasizes how Hal's native nobility has transcended outward show. In his essay "Invisible Bullets: Renaissance Authority and Its Subversion," Stephen Greenblatt has argued, "*1 Henry IV* confirms the Machiavellian hypothesis of the origin of princely power in force and fraud even as it draws its audience irresistibly toward the celebration of that power."[21] Given the political dynamics of the entire play, this view is largely accurate, but what makes Hal's triumph over Hotspur so irresistible is the way Shakespeare has altered our perception of princely power.

If Hal's challenge to Hotspur substitutes a purer version of theatrical display for the king's impure version, Hal's triumph over Hotspur moves into a different dimension altogether, a dimension in which power is paradoxically uncelebrated. The other characters do not witness Hal's victory: it is not seen, and hence cannot be regarded. Nor does it appear in the regard of history: the climax of *Henry IV, Part 1*—Hotspur's death at the hands of Prince Hal—does not appear in the accounts of the Battle of Shrewsbury (it is only suggested by Daniel's *Civil Wars*). Only we the audience see it, and thus only we recognize what Hal gives up when he lets Falstaff claim the honor rightfully his.

Hal's magnanimity therefore reverses the ongoing conception of princely theatricality construed by the king as that "extraordinary gaze / Such as is bent on sunlike majesty" by an admiring audience (III.ii.78–80). Hal does not have an audience on stage. Yet, at the same time, Hal's magnanimity reinforces this conception of majesty, for *we* see it, and because *only* we see it, we are uniquely privileged. We have already seen Hal mock "the parcel of a reckoning," and when we see him letting Falstaff take the credit we may be reminded that Hal, unlike his father, did not gain his title by fraud even if he has had to help keep it by force. In these terms, Hal proves he is a "true" prince precisely because he can afford to let the glory go. Or so we can speculate—even as privileged spectators, we still know nothing about Hal's private self, about his real motives, or about his "inward intention."

Hal begins Act V by giving a challenge in which he embodies to a preeminent degree the theatrical conception of kingship. His Return to Chivalry is a splendid performance, as Vernon testifies. By the close of Act V, however, Hal stands in a different relation to that conception. He is not recognized by those on stage as the worthy successor to Hotspur, "the theme of honour's tongue," and if Shakespeare had chosen to stage a Triumph of Fame, the leading figure after Fame or Renown would be not Hal but Falstaff. On the contrary, Hal has become Best Dessert, the emblematic figure "that liveth out of view, / Or soone by Envie, is commaunded downe." By this kind of theatrical inversion, Shakespeare has made Hal's

circumstances and outward parts be the more impressive in their theatrically studied unimpressiveness. They derive their force from a kind of
negative definition, from what they are not: the splendid display briefly
visible in the chivalric pageantry of the challenge and imaginatively represented in Vernon's speech to Hotspur about Hal and his men "glittering in
golden coats like images."

If in delivering the challenge Hal became "like a prince indeed," by
overcoming Hotspur Hal has translated appearance into actuality: he has
become a prince in deed. Hal's is a triumph of honor precisely because he
is not accorded any public triumph, and this omission is altogether fitting—if ultimately ironic—for the prince *sine pluma*. In Shakespeare's
theater we see that Hal's victory over Hotspur went unrecorded in history
for the simplest of reasons: no one saw it.

Notes

1. *I Henry IV* (III.ii.149–50). This and subsequent references are to *King Henry IV, Part 1*, ed. A. R. Humphreys (London: Methuen, 1966).

2. John Florio, *A Worlde of Wordes* (London, 1598), *"Trionfo"* (p. 433). See also D. D. Carnicelli's useful discussion of triumphs in his introduction to *Lord Morley's "Tryumphes of Fraunces Petrarcke": The First English Translation of the "Trionfi"* (Cambridge, Mass: Harvard University Press, 1971), pp. 54–56; and Gordon Kipling, "Triumphal Drama: Form in English Civic Pageantry," *Renaissance Drama,* n.s., 8 (1977): 37–56.

3. John Dover Wilson, *The Fortunes of Falstaff* (Cambridge: Cambridge University Press, 1945), p. 64. Wilson observes about Hal: "As a 'truant to chivalry,' he has first to prove himself a soldier and a leader; and this he accomplishes on the field Shrewsbury" (p. 64). In my view, however, the action is rather more complex.

4. *The First English Life of King Henry the Fifth* (1513), ed. Charles L. Kingsford (Oxford: Clarendon Press, 1911), p. 83; this is a translation of Tito Livio's *Vita Henrici Quinti*. Stow used this source but not the account of this challenge. Holinshed's *Chronicle* (ed. Allardyce Nicoll and Josephine Nicoll, Everyman Library [London: J. M. Dent, 1955]) gives the traditional motive of avoiding "the de-struction of Christian people" and the "effusion of Christian bloud" but sub-stitutes for the challenge a demand for restitution (p. 76).

5. Johan Huizinga, *Homo Ludens* (Boston: Beacon Press, 1955), p. 92. Com-pare his *Waning of the Middle Ages* (Garden City, N.Y.: Doubleday, Anchor Books, n.d.), pp. 96–98. My examples come from Raymond L. Kilgour (who agrees with Huizinga about the "empty" ceremonial), *The Decline of Chivalry As Shown in the French Literature of the Late Middle Ages* (1937; rpt. ed., Gloucester, Mass.:

Smith, 1966), pp. 10–11. See also George Nelson, *Trial by Combat* (Boston: G. A. Jackson, 1909).

6. On the Renaissance revival of chivalry, see Roy Strong, *Splendor at Court: Renaissance Spectacle and the Theatre of Power* (Boston: Houghton Mifflin, 1973), pp. 36–37; Sydney Anglo, *Spectacle, Pageantry, and Early Tudor Policy* (Oxford: Clarendon Press, 1969), pp. 98ff.; Gordon Kipling, *The Triumph of Honour: Burgundian Origins of the Elizabethan Renaissance* (Leiden: Leiden University Press for Sir Thomas Browne Institute, 1977).

7. Montaigne, *Essays,* book 3, chap. 7, trans. John Florio, Everyman Library (London: J. M. Dent, 1946), 3:153.

8. Stephen Orgel, *The Illusion of Power: Political Theater in the English Renaissance* (Berkeley and Los Angeles: University of California Press, 1975), p. 42. Orgel also gives the beginning of my quotation from James I.

9. *The Basilicon Doron of King James VI,* ed. James Craigie, S.T.S., 3d ser., 16 (Edinburgh: W. Blackwood and Sons, 1944), 1:163. This "true olde saying" appears in both the 1599 and 1603 editions.

10. See J. D. Schuchter, "Prince Hal and Francis: The Imitation of an Action," *Shakespeare Studies* 3 (1967): 129–37; Sheldon P. Zitner, "Anon, Anon; or, A Mirror for a Magistrate," *Shakespeare Quarterly* 19 (1968): 63–70; John Shaw, "The Staging of Parody and Parallels in '1 Henry IV,'" *Shakespeare Survey* 20 (1967): 61–73.

11. Niccolo Machiavelli, *The Prince,* trans. A. Robert Caponigri, Gateway Edition (Chicago: Henry Regnery, 1963), p. 118.

12. Desiderius Erasmus, *The Education of a Christian Prince (Institutio Principis Christiani),* trans. Lester K. Born (New York: W. W. Norton, 1968), p. 150. Compare what Reynaldo protests about Laertes in *Hamlet,* II.i.20ff.

13. Aristotle, *Nicomachean Ethics,* 4. 3 (1124^a), from *Introduction to Aristotle,* ed. Richard McKeon (New York: Random House, 1947), pp. 384–85. William B. Hunter discusses Hal as embodiment of the Aristotelian mean in "Falstaff," *South Atlantic Quarterly* 50 (1951): 86–95.

14. Fredson Bowers, "Hal and Francis in *King Henry IV,* Part 1," *Renaissance Papers 1965* (1966), pp. 15–20. See also his essay "Theme and Structure in *King Henry IV,* Part 1," in *The Drama of the Renaissance: Essays for Leicester Bradner,* ed. Elmer M. Blistein (Providence, R.I.: Brown University Press, 1970), pp. 42–68.

15. See Raymond H. Reno, "Hotspur: The Integration of Character and Theme," *Renaissance Papers 1962* (1963), pp. 17–25.

16. James Black, "A World of Figures Here," in *Shakespeare: The Theatrical Dimension,* ed. Philip C. McGuire and David A. Samuelson (New York: AMS Press, 1979), p. 170.

17. See the sixteenth-century tournament song about passing "the tyme of youth joly" quoted by Joycelyne G. Russell, *The Field of Cloth of Gold* (New York: Barnes and Noble, 1969), p. 108. The mock battles of pageant dramatists might also apply to these lines: see David M. Bergeron, *English Civic Pageantry 1558–1642* (Columbia: University of South Carolina Press, 1971), p. 46. On princes' tournament victories, see Strong, *Splendor at Court,* p. 44.

18. Commentary is legion, but see Kipling, *Triumph of Honour,* pp. 28–29, 163; on "Counterfeit Countenance" see William O. Harris, *Skelton's "Magnyfycence" and the Cardinal Virtue Tradition* (Chapel Hill: University of North Carolina Press, 1965), pp. 89–90; on Blunt, see Alan C. Dessen, "The Intemperate Knight and the Politic Prince: Late Morality Structure in *1 Henry IV,*" *Shakespeare Studies* 7 (1974): 167.

19. An even greater display of plumes is apparent in Hilliard's portrait of George Clifford, third earl of Cumberland, painted about 1590. Clifford succeeded Sir Henry Lee as the stager of the Accession Day tilts, and this portrait of the queen's champion features plumes both on his hat and on the helmet of his armor. On the elaborate armor so important in ceremonial chivalry, see Frances A. Yates, "Elizabethan Chivalry: The Romance of the Accession Day Tilts," *Journal of the Warburg and Courtauld Institutes* 20 (1957): 4–25.

20. Herbert Hartman, "Prince Hal's 'Shew of Zeale,' " *PMLA* 46 (1931): 720–23. In "Virtue and Kingship in Shakespeare's Henry IV," *English Literary Renaissance* 5 (1975), Sherman H. Hawkins suggests that Hal's gesture is modelled on that of Alexander to Darius, as recorded by Plutarch (331, n. 58).

21. Stephen Greenblatt, "Invisible Bullets: Renaissance Authority and Its Subversion," *Glyph* 8 (1981): 57.

Part Three

"Exeunt with a Dead March": Funeral Pageantry on the Shakespearean Stage

Michael Neill

At the end of Thomas Preston's *Lamentable Tragedy . . . of Cambyses, King of Persia* (circa 1558–69), three Lords are left to moralize in Preston's inimitably jigging vein over the corpse of their unlucky monarch:

> *1 Lord.* A just reward for his misdeeds the God above hath wrought,
> For certainly the life he led was to be counted naught.
> *2 Lord.* Yet a princely burial shall he have, according to his estate;
> And more of him here at this time we have not to dilate.
> *3 Lord.* My lords, let us take him up and carry him away.
>
> [x.249–53]¹

At first sight these lines may appear to do little more than provide a fairly predictable solution to one of the most basic practical problems of an uncurtained stage—that of clearing away the corpses after a scene of climactic butchery. For an audience schooled in the idiom of Renaissance pageantry, however, this simple processional exit—two men bearing a corpse and a third following in an attitude of mourning—will have had an eloquence beyond Preston's limping fourteeners. For the actors are to compose, as the Second Lord makes clear, a rudimentary version of a royal funeral cortège—reminding the audience of those rites of "princely burial" that partly offset God's leveling judgment with a symbolic reassertion of earthly degree ("according to his estate"). It is a device which, in its hieratic fashion, returns the play from the morality world of Ambidexter's mocking farewell, to the social reality proper to that realm of "tragical history" proclaimed by the Epilogue. For all the crudeness of its execution, it anticipates what was to become the standard form of tragic ending in the Elizabethan and early Jacobean period—a form already well established by the time of Kyd's *Spanish Tragedy* (circa 1587–90):

> *The trumpets sound a dead march, the* KING *of Spain mourning after his brother's body, and the* KING *of Portingale bearing the body of his son.* [IV.iv.266,S.D.][2]

Often the stage funeral was no more elaborate than this—a corpse, two pallbearers, a token mourner or two, and the doleful sounding of a funeral march; at other times dramatists would ask the companies to stretch their resources to the full to create as nearly as possible the illusion of a magnificent public funeral.[3] In either case, the power and meaning of the stage spectacle drew on a major tradition of street pageantry—one whose rituals and conventions bore a complex and interesting relationship to those of tragedy itself. Funeral obsequies are the pageant theater of death and mourning; tragedy (as the rough working definitions of the Elizabethans constantly remind us) is above all a drama of death: the funeral constitutes, I would suggest, an important and largely neglected area in the study of pageantry on the English stage.

Of all those lavish forms of organized public display that adorned the streets of Shakespeare's England, the funerals of princes, great nobles, powerful gentry, and wealthy merchants were necessarily the most common;[4] reminders of their pomp, in the form of monuments, tombs, hearses, hatchments, and heraldic accouterments, decorated every church in the land; the tombs of the great formed a kind of permanent "show" in themselves, rivaled only (in the case of Westminster Abbey) by those wooden or wax portrait effigies originally displayed on the coffins of princely funerals.[5] In spite of their religious context, funeral rites were primarily pieces of secular ostentation, "symbolic justifications of rank and status," organized according to elaborate rules by the College of Heralds: "Though the service took place in church, the master of ceremonies was not the parson, but the heralds, and the affair was characterised more by the rituals of antiquarian feudalism than those of Christianity. It was, remarked the Separatist Henry Barrow, "as if Duke Hector, or Ajax, or Sir Launcelot was buried."[6] From the perspective of an Elizabethan herald like Sir William Segar, Garter King of Arms, funeral "shewes" belonged to precisely the same order of pageantry as coronations, royal weddings, entries, and progresses—all were forms of "Triumph."[7] Every detail of the funeral procession, from the display of knightly arms, banners, and heraldic devices to the arrangement of successive groups of paupers, yeomen, household servants, serving gentlemen, client gentry, and noble mourners with their followers, was designed to proclaim not just the power, wealth, and status of the dead man, but his place inside a fixed and unassailable social order, to which the rituals of the church gave ultimate sanction and the inscriptions and iconography of his tomb bore lasting testament (figure 1).[8] Segar, who devotes an entire chapter of his treatise on honor to the "order to be . . . kept" in funerals, gives a particularly clear sense of this social symbolism:

> We see that at the buriall of our Princes and persons of honour all their friends and domesticall servants doe assemble, and carrie in their hands all the Armes, Pennons and other Hatchments appertaining unto the defunct . . . ech man [is] to march in such place, as is meete for his estate. The Heralds therefore by their skill and care, are to take a List or Rolle of all Mourners, then to marshall them into severall classes by their divers titles, as Gentlemen, Esquires, Knights, Barons, Vicounts, Earles, &c. ever preferring her Majesties officers and servants before all others. . . . And if none . . . be there present, then every one to proceede according to his antienty *in pari dignitate.* [pp. 252–53]

Segar even argues that, to avoid inappropriate expense and to preserve a proper decorum, the queen or earl marshall should

> prescribe a certaine number of Mourners to every degree, and that no man of greater title than the defunct should be permitted to mourne, so as the chiefe mourner may ever be *in pari dignitate* with the defunct, and all the rest of meaner qualitie. [p. 253]

In addition to this somewhat bureaucratic preoccupation with the minutiae of hierarchical ordering, the heralds must exhibit a proper care for celebrating the defunct's personal honor and exalted rank; the funeral procession should constitute a kind of heraldic biography:

> *Nota,* That an Officer of Armes weareth the Kings coate at th'enterrements of Noblemen, and others of dignitie and Worship, not onely for the ordering of the funerals, and marshalling of the degrees . . . but to the intent that the defunct may be knowen to all men to have died honourably in the Kings allegeance, without spot or infamie, or other disworship to his Name, Blood & Family: and that his heire, if he have any, or next of whole blood, or some one for him (which commonly is the chief mourner) may publikely receive in the presence of all the mourners, the Coate armor, Helme, Creast, and other Atchievements of honour belonging to the defunct: whereof the King of Armes of the Province is to make record, with the defuncts match, issue and decease for the benefit of posterity. [p. 253]

The well-known portrait of Sir Henry Unton, now in the National Portrait Gallery, London, provides an eloquent pictorial gloss on Segar's

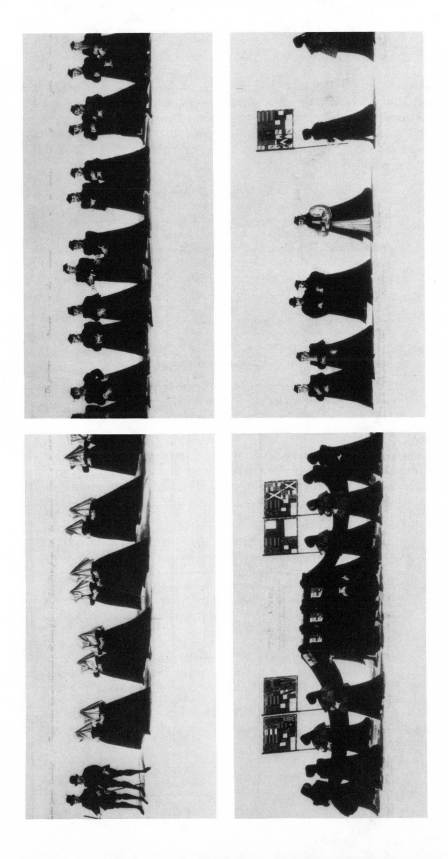

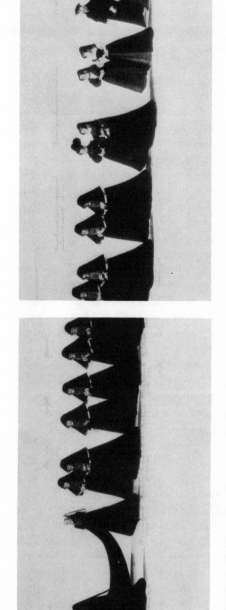

Figure 1. The funeral procession of Lady Lumley. (British Library, Add. Ms. 35324; reproduced by permission of the British Library.)

funeral instructions (figure 2). The portrait, commissioned by Unton's widow after his death in 1596, is both a *memento mori* and a memorial— the domestic equivalent of that splendid church monument toward which its narrative leads.[9] The picture enshrines the history of an entire life, seen retrospectively: as it might be, the narrative of the funeral sermon being preached in Faringdon church on the left of the painting. The composition is dominated by an outsize portrait figure of Sir Henry, the diplomatist at his desk, caught at the instant of writing a dispatch to his royal mistress. But the semblance of arrested life is misleading: for the image is superimposed on the biographical narrative, not a part of it; the funeral black of Sir Henry's costume and of the drapes behind him remind us that it is the portrait of a man already dead. Like the bust effigies of tomb sculpture that it resembles,[10] it is an ideal image, summarizing a life already lived—a point emphasized by the flanking figures of Fame and Death making their rival claims for the dead hero much as they might in any church monument (and as Fame indeed does in the lunette of Unton's arched tomb below). The hangings that frame the portrait also seem to draw upon the vocabulary of memorial sculpture, where parted curtains functioned as a familiar symbol of resurrection.[11] This portrait, as Roy Strong notes, divides the picture space into a sunlit world of life and business, and the night world of death, its darkness, silence, and emptiness broken only by the crowded funeral service and the brightly illuminated tomb. But strictly this division affects only the upper two-thirds of the painting; cutting off one narrative sequence at its height, it leaves another, visually more compelling, intact. For the foreground asks to be read in terms of a single ineluctable movement from cradle to grave, only fleetingly diverted by the harmonious circling of the masque dancers in Sir Henry's hall at Wadley. To this grim progress, the great events of Unton's life, as scholar, traveler, soldier, and diplomat, appear to form no more than a picturesque but remote background: they become in the strictest sense marginalia, ornaments of a life properly comprehended in death. The effect is emphasized by a continuous line of masonry, beginning as the outer wall of the house in Ascott-under-Wychwood where Unton was born, continuing through the house and park wall at Wadley to the walls of Faringdon churchyard and the vault beneath Sir Henry's monument in the Unton chapel. Along the wall are spectators—witnesses of a life whose meaning is concentrated in the funeral pageant before them.[12] The funeral procession itself stretches fully two-thirds of the picture's length, emerging from the porch of Wadley even as the wedding revels continue in the hall above. Through the mourning black worn by Unton's mother and bride and by other principals in the action, the procession can even seem to include the life:[13] it is as though funeral provided the occasion for

Figure 2. Sir Henry Unton. (Reproduced by permission, of the National Portrait Gallery, London.)

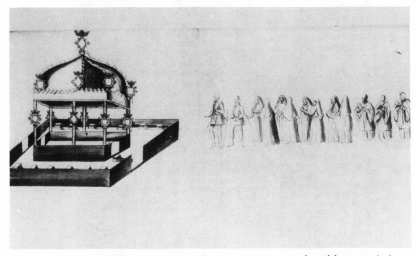

Figure 3. Hearse. (British Library, Add. Ms. 35324; reproduced by permission of the British Library.)

biography. Death, Montaigne wrote, "is the condition of your creation: death is part of your selves. . . . The first day of your birth doth as well adress you to die, as to live. . . . The continuall worke of your life, is to contrive death; you are in death, during the time you continue in life: for, you are after death, when you are no longer living . . . and death doth more rudely touch the dying, than the dead, and more lively and essentially"; the day of death "is the master-day, the day that judgeth all others. . . . To death doe I referre the essay of my studies fruit."[14] The Unton portrait interprets this familiar sentiment pictorially; but, because of its heraldic perspective,[15] its "master-day" is that of the funeral rather than death itself. Unton was buried, according to a College of Arms memorandum, "with a Baron's hearse, and in the degree of a Baron, because he died Ambassador Leger for France."[16] The portrait (recording the family's pride in this distinction) gives some idea of what this "degree" entailed: the cortège winds its way into a church hung with blacks, emblazoned with the Unton escutcheon; the coffin, placed at the symbolic center of the procession, is preceded by a somber parade of mourners in ascending order of rank; immediately before the pallbearers marches the heralds' party— black-clad figures carry great banners ("streamers") displaying the armorial bearings of Sir Henry's family and the cross of Saint George, the three heralds themselves stand out from the rest of the company in their

Figure 4. Part of the funeral procession of Queen Elizabeth. (British Library, Add. Ms. 35324; reproduced by permission of the British Library.)

resplendent coat armor, and the last of them carries Unton's achievements, including the great crested helm which is to be mounted above the tomb; behind the bier walk the chief and principal mourners with their friends and servants in descending order of rank—a long line that reaches back to Wadley.[17] The funeral is a conclusive statement, the abstract record of a life achieved, a Triumph of Fame whose meaning is enshrined forever in that illuminated marble monument of which the picture itself provides a kind of exegesis. But it is not simply the record of an individual life; as the elaborately proclaimed concern for family honor and the proprieties of degree reveal, it is also a piece of propaganda—the symbolic celebration and justification of an entire social order.

A great Elizabethan funeral of this kind was both biographical drama and political theater. Something of the emotive power of this pageant genre is suggested by the strong interest taken in it by the queen. Her own funeral (part of which is shown in figure 4) was among the more splendid public spectacles of her reign. The encouragement (often amounting to virtual blackmail or open compulsion) that Elizabeth and Burleigh gave to the maintenance of this lavish and costly form of display suggests that they saw it as an indispensable symbolic accompaniment to their systematic under-pinning of place and prerogative.[18] Certainly the ideological content of funerals was well understood by a man like John Weever, the historian of funerary monuments, who deplored the decline of elaborate obsequies in the 1620s as a serious neglect of decorum and a threat to the proper ordering of society.[19]

The stage funeral, then, can never have been a merely neutral piece of action; as with other forms of pageantry, its gestures and decor carried with them a freight of social and political meanings on which the drama-tists were bound to draw. It is not, of course, always easy to determine how far the players sought to match the pompous dignity of public obse-quies in the funeral processions that moved across their stages. But cer-tainly the theatrical companies, by virtue of their semifictive status as household servants, would have been directly acquainted with the pro-tocol of such events—Shakespeare's troupe, for instance, will have had their allotted place in the grand funeral of their patron, Lord Hunsdon, in 1596 (compare figure 5). In such plays as Marston's *Antonio's Revenge,* the unusually full stage directions, evidently deriving from an autograph manuscript used in the theater,[20] give us a glimpse of a dramatist mobi-lizing all the resources of his company to evoke the splendor of the real event:

> *The cornets sound a sennet.*
> *Enter two mourners with torches, two with streamers,* CASTILIO *and* FOR-
> OBOSCO *with torches, a Herald bearing Andrugio's helm and sword, the*
> *coffin,* MARIA *supported by* LUCIO *and* ALBERTO, ANTONIO *by himself,*
> PIERO *and* STROTZO *talking,* GALEATZO *and* MATZAGENTE, BALURDO *and*
> PANDULPHO; *the coffin set down, helm, sword, and streamers hung up, placed*
> *by the Herald, whilst* ANTONIO *and* MARIA *wet their handkerchiefs with*
> *their tears, kiss them, and lay them on the hearse, kneeling. All go out but*
> PIERO. *Cornets cease and he speaks.* [II.i.1,S.D.][21]

Clearly the more-or-less improvised funeral processions into which the ceremonies of mourning are telescoped at the end of most tragedies cannot have been mounted with such elaboration. Nevertheless, however cur-tailed and hieratic their treatment, they must have always been con-structed with an awareness of the rich potential significance of funeral decorum. Indeed it is apparent that in a number of plays the stinting or abruption of the ceremonies is being used for dramatic effects that cru-cially depend on the audience's sensitivity to this decorum.

The drama did more than simply incorporate episodes of funeral pag-eantry into its action: the very decor of the tragic stage was shaped by the

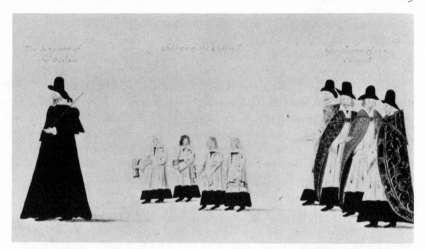

Figure 5. Part of the funeral procession of Queen Elizabeth, showing boy actors from the Children of the Chapel Royal. (British Library, Add. Ms. 35324; reproduced by permission of the British Library.)

conventions of funeral. When the mourning Bedford, in the opening lines of *1 Henry VI*, proclaims, "Hung be the heavens with black, yield day to night" (I.i.1), his metaphor depends on the actual dressing of the stage for what Marston called the "sullen . . . scene" and "black visag'd shows" of tragedy (*Antonio's Revenge*, Prologue, ll. 6, 20). The players decked their stage with black hangings and curtains derived from the "blacks" of funeral custom and designed to prepare the audience's emotions for the ensuing drama of death: "The stage is hunge with blacke; and I perceive / The Auditors prepar'de for Tragedie." The effect of this proleptic announcement of catastrophe was to supply a continuous visual commentary on the action, often creating (particularly in scenes of romantic intrigue and so-called "comic relief") a sharply ironic effect.[22] At the same time it fostered a sense of funeral as the proper and expected end of this kind of drama, so that the final procession of mourners with its accompanying "dead march" came to occupy in tragedy precisely the place accorded in comedy to wedding revels and the final dance of reconciliation. As early as 1583, indeed, we find Sidney using "hornpipes and funerals" as natural metonymies for the opposing genres which "mongrel tragi-comedy" grafted so indecorously together.[23] If in comedy the music and circulating movements of the dance reasserted that transcendent harmony of the universe which the follies of mankind had temporarily disguised, in tragedy the "dead march" and solemn procession served to reaffirm that hierarchic sense of "fair sequence and succession" which the disorders of sin or rebellion had temporarily disrupted.[24] At a deeper level, these two rituals of order arguably correspond to metaphors embedded in the structure of these opposing genres. For if the comic dance suggests a "whirligig of time," that sense of seasonal rotation and renewal (appropriate to the marriage festivals of romantic comedy in particular) in which all things turn and return, the funeral procession answers to the alternative sense of time as ineluctable linear process. The tragic action moved from its opening spectacle of blackness to its concluding ritual of death rather as a funeral moved from the dead man's house with its black-hung rooms, windows, staircases, and funeral bed, to the graveside in the black-draped church; and because in tragedy the anticipated obsequies were normally those of the hero himself, the final procession became a reenactment in little of the plot's remorseless progress to the grave.[25] As *The Spanish Tragedy* with its Babylonical catastrophe, *King Lear* with its intimation of "the promised end," and *Dr. Faustus* with its agonized paraphrase of Revelation remind us, there is frequently a profound suggestion of apocalypse about the endings of tragedy.[26] The funeral procession is not simply an incarnation of earthly order, but an intimation of the process that will ultimately sweep that order away forever: against the elaborately arranged hierarchy of its processional form funeral sets the leveling anonymity of its mourning blacks—symbolically confounding the meticulous hierarchies of costume enshrined in what Keith Thomas has dubbed "the vestimentary system." The poignancy of funeral ceremony derives exactly from this sense that all its pompous ritual is only a mask for that procession to dusty death which haunts Macbeth's imagination; it enacts a line of tragic succession which stretches implicitly to the "crack of doom," beyond the immediate catastrophe to "the promised end": each of us, great and humble, it covertly insists, must follow.

The dramatic equivalent of this concealed metaphor is most clearly displayed in a consciously processional play such as Marlowe's *Tamburlaine,* whose plot unfolds like a sequence of pageant tableaux in a triumphal entry: "All sights of power to grace my victory."[27] In *Part 1* Tamburlaine's symbolic dressing of the stage in white, blood red and black usurps the language of funeral pageantry:

> Black are his colours, black pavilion;
> His spear, his shield, his horse, his armour, plumes,
> And jetty feathers menace death and hell. [*1 Tamburlaine*, IV.i.59–61]

In the second part, however, his parade of victorious spectacles is given new meaning by the introduction of a hearse, containing the embalmed body of Zenocrate. This ambivalent property becomes a prominent feature of the hero's train from the moment of her death in Act II, scene iv—

> Where'er her soul be, thou shalt stay with me,
> Embalm'd with cassia, ambergris, and myrrh,
> Not lapp'd in lead, but in a sheet of gold,
> And till I die thou shalt not be interr'd. [2 *Tamburlaine,* II.iv.129–32]

—until his own death at the end of the play:

> Now fetch the hearse of fair Zenocrate;
> Let it be plac'd by this my fatal chair,
> And serve as parcel of my funeral.   [2 *Tamburlaine,* V.iii.210–12]

Less the intended symbol of her immortality than a mocking counterpart to Tamburlaine's triumphal chariot, the hearse can make us see the whole drama as a concealed Triumph of Death, with Tamburlaine as the unwitting driver of Death's funeral car:[28]

> Where Belus, Ninus, and great Alexander
> Have rode in triumph, triumphs Tamburlaine,
> Whose chariot wheels have burst th'Assyrians' bones,
> Drawn with these captive kings on heaps of carcasses.
>   [2 *Tamburlaine,* V.i.69–72]

The recollection of those Triumphs of Death in which Death's black-draped chariot rumbled over the bones and corpses of a helpless mankind is unmistakable (figure 6): for here, as the Prologue announced, "death cuts off the progress of his pomp, / And murderous Fates throws all his triumphs down" (ll. 4–5); and in the splendid tableau and procession that wind up the play, throne, chariot, and hearse, those parcels of the conqueror's funeral triumph, become sights of power to grace the victory of King Death.[29] *Tamburlaine* makes perhaps the most elaborate use of funeral pageantry of any play in the period, but (like other pageant devices in the play) the familiar rituals are turned awry by the iconoclastic thrust of Marlowe's imagination. The tragedy concludes with an appeal to the apocalyptic paradigm ("Meet heaven and earth, and here let all things end," V.iii.249), but in a context that affirms neither the temporal order of society nor the providential ordering of history. Instead both schemes are subject to a fierce sense of nature's self-consuming destructiveness: "Earth hath spent the pride of all her fruit, / And heaven consum'd his choicest living fire" (V.ii.250–51). It is the note of mingled pessimism and defiance struck by Marlowe's own motto: *Quod me nutrit, me detruit.*[30]

The printed text of 2 *Tamburlaine* supplies no final stage direction, but it is clear from the preceding action and from Amyras's epitaph that Marlowe meant to end the play (as he had ended *Part 1*) in a grand funeral procession. In this part, however, the last of Tamburlaine's triumphs proves to be only the concluding show of a grim progress which began with the death of his queen in Act II. Act III, scene ii opens with Zenocrate's funeral procession, its mournful ostentation tellingly set against the coronation pomp of Callapine in the previous scene:

> [*Enter*] Tamburlaine *with* Usumcasane, *and his three sons* [Calyphas,
> Amyras *and* Celebinus]; *four bearing the hearse of* Zenocrate; *and the drums
> sounding a doleful march; the town burning.*

These rites conclude in the expected fashion with the consecration of a monument to the dead queen:[31]

> *Calyphas.* This pillar plac'd in memory of her,
>   Where in Arabian, Hebrew, Greek, is writ,
>   *This town being burnt by Tamburlaine the Great,*
>   *Forbids the world to build it up again.*
> *Amyras.* And here this mournful streamer shall be place'd
>   Wrought with the Persian and Egyptian arms,
>   To signify she was a princess born,
>   And wife unto the monarch of the East.
> *Celebinus.* And here this table as a register
>   Of all her virtues and perfections.
> *Tamburlaine.* And here the picture of Zenocrate,
>   To show her beauty which the world admir'd.
>   [*2 Tamburlaine*, III.ii.15–26]

For all its heraldic orthodoxy, however, this is a funeral without an interment, and the spectacle of the burning town recalls the promises of a Prologue that seem to invite us to see the whole of Tamburlaine's subsequent military career as a continuation of its obsequies:

> But what became of fair Zenocrate,
> *And with how many cities' sacrifice*
> *He celebrated her sad funeral,*
> Himself in presence shall unfold at large.
>   [*2 Tamburlaine*, Prologue, ll. 6–9 (my italics)]

The repetition of this episode in minor key, with the death of Olympia in Act IV, reinforces the sense of unfolding funeral pageant:

> *Theridamas.* Infernal Dis is courting of my love,
>   Inventing masques and stately shows for her,
>   Opening the doors of his rich treasury
>   To entertain this queen of chastity,

Figure 6. "The Triumph of Death," Florentine School, fifteenth century. (Courtesy of the Pinacoteca, Siena.)

Whose body shall be tomb'd with all the pomp
The treasure of my kingdom may afford. [*2 Tamburlaine*, IV.ii.93–98]

Chastity, in the scheme of Petrarch's *Trionfi*, triumphed over Love, but Death triumphed over Chastity: those "masques and stately shows" are the pageants of Death's Triumph, for which Theridamas's promised "pomp" only provides an earthly shadow.

In so far as funeral is the expected *end* of tragedy, the deliberate displacement of a funeral episode can have (as Marlowe surely intended it to have in the third act of *2 Tamburlaine*) a curiously disturbing effect.[32] Even more striking in this respect is Shakespeare's decision to open the first part of *Henry VI* with a funeral. Bedford's oration ("Hung be the heavens with black") immediately marks the stage's resemblance to a funeral church: the play begins, as it were, with the ending of another (unwritten) tragedy, and the solemn burial of its hero-prince, Henry V. It is one of many devices by which, throughout this tetralogy, the dramatist reinforces our sense of a plot larger than that of any single play; but it has the effect, too, of putting us in a world whose significant history is somehow already past, a world intensely conscious of ending. An analogous effect is created in the final play of the series, *Richard III,* whose second scene is built around the funeral of the murdered Henry VI—though here it is complicated by the stunted character of the rites accorded the dead king and by Richard's contemptuous abruption of them, a black-comic anticipation of Claudius's blasphemous mingling of "mirth in funeral and dirge in marriage."[33]

In *Titus Andronicus,* whose whole first act is dominated, visually and dramatically, by the image of the Andronicus family monument, Shakespeare once again introduces his tragedy with the rites of funeral. After a brief dramatized prologue, sketching in the political background to the action, we are confronted with a procession which is simultaneously a military triumph *all'antica* and a funeral:[34]

> *Sound drums and trumpets, and then enter . . . two of Titus's sons; and then two Men bearing a coffin covered with black; then . . . two other sons; then* TITUS ANDRONICUS; *and then* TAMORA *the Queen of the Goths, with her three sons,* ALARSUS, DEMETRIUS *and* CHIRON, *with* AARON *the Moor, and others as many as can be; then set down the coffin*[35] *and Titus speaks.* [I.i.69, S.D.]

The spectacular intention of the entry is underlined by that "*as many as can be*": neither the displacement nor the spectacle are arbitrary effects, but designed to imprint a key image upon the audience's memory. The rites performed at the tomb, the sacrifice of Alarbus, and the interment of Titus's sons amount both to a symbolic enactment of those traditional

Roman values of piety and order for which Titus stands, and an intimation of the latent barbarity by which this civilization will be consumed. The five-hundred-year-old tomb itself is an embodiment of this contradiction: described by Titus as "sacred receptacle of my joys, / Sweet cell of virtue and nobility" (I.i.92–93) it is the monumental repository of Roman honor; but it is also, by its quenchless thirst for human life, an anticipation of that "detested, dark, blood-drinking pit" which takes its place in Act II.[36] The dumping of Bassianus's body and the entrapment of Quintus and Martius are presented as a kind of ghastly mock burial; so that the pit becomes a second grave, and tomb and pit together can be seen to represent that destructive grip of the past upon the present which is a standard theme of revenge tragedy.[37] By the end of the play the monument will have swallowed Titus and most of his kin as surely as the "swallowing womb" of earth will have devoured Tamora and hers.

Where the action of *Titus* is carefully framed by two sets of obsequies, *Julius Caesar* follows the pattern of *2 Tamburlaine* by falling into two halves, each of which is rounded with a funeral.[38] But in this case the division is one that corresponds to the play's double nature as both the Tragedy of Julius Caesar and the Tragedy of Marcus Brutus. With the entry of Caesar's funeral procession and the delivery of Antony's oration over the body, the play reaches the natural conclusion of its titular tragedy. But the decorum of the last rites is overturned by Antony's rhetoric; and, in place of the processional reassertion of political order, the scene issues in the anarchic violence of the mob:

> *1 Plebeian.* We'll burn his body in the holy place,
>   And with the brands fire the traitors' houses.
>   Take up the body.   [*Julius Caesar,* III.ii.254–56]

It is a wild travesty of civilized funeral custom, which marks not the expected end but a terrible new beginning:

> *2 Plebeian.* Go, fetch fire.
> *3 Plebeian.* Pluck down benches.
> *4 Plebeian.* Pluck down forms, windows, anything.   [III.ii.257–59]

After this, the magnanimous epitaph and pious funeral instructions uttered by the victorious Antony and Octavius over the body of Brutus ("According to his virtue let us use him, / With all respect and rites of burial. / Within my tent his bones tonight shall lie, / Most like a soldier, order'd honourably," V.v.76–79) can hardly escape the taint of political interest. Those "rites of burial" which are represented for the audience by the parting procession of soldiers stand exposed as the conservative public face of a social order founded upon violent innovation. A similar ambivalence compromises Aufidius's public show of magnanimity in the rites he grants to his butchered antagonist in *Coriolanus*.

> *Aufidius.* My rage is gone,
>   And I am struck with sorrow. Take him up,
>   Help, three o'th'chiefest soldiers; I'll be one.
>   Beat thou the drum, that it speak mournfully;
>   Trail your steel pikes. Though in this city he
>   Hath widowed and unchilded many a one,
>   Which to this hour bewail the injury,
>   Yet shall he have a noble memory.
>   Assist.
> *Exeunt, bearing the body of Coriolanus. A dead march sounded.*
>   [V.vi.147–55]

It is a tribute to heroic fame contrived by a man whose actions have conclusively destroyed the last shreds of those values on which such fame might rest.

As the travesty-funeral of Caesar shows, the form of stage funerals is as crucial as their placement to dramatic meaning. Henry V's funeral at the beginning of *1 Henry VI* is designed both to memorialize a heroic past and to enact the forms of political order that the subsequent action will shatter. Shakespeare clearly intended that it be staged with an appropriately spectacular emphasis: the coffin, it would appear, was to be placed on a funeral car, recalling the pageantry of King Death:

> [*Exeter.*] Upon a wooden coffin we attend:
>   And death's dishonourable victory
>   We with our stately presence glorify,
>   Like captives bound to a triumphant car.   [I.i.19–22]

The retinue of mourning nobles in their funeral blacks (l. 17) pass over the stage to the somber music of a Dead March (I.i.1., S.D.), accompanied by the Heralds in their glittering coat-armor (l. 45) and displaying, in the prescribed fashion, the arms and chivalric achievements of the dead hero. In accordance with its memorial function, the ceremony is to culminate in the formal offering of knightly arms to the shade of the king. The ceremonies, however, are violently interrupted by the arrival of a Messenger announcing (in fittingly heraldic terms) the imminent collapse of Henry's empire in France:

> Cropp'd are the flower-de-luces in your arms;
>   Of England's coat one half is cut away.   [I.i.80–81]

Left unfinished, this broken pageant becomes a prophetic anticipation of the disastrous course of the play's action. In *Richard III*, by contrast, the pathetically stunted retinue of Henry VI's corpse—"Halberds" and three mourners (I.ii.1, S.D.)—is a ritual display of humiliation (carried to its comic extreme by Richard's wooing over the hearse) which announces an already shattered frame of order. In a similar way, Bolingbroke's attempt in *Richard II* to cobble together a proper funeral for the casually produced coffin of the murdered king ("March sadly after; grace my mournings here / In weeping after this untimely bier," V.vi.51–52) perfectly enacts his hopeless desire to restore those ancient forms of sequence and succession which his own hand has destroyed. The perfunctory and inadequate nature of his gesture is readily shown by a comparison with (for example) the much more careful decorum of the funeral contrived by the pious young Edward III at the end of Marlowe's *Edward II*: "Go fetch my father's hearse, where it shall lie, / And bring my funeral robes. . . Help me to mourn, my lords" (V.vi.94ff.)—though Marlowe makes his own characteristically sardonic comment on the rites by having the new king adorn the hearse with the severed head of his father's murderer, Mortimer.

The attempts of politicians like Henry IV and Octavius to pageant out a restored order in the funeral processions of their rivals draw on a vocabulary of political theater that other plays make quite explicit. Tamburlaine, for instance, crowns the contemptuous killing of his cowardly son, Calyphas, by devising a cruel burlesque of military funeral:

> Ransack the tents and the pavilions
> Of these proud Turks, and take their concubines,
> Making them bury this effeminate brat;
> For not a common soldier shall defile
> His manly fingers with so faint a boy.   [2 *Tamburlaine,* IV.i.158–62]

Similarly, in *Titus Andronicus,* the grisly black comedy of revenge is carried through a series of grotesque mock funerals, climaxing in the banquet scene of Act V: the first of these is the procession arranged by Titus at the end of Act III, scene i, where the Andronici solemnly bear off the severed heads of Quintus and Martius and Titus's own severed hand in a grim reenactment of the funeral rite of Act I, scene i with its sacrificial "lopping" of Alarbus's limbs; the second is the "funeral" mockingly prescribed for the Nurse by Aaron in Act IV:

> You see I have given her physic,
> And you must needs bestow her funeral;
> The fields are near, and you are gallant grooms.
>
> . . . .
> *Exeunt Demetrius and Chiron, bearing off the dead Nurse.*   [IV.ii.163–72]

Then in Act V, scene ii, Titus is made to preface his sacrifice of Demetrius and Chiron with a speech whose hideous wordplay converts his forthcoming banquet into the most monstrous funeral parody of all:

> Hark, villains! I will grind your bones to dust,
> And with your blood and it I'll make a paste;
> And with the paste a *coffin* I will rear,
> And make two pasties of your shameful heads;
> And bid that strumpet, your unhallowed dam,
> Like to the earth, swallow her own increase.
>
> [V.iii.187–92 (my italics)]

It is clear, I think, that the processional entry of Titus and his family bearing these pastry "coffins" in the following scene is meant to be staged as parodic reenactment of the funeral of Titus's sons in Act I, scene i:

> *Trumpets sounding, enter* TITUS *like a cook, placing the dishes, and* LAVINIA
> *with a veil over her face; also* YOUNG LUCIUS, *and others.*   [V.iii.25, S.D.]

Finally the triumphant Lucius, in the closing episode of the play, defines his new order by setting forth, with methodical grimness, the funeral arrangements for the victims and perpetrators of the play's holocaust; the emperor, with due deference to his rank, is to be honored with "burial in his father's grave" (V.iii.191–92); Titus and Lavinia, more solemnly, "shall forthwith / Be closed in our household's monument" (ll. 193–94); Aaron, in a vicious mock interment that mirrors his treatment of Titus's sons, will be set to "starve breast-deep in earth" (l. 179), while the barbarous Tamora's corpse will be cast into the wilderness where it belongs: "No funeral rite, nor man in mourning weed, / No mournful bell shall ring her funeral" (ll. 196–97). If Aaron is to be starved in the hungry maw of the earth, Tamora, who came to embody the blood-greed of earth's swallowing womb, will now be left "not where [she] eats, but where" (in Hamlet's phrase) " 'a is eaten"—as "prey" for "beasts and birds" (l. 198). As Act I's bitter quarrel over Mutius's right to funeral and interment in the family tomb reminds us, the contemptuous treatment meted out to these bodies amounts (for an age which preserved the ancient superstition that happiness beyond the grave was somehow contingent on proper burial) to a form of damnation.[39] In their grand-guignol fashion these antifunerals can be seen to anticipate the silent oblivion to which Shakespeare consigns the corpses of Richard III and Macbeth—villain-heroes whose tragedies conspicuously deny them the pomp of funeral, replacing it with the coronation march of a triumphant rival.

Rather different in their effect are the equally unorthodox endings of *Troilus, Timon, Othello,* and *King Lear.* In the first of these the fact that the hero remains alive, the solemn orator of a rhetorical false ending whose monumental attitudinizing is undercut by Pandarus's mocking epilogue, reinforces the play's sense of ending where it began, "in the middle." In *Timon,* on the other hand, the hero's self-interment in a "rude tomb," placed on the seashore, exposed to the destructive battery of the "turbulent surge" (V.i.213ff.) and engraved with characters too cryptic to be deciphered by any but Alcibiades (V.iii.5–8), seems designed to court an enigmatic oblivion; significantly, in the final scene Alcibiades, even in the absence of a body, is driven to contrive a funeral rite of sorts to revive the "memory" of the man he thinks of as "noble Timon" (V.iv.65–85). In *Othello* on the other hand, the profoundly private quality of the tragedy (to which the ostentation of public funeral would be palpably inappropriate) is signaled by the merciful reticence of Lodovico's simple instruction to draw the curtains of a bed upon the spectacle of death ("Let it be hid," V.ii.368): it is a more compassionate version of the annihilation despairingly courted by *Malfi's* Cardinal ("let me / Be laid by, and never thought of," *Duchess of Malfi,* V.v.89–90). Yet even here there are hints of monumental grandeur: Othello's picture of the sleeping Desdemona with her skin "smooth as monumental alabaster" (V.ii.5) plays on the audience's recollection of those great tester tombs where the effigies of husbands and wives lie as though frozen upon their beds of state—a suggestion intensified when at last Othello's body lies beside hers; and what, after all, is Othello's last great speech but an attempt to pronounce his own funeral oration, to tell his "story" as Horatio tells Hamlet's? No such ritual consolations, however, can be allowed to modify the starkness of *Lear;* the ending of this tragedy, though the final "Exeunt with a dead march" indicates a form of funeral procession, is one which asks to be staged with a bareness fitting to a world laid waste. There is no talk here of "princely burial" or "degree," no attempt at the formal magnanimity of a funeral oration, only Albany's terse "bear them from hence" and Edgar's painfully insufficient "Speak what we feel, not what we ought to say" (V.iii.318, 324). If this scanted ceremony speaks of a kingdom made wilderness, elsewhere, in *Cymbeline,* we find a wilderness made civil through the careful devising of burial rites for Imogen/Fidele and Cloten (IV.ii.196–291). It is Belarius's firm sense of the ceremonious marks of degree due even to a Cloten which shows him, cave-dweller though he is, as the play's true champion of courtly values:

> Though mean and mighty rotting
> Together have one dust, yet reverence—
> That angel of the world—doth make distinction
> Of place 'tween high and low. Our foe was princely;

And though you took his life, as being our foe,
Yet bury him as a prince.   [*Cymbeline,* IV.ii.247–52]

And it is Guiderius's and Arviragus's decorous improvisation of a pastoral
equivalent of church obsequies for "Fidele" that helps to confirm their
princely natures. It shows their instinctive feeling for that "very good
order" emblematized in the funeral with which the pious Charalois, for
instance, restores the memory of his disgraced father in Massinger's *The
Fatal Dowry.*

By contrast, in the drama of playwrights like Dekker, Marston, and
Webster, with their ingrained suspicion of courtly values, funeral pageantry may come to stand for the empty pride and hypocrisy of the court
world. The strikingly elaborate funeral procession which opens *1 Honest
Whore,* with its hearse, coronet, scutcheons, and garlands, is merely a
tyrannical prince's device to keep his daughter from an "unworthy" lover.
Similarly in *Antonio's Revenge* the high pomp of Andrugio's funeral at the
beginning of Act II is intended to point up, with bitter irony, Duke
Piero's contempt for its ceremonial meanings:

Rot there, thou cerecloth that enfolds the flesh
Of my loathed foe; moulder to crumbling dust;
Oblivion choke the passage of thy fame!
Trophies of honoured birth drop quickly down;
Let naught of him, but what was vicious, live.   [II.i.1–5]

And in Webster's radically anticourt tragedy, *The White Devil,* the pomp of
noble funerals becomes one of the ruling metaphors of glittering false-
hood—a grimly ironic epitome of "courtly reward and punishment":

Be thy life short as are the funeral tears
In great men's [palaces].   [I.ii.302–3][40]

Cornelia's curse, in Webster's characteristic fashion, is woven into the
action of the play—first through the dumb-show processions and Brachiano's sardonic commentary following the deaths of Isabella and Camillo
(II.i.23–24, 37–38), and then through Vittoria's short-lived "howling"
at Brachiano's own deathbed. The last act carefully contrasts the pompous
black farce of Brachiano's death (climaxing in a grotesque parody of extreme unction carried out by revengers in the guise of Capuchin friars,
V.iii.121ff.) with the lyric simplicity of Marcello's funeral preparations
(V.iv.75–112). The contrast is emphasized by the visual resemblance of
the two tableaux, each of which (perhaps making use of the same bed-
property) is revealed by the drawing of a curtain (V.iii.83, S.D.; V.iv.65,
S.D.), and each of which presents a group of mourning women around a

dead, or dying, body. But where Marcello's corpse, in what becomes a moving secular version of the pietà, remains at the center of the composition (until the closing instruction to "shut up shop"), Brachiano's is relegated contemptuously to the background by the courtship of Zanche and Francisco. Webster's choice of a scene of domestic grief to replace the public ostentation of funeral in the final act of his play is deliberate and revealing: it speaks of a world where the forms of ritual display, no longer answering to any profound intimation of social order, are felt to be inadequate, or even inimical, to the intensity of private emotion. By the end, the elaborate decorum of courtly ceremonial is reduced to the curt order of a slaughterhouse: "Remove the bodies" (V.vi.300).[41]

To look at Cornelia's mourning scene ("There's rosemary for you—and rue for you," V.iv.76) is to be reminded that *Hamlet* is among the many sources of Webster's brilliant patchwork. The tension between forms and feelings, public order and private affect is a more consistent theme, obviously, in Shakespeare's play; but in *Hamlet,* as in *The White Devil,* the language of funeral pageantry becomes an object of furious scrutiny. Of all Shakespeare's plays, it is naturally *Hamlet,* with its obsessive meditation on death, in which the properties of funeral custom figure most prominently. The play opens a mere two months after the death of King Hamlet and little more than a month after his interment; but we are introduced to a court that has already abandoned the ceremonies of mourning for revels of marriage. The prince alone maintains those "customary suits of solemn black," proclaiming an "obsequious sorrow" which keeps him like the follower of some interminable funeral cortège, seeking his "noble father in the dust" (I.ii.71–92). The propriety of his mourning display is affirmed by the dressing of the stage;[42] but for Claudius, Hamlet's willful ostentation of the "trappings" of funeral pageantry is not merely an implied insult to his wedding celebrations, but a denial of that due succession publicly asserted by Old Hamlet's funeral procession:

> But you must know your father lost a father;
> That father lost lost his; and the survivor bound,
> In filial obligation, for some term
> To do obsequious sorrow. But to persever
> In obstinate condolement is a course
> Of impious stubbornness; 'tis unmanly grief;
>
> . . . .
>
> To reason most absurd; whose common theme
> Is death of fathers, and who still hath cried,
> From the first corse till he that died to-day,
> "This must be so." We pray you throw to earth
> This unprevailing woe.   [*Hamlet,* I.ii.89–107]

In this world, however, where graves open to give up their dead, the past is less easily buried. For Claudius, sorrow is not something to feel, but something to "do" (l. 92), a thing to be enacted in a public ritual, nothing more. For Hamlet, though, the ritual is already rendered void by his mother's betrayal of it ("A little month, or ere those shoes were old / With which she followed my poor father's body," ll. 147ff.), and by that perverted "thrift" through which marriage "followed hard upon" the heels of funeral, creating the obscene confusions of "mirth in funeral" and "dirge in marriage."[43] Hamlet's distress at his father's contemptuously huddled obsequies will be mirrored later in the play by Laertes' fury at the "hugger-mugger" interment of Polonius; to Laertes the callous neglect of honor and degree seems to give as much pain as the murder itself:

> His means of death, his obscure funeral—
> No trophy, sword, nor hatchment, o'er his bones,
> No noble rite nor formal ostentation—
> Cry to be heard. [*Hamlet* IV.v.209–12]

The full intensity of his bitterness is comprehensible only once it is recognized that this neglect amounts to an act of calculated public oblivion: it is, above all, that oblivion which cries "to be heard" in the barbaric commemoration of revenge. Laertes' anger recalls Hamlet's savage gird to Ophelia:

> O heavens! die two months ago, and not forgotten yet? Then there's hope a great man's memory may outlive his life half a year; but by'r lady, 'a must build churches, then; or else shall 'a suffer not thinking on, with the hobby-horse, whose epitaph is "For O, for O, the hobby-horse is forgot!" [II.ii.125–30]

Finally in Act V both of these vindicative memorialists will be compelled to witness the "maimed rites" of Ophelia, denied the "sage requiem" and full service of the dead which Laertes insists is her due, and laid (like her father) not in the church tomb to which her rank entitles her, but in the common graveyard, to be commemorated only by the "living monument" of Gertrude's vague promise (V.i.291).[44] It is in the context of these variously aborted funeral shows and the violent emotion attaching to them that we are meant to respond to "the soldier's music and the rite of war" (V.v.391), the full military funeral that Fortinbras decrees for Hamlet. More powerfully than in any other play, funeral pageantry functions here as a sign of human order rescued from the jaws of chap-fallen death itself—not simply the social order enacted in the military procession (for that cannot wholly escape the taint of a conqueror's interest), but the monumental ordering of art. For beyond the rather barren plot narrative that Horatio offers by way of epitaph is the larger "story" of the play itself. *Hamlet, Prince of Denmark* is its hero's own "living monument":[45] Shakespeare's tragedy comprises, to pun on Fortinbras's claim, his "rites of memory."

Memory, of course, as a number of recent essays have shown, is one key to this play's meaning;[46] and the nature of its obsession with funerals, graves, and rituals of commemoration can help to explain why this should be so. The principal agent of memory in the play is the Ghost: a Ghost that distinguishes itself from most of its proliferating sixteenth- and seventeenth-century kind by a melancholy yearning to be remembered: "Adieu, adieu, adieu! Remember me!" (I.v.92). More even than the history of Claudius's iniquity, it is the desperate pathos of this appeal (with its echoes of the *memento mori* tradition) that possesses Hamlet's imagination (ll. 92–112): the revenge itself is conceived less as a piece of retributive justice than as a proof of remembrance.[47] It is as though only such an act, absolute and irreversible, can escape the transience of feeling and intention, the hollowness of mere words and ritual gestures, to provide unequivocal demonstration of a love capable of surviving the grave:

> [*Ghost.*] If thou didst ever thy dear father *love*—
> *Revenge* his foul and most unnatural murder.
> . . . .
> *Hamlet.* Haste me to know't, that I with wings as swift
>   As meditation or the thoughts of *love*,
>   May sweep to my *revenge*.   [I.v.23–31 (my italics)]

When the Ghost returns in Act III (as though conjured up by Hamlet's attempt to reawaken Gertrude's forgotten love for her husband), its first words once again evoke this unappeasable longing for love and remembrance: "Do not forget" (III.iv.110). Significantly, it is the same emotion which (in Hamlet's version of "The Murder of Gonzago") possesses the Player King when he contemplates the state of things after his death (III.ii.168–210).[48] There is seemingly no limit to the love which the dead seek to exact from the living; and consequently (as Hamlet's "Hecuba" and "How all occasions" soliloquies insist) no impiety more dreadful than "bestial oblivion." Ironically, this is exactly the basis of Claudius's appeal to Laertes when he tries to work him to revenge against Hamlet:

> *King.* Laertes, was your father dear to you?
>   Or are you like the painting of a sorrow,
>   A face without a heart?

. . . .
Not that I think you did not *love* your father;
But that I know love is begin by time,
And that I see, in passages of proof,
Time qualifies the spark and fire of it.
. . . .
What would you *undertake*
To show yourself in *deed* your father's son
More than in words?   [IV.iii. 107–26 (my italics)]

This insistence that the proofs of love and remembrance are to be found in
deeds alone is made for the last time at Ophelia's grave; but this time it is
given a bitterly ironic twist:

I *lov'd* Ophelia: forty thousand brothers
Could not, with all their quantity of love,
Make up my sum. What wilt thou *do* for her?
. . . .
'Swounds, show me what th'owt *do*:
Woo't weep, woo't fight, woo't fast, woo't tear thyself,
Woo't drink up eisel, eat a crocodile?
I'll *do*'t.   [V.i.263–71 (my italics)]

By now (and this is Hamlet's point) the Herculean deeds themselves have
been reduced to mere words, no better than the drab's bombast of the
Hecuba soliloquy: "Nay and thou'lt mouth, / I'll rant as well as thou" (ll.
277–78). In the end, as the graveyard seems to have taught the prince,
there is nothing to be *done* for the dead: we can no more satisfy their
importunate demand for love, than they can answer our impertinent questions about death.

For, apart from its restless longing for remembrance, the most striking
feature of the *Hamlet* Ghost is its enigmatic, even secretive nature. It can
disinter the past, but of its own present it can reveal almost nothing—at
most the vague claim to issue from a purgatory which, for most of Shakespeare's audience, was no longer supposed to exist:

But that I am forbid
To tell the secrets of my prison house,
I could a tale unfold whose lightest word
Would harrow up thy soul, . . .
. . . .
But this eternal blazon must not be
To ears of flesh and blood.   [I.v.12–22][49]

Traditionally the pains of hell and purgatory, far from being secret, had
been paraded as a warning to the living. To sense the oddity of the prohi-

bition we have only to look at one of Shakespeare's models, the Ghost of Andrea in Kyd's *Spanish Tragedy,* whose eloquent and richly embellished account of his underworld experiences takes up nearly seventy lines of the Induction. It is often supposed that there is something inconsistent about Hamlet's description of death as "The undiscover'd country, from whose bourn / No traveller returns" (III.i.79–80). Actually Andrea had been exactly that sort of traveller, a voluble Hakluyt of the underworld; but in the case of the *Hamlet* Ghost the question of its origin, like that of its nature ("spirit of health or goblin damn'd") remains occluded to the end. It can do nothing therefore to alleviate those puzzles of the will which attend the obscure "dread of something after death": it exists perhaps only as a discarnate force of longing. Yet there are other suggestions about this Ghost which make it appear surprisingly substantial and suggest that it comes, if anywhere, quite literally "from the grave," as Horatio says (I.v.125). When Hamlet calls it "dead corse" (I.iv.52) the description suggests that (despite its "complete steel") this Ghost is cadaverlike, resembling one of those *transi* tomb effigies in which the signs of mortal decay have already appeared:

> *Hamlet.* Let me not burst in ignorance, but tell
> Why thy canoniz'd bones, hearsed in death,
> Have burst their cerements; why the sepulchre
> Wherein we saw thee quietly enurn'd
> Hath op'd his ponderous and marble jaws
> To cast thee up again.   [I.iv.46–51][50]

This ghostly rising, drawing on the old resurrection iconography of the Last Judgment, is a kind of funeral in reverse, as the corpse successively throws off cerecloths and coffin to break through the marble doors of the tomb itself. When referred to this charnel image, Hamlet's reiterated determination to "follow it" (I.iv.63, 68, 79, 86) develops a large and sinister suggestiveness—it is a purposeful reenactment and redirection of the pieties of "obsequious sorrow," the ritual following of the funeral procession. It reaches its inevitable conclusion in the graveyard of Act V, where actual bones take the place of the ghostly cadaver. Indeed Hamlet's quizzing of the skulls (V.i.75ff.)—in particular that of Yorick, the father figure who "hath borne me on his back a thousand times" (ll. 182–83)— is the exact counterpart of his questioning of the Ghost; except that all questions are now reduced to a single traditional graveyard conundrum, "*Ubi sunt . . . ?*" The skull is at once more eloquent and even more enigmatic than the Ghost: if there is an answer to that riddle, beyond the reductive materialism of the "quintessence of dust" which stops a beer barrel, the play finds it only in the reaches of memory. Life, this scene (like Unton's portrait) declares, is merely a procession to the grave: the gravedigger began his work on "that very day that young Hamlet was born" (V.i.143–44) and in this violently foreshortened temporal perspective "A man's life [indeed] is no more than to say 'one' " (V.ii.74). But that grim procession can also become a species of triumph, which finds its proper extension in the "living monuments" of memory.

Through its hero's preoccupation with death, decay, and the sovereign preservative of memory, *Hamlet* was, I believe, tapping a profound source of post-Reformation *angst*. The play succeeds in laying open a theme that is buried deep in the structures of revenge tragedy, a theme that can be identified as the literary expression of that same troubled mentality that led to the great sixteenth-century elaboration of funeral rites and burial customs. Among those things which the Reformation swept away forever was the whole vast industry of intercession: indulgences, prayers of intercession, and masses for the dead. What would have struck a visitor to any church in Catholic Europe from the twelfth to the eighteenth centuries would have been "not so much the plowing of the ground by the gravediggers as the uninterrupted series of Masses said in the morning at all the altars by priests for whom this was often the only source of income."[51] With the Reformation this whole liturgy of remembrance fell silent; it was no longer possible for the living to intervene on behalf of the dead; each man's death had become (as *Dr. Faustus* vividly demonstrates) a private Apocalypse, whose awful Judgment could never be reversed.[52] The dead might still call upon the duty, love, and pity of the living,[53] but the new theology rendered all such emotion painfully ineffectual, as Sir Thomas Browne discovered. Among those heresies by which he confessed himself tempted in his "greener studies" he included

> a third . . . which I did never positively maintaine or practice, but have often wished it had been consonant to Truth, and not offensive to my Religion, and that is the prayer for the dead; whereunto I was inclined from some charitable inducements, whereby I could scarce containe my prayers for a friend at the ringing of a Bell, or behold his corpes without an oraison for his soule: 'Twas a good way me thought to be remembered by Posterity, and farre more noble then an History.[54]

The terrible frenzies of the revenger, that berserk memorialist, can be read as one response—at the level of grandiose fantasy—to the despairing impotence revealed in Browne's confession. Arguably those funeral monuments which increasingly cluttered the churches of sixteenth- and seventeenth-century England, represent another: that extraordinary imaginative stroke, whereby Marston's Antonio is made to sacrifice Julio in a savage parody of the Requiem Mass,[55] at the murdered Andrugio's altar-tomb, makes the connection with brutal directness. Unlike earlier tombs (as satirists like Webster did not fail to observe), the great memorials of this period are almost exclusively retrospective in their appeal;[56] "wholly bent upon the world," they are conspicuously worldly substitutes for the liturgical memento of the Mass. The more splendid their marble sculpture, the richer their gilt and painting, the more elaborate their heraldic ornament, the more eloquently these shrines of memory speak of a species of immortality which it remained in the power of the living to assist.[57]

The monument, as a kind of perpetual pageant or hearse, can be regarded as the climactic episode of a funeral show. Through their pomp and heraldry, their portraits of wives and children, their records of ancestry and descent, the tombs of the great (designed as they often were by the heralds themselves) preserved the social propaganda of funeral—a fact that helps to explain the iconoclastic fury with which they were treated in troubled times; but they also make a more personal assertion, for (as John Weever put it) "every man desires a perpetuity after death by these monuments."[58] In the drama, the monument with its artifice of eternity stands in the same relation to the play-as-finished-artifact, as the funeral to the play-as-unfolding-plot; and it has the same emblematic relation to the completed action as the tomb in Sir Henry Unton's portrait. In certain plays it becomes the iconographic and even the emotional focus of the whole action. *Romeo and Juliet,* Shakespeare's second tragedy, takes over from his first, *Titus,* the stage image of a family sepulcher, which once again acts as a visible sign of the tyranny of the past, and of Death's inevitable Triumph. But the Capulet tomb is also a "triumphant grave" (V.iii.83) in another, more positive sense: for, by the end of the play, the lovers on their bed of death have begun to resemble monumental figures of tomb sculpture, anticipating the "statues in pure gold" which the penitent fathers will raise to the memory of their children. Fame's triumph over Death remains nevertheless uncertain and equivocal in the charnel tomb of *Romeo and Juliet.* In the mature love tragedy that Shakespeare wrote a dozen years later, however, the Triumph of Fame, embodied in Cleopatra's monument, is absolute. *Antony and Cleopatra* ends in the prescribed fashion with instructions for a funeral:

> Take up her bed
> And bear her women from the monument.
> She shall be buried by her Antony;
> No grave upon the earth shall clip in it
> A pair so famous.
> . . . .

> Our army shall
> In solemn show attend this funeral,
> And then to Rome. Come, Dolabella, see
> High order in this great solemnity.   [V.ii.353–63]

For the last time in this urgently demonstrative play, we are being asked to "behold and see"; by now, however, we should be accustomed to discovering that *what* we see is seldom what the presenter intends. The projected funeral triumph, for all its public display of magnanimity, is too much the substitute for that military triumph, adorned with the captive figures of Antony and his Egyptian queen, of which Caesar has been balked.[59] The most compelling image, when all is done, remains that of Cleopatra's monument and the tableau of marble constancy that she composes within it. Here the monument is not confined to one of those tomb properties that appeared in so many plays; it is represented now by the entire stage, dominated by a façade which bore more than a passing resemblance to a triumphal arch.[60] It is a setting that emblematizes, more splendidly than in any other play, the old trope of poetry-as-monument.[61] To the extent that it stands for a kind of transcendence, a triumph over the destructive agencies of Time and Death, it is perhaps this magnificent spectacle that most contributes to the often felt connection between *Antony and Cleopatra* and the tragicomic romances that followed it. It suggests (as the tombs and monuments of *Pericles* and *The Winter's Tale,* those dramas of resurrection, can also suggest) a bridge between the worlds of tragedy and comedy, between dirge and marriage, funeral and revels.[62]

Notes

1. Quoted from Russell A. Fraser and Norman Rabkin, eds., *Drama of the English Renaissance* (New York: Macmillan, 1976). Except where otherwise indicated, all non-Shakespearean plays are cited from this text.

2. The stage direction is incomplete, since the bodies of Hieronimo, Bel-Imperia and Lorenzo have also to be removed. Presumably they too are carried in the procession—though one or more might conceivably be concealed behind the curtain of the "arbour" where Horatio's body hangs. For general discussion of the method of removing bodies from the stage, see E. K. Chambers, *The Elizabethan Stage* (Oxford: Clarendon Press, 1923), 3:80.

3. Early examples of full pageant funerals occur in the Inns of Court tragedies *Gorboduc* (1562) and *Jocasta* (1566), though in neither case is the funeral incorporated in the action, being confined to allegorical dumb shows before the acts. The *Jocasta* procession, involving two coffins and sixteen mourners, is particularly elaborate.

4. For discussion of the development of funeral rites through the late Middle Ages and Renaissance, see Malcolm Vale, *War and Chivalry* (London: Duckworth, 1981), pp. 88–99; Philippe Ariès, *The Hour of Our Death,* trans. Helen Weaver (London: Allen Lane, 1981), pp. 164–68; and Lawrence Stone, *The Crisis of the Aristocracy 1558–1641* (Oxford: Oxford University Press, 1965), chap. 10, sec. 7, "Funerals and Tombs."

5. See Ariès, *The Hour of Our Death,* pp. 170–71; and Michael Neill, "Monuments and Ruins as Symbols in *The Duchess of Malfi,*" *Themes in Drama* 4 (1981): 71–87.

6. Stone, *The Crisis of the Aristocracy,* pp. 586, 573. Two fine illuminated manuscript rolls in the British Library (Add. Mss. 45131 and 35324) illustrate the heralds' practice of drawing up "remembrances" of these events in order to instruct their successors in the proper order to be kept in marshaling the procession and in the niceties of its heraldic pageantry. The former includes sketches which show how the heralds' part in designing funeral and "hearse" naturally extended to include the more permanent display of monuments and tombs.

7. Sir William Segar, *Honor Military, and Civill, Contained in Foure Bookes* (London, 1602), p. 138: "Triumphs have bene commonly used at the Inauguration and Coronation of Emperors, Kings and Princes; at their Mariages, Entry of cities, Enterviewes, Progresses and Funerals. Those pompous shewes, were first invented and practised by the Romanes." Erwin Panofsky, *Tomb Sculpture: Its Changing Aspects from Ancient Egypt to Bernini,* ed. H. W. Janson (London: Thames and Hudson, 1964), p. 46, writes of the Christian dead that "every one of them was an Anointed, and, in a sense, a *triumphalis.*" The triumphal nature of Renaissance funerals was frequently reflected in the architecture of tombs; thus Francis I's tomb was designed as a triumphal arch, its reliefs celebrating victories and battle and featuring a formal triumph *all'antica* (Panofsky, *Tomb Sculpture,* p. 80; cf. also pp. 83–85). In effect the tomb stood in the same relation to the funeral pageant as the triumphal arch to the military triumph.

8. For discussion of the strong family emphasis in sixteenth- and seventeenth-century funerary monuments (many of which were family tombs) see Ariès, *The Hour of Our Death,* pp. 74–77, 254–58, 288–93; and Lawrence Stone, *The Family, Sex, and Marriage in England 1500–1800* (London: Weidenfeld and Nicholson, 1977), pp. 135, 225–26.

9. For an invaluable analysis of this portrait, see Roy Strong, *The Cult of Elizabeth: Elizabethan Portraiture and Pageantry* (London: Thames and Hudson, 1977), chap. 3. Strong describes memorial portraits of this kind as occupying "a curious hinterland between the living portrait and the funeral or tomb effigy"; the Unton picture is both " a *memento mori* . . . [and] a Triumph of Fame" (p. 84).

10. Strong (*The Cult of Elizabeth,* p. 85) compares it with the half-figures on the tombs of Shakespeare and Stow—both of whom are presented in the act of writing. There is, Ariès argues, a close connexion between the emergence of realistic tomb sculpture and the development of the portrait genre in painting (*The Hour of Our Death,* pp. 257–63). Cf. also Stone, *Family,* p. 226. For further discussion of the memorial portrait genre, see Eric Mercer, *English Art, 1553–*

1625 (Oxford: Oxford University Press, 1962), pp. 162–65; the genre includes the curious revenge memorials of Darnley (1567) and Moray (1591).

11. See George R. Kernodle, *From Art to Theatre: Form and Convention in the Renaissance* (Chicago: University of Chicago Press, 1944), pp. 53–58, 151, Mercer, *English Art*, pp. 246, 251; the emblematic significance of the drawn curtains is clearly relevant to the "resurrection" scenes of *The Winter's Tale* (where Paulina draws the curtain to reveal the living monument of Hermione) and *The Tempest* (where Prospero similarly discloses the living figures of the supposedly dead Ferdinand and Miranda); it must also have an ironic bearing on the parallel "discoveries" by revengers like Hieronimo and Hoffman of corpses symbolically revived by their acts of vengeance.

12. The witnesses (others of whom sit under trees to which are attached escutcheons bearing epitaphs and mottoes) act as a kind of surrogate for the viewer of the painting. In this their function is not unlike that of the scholars in *Dr. Faustus,* a play which, with its curiously compressed time scheme, has something in common with the Unton portrait. In Marlowe's prologue the hero's entire life from birth to untimely death ("Now is he born . . . heavens conspired his overthrow," ll. 11–22) is mysteriously conflated in the figure of the doomed scholar at his desk ("And this the man that in his study sits," l. 28): the Prologue, of course, introduces a play in which the twenty-four years of Faustus's career as a conjuror are wittily contracted to the twenty-four hours classically allowed to the action of a play. This telescoping is made theatrically possible by the fact that the action (as in the Unton portrait) is seen in some sense retrospectively—from the perspective of a damnation already achieved.

13. Strong (*The Cult of Elizabeth,* p. 104) denies the traditional identification of the masque with Unton's wedding feast, on the grounds that no Elizabethan bride would wear black. I believe that (like most of the principals in this and other scenes) she does so for the same reason that her mother-in-law wears black as she nurses the infant Henry in a birth chamber that is already hung with funeral blacks: the life is seen from the perspective of the funeral; it is as though Lady Unton were already the black-clad "figure cut in alabaster / Kneels at her husband's tomb" (*Duchess of Malfi,* I.i.458–59).

14. Montaigne *Essays,* trans. John Florio (London: Dent, 1965), I.xix, p. 87; xviii, p. 72. Cf. also "Death's Duel," the sermon Donne preached in anticipation of his own funeral: "Our *criticall* day is not the very day of our death: but the whole course of our life . . . from *wombe* to the *grave* . . . we passe from *death* to *death*" (quoted from *The Sermons of John Donne,* ed. G. R. Potter and E. M. Simpson [Berkeley and Los Angeles: University of California Press, 1953–62], 10: 241). Herbert's poem "Mortification" methodically analogizes the whole progress of man's life to a funeral ritual—beginning with the dressing of the infant in those "little winding sheets," his swaddling clothes, and concluding with the 'herse' that awaits his bier in the church. For further discussion of this motif, see Theodore Spencer, *Death and Elizabethan Tragedy* (Cambridge, Mass.: Harvard University Press, 1936), pp. 59ff. and 146ff.

15. Strong (*The Cult of Elizabeth,* p. 85) makes the attractive suggestion that the painting may actually have been the work of one of the heralds involved in the funeral: "The meticulous rendering of the funeral procession and of the numerous and complex coats of arms suggests that the picture may well be the work of a herald, whose task it would have been to supervise the correct rendering of his achievements, both during the funeral ceremonies and upon his monument." An inscription above the nursery scene deciphered by Strong, continues the heraldic emphasis by carefully tracing Sir Henry's descent from the Seymour family and his consequent connection with the royal house.

16. Quoted in Strong, *The Cult of Elizabeth,* p. 99. The term "hearse" may need some explanation: it refers here to the elaborate temporary structure (resembling a tester-tomb), decorated with heraldic banners and devices, with candles and with epitaphs, in which the coffins of the great were placed while they lay in the church (figure 3). In theatrical stage directions it more commonly refers to the bier or to the coffin itself. When necessary in the following discussion I distinguished the first type as a "fixed hearse."

17. Stone's description (*Crisis,* pp. 574–75) of the earl of Derby's funeral in 1572 gives some notion of the kind of splendid ceremony which the painting seeks to evoke:

> First came 100 poor men fitted out in blacks for the occasion. . . . Behind them marched the choir of 40 in their surplices, followed by an esquire on horseback bearing the late Earl's standard. Next came 80 gentlemen of the Earl, his 2 secretaries, 2 chaplains, and 50 knights and esquires, the preachers, the Dean of Chester, the three chief officers, and an esquire on horseback carrying the great banner. At this point appeared the splendid spectacle of four heralds riding horses with black trappings ornamented with escutcheons reaching to the ground. First came Lancaster wearing the Earl's coat of arms in damask, and carrying his parcel-gilt steel helmet with its pointed and gilded crest, followed by Norroy with the Earl's shield of arms within a garter and topped by a coronet, Clarenceux with the Earl's sword carried pommel upwards, and finally Garter carrying another coat of arms. The heralds directly preceded the black-draped chariot within the coffin, drawn by four horses and surrounded by ten hooded esquires on horseback, some carrying bannerols with the arms of distinguished families whose blood was mingled with that of the Stanleys. Behind the chariot walked the chief mourner, the new Earl, with his two ushers, his two sons, and eight other distinguished mourners headed by Lord Stourton. The tail of this great procession was composed of 500 yeomen and all the servants of the gentlemen taking part in the ceremony.
>
> On arrival at the church, the coffin was removed from the chariot by eight gentlemen and solemnly borne inside. The church itself was in heavy mourning, the pulpit, the communion table, and the arches of the aisles being swathed in black drapes. In the centre stood the hearse upon which the coffin was laid . . . a gigantic affair 30 ft. high, 12 ft. long, and 9 ft. wide, covered with black taffeta and velvet, and adorned with numerous heraldic escutcheons. The funeral service opened with Norroy pronouncing the names and titles of the deceased. . . . [After a sermon and the reading of the gospel and epistle]

the new Earl then offered the heralds a piece of gold for the deceased, and was himself solemnly offered by the chief mourners the late earl's arms, sword, target, standard and banner. After the other mourners down to the yeomen had made their offering to the deceased, the majority of the congregation again formed up two by two and marched off home, leaving the burial itself to be conducted by two of the heralds, the twenty-odd esquires, gentlemen, yeomen and officers of the late Earl. These latter broke their staves of office over their heads and threw them into the open grave before the earth was shovelled in.

The cost of such displays and the feasting that followed them was phenomenal—often as much as a whole year's income for a great household. No less than £1,097 was laid out on Lord Hunsdon's funeral in 1596, of which £836 went on funeral blacks, and £100 to the heralds for supplying hearse, banners, standards, escutcheons and achievements (Stone, *Crisis,* p. 784). Cf. also the magnificent funeral accorded to Sir Philip Sidney in 1587, described in M. W. Wallace, *The Life of Sir Philip Sidney* (Cambridge: Cambridge University Press, 1915), pp. 394–96; Sidney's body, like Unton's, was ferried across the channel in a ship dressed in black sails, tackling, and furniture. Walsingham, who appears to have thought a monument superfluous, nevertheless "spared not any cost to have this funeral well *performed*" (p. 394, my italics).

18. Stone, *Crisis,* p. 578.

19. John Weever, *Ancient Funerall Monuments* (London, 1631), pp. 17–18; Lady Unton's desire in 1634 to be buried "without any pomp or solemnity, and with as small charge as may be, in the night" (quoted in Strong, *Crisis,* p. 108) is an example of the changing fashion which Weever decried. Cf. also Segar, *Honor Military, and Civill,* chap. 27 passim. Weever (pp. 10–11, 37–41) and Segar (chap. 28) also show a common concern for the social meaning of monuments, which an ordered society must be careful to preserve—"A matter of more consequence, then every one marketh," as Segar puts it (p. 254).

20. John Marston, *Antonio's Revenge,* ed. Reavley Gair, Revels Edition (Manchester: Manchester University Press, 1978), p. 2; all citations from the play are to this edition.

21. *A Warning for Fair Women,* ed. Charles D. Cannon (The Hague: Mouton, 1975), Induction, ll. 82–83. Chambers (*The Elizabethan Stage,* 3:79) gives a full list of contemporary references to this practice, making it clear that it was standard in both public and private playhouses, as well as in the court theaters. Cf. also M. C. Bradbrook, *Themes and Conventions of Elizabethan Tragedy,* 2d ed. (Cambridge: Cambridge University Press, 1980), pp. 16–17; and Michael Hattaway, *English Popular Theatre* (London: Routledge and Kegan Paul, 1982), p. 20. The black hangings, as several of the passages cited by Chambers show, had the effect of consigning tragedy to an imaginative night world—a fact that helps to account for the popularity of "night-pieces" or "nocturnals" in tragic drama. In Marston's *Insatiate Countess,* for instance, the onset of night immediately evokes the tragic spectacle of blackness: "The stage of heav'n, is hunge with solemne black, / A time best fitting to act tragedies" (cited from *The Plays of John Marston,* ed. W. Harvey Wood (Edinburgh: Oliver and Boyd, 1934–39), 3:65). Vindice's

invocation of Night in *The Revenger's Tragedy* makes explicit the triple connexion of nocturnals, black hangings and funeral decor: "Night, thou that lookest like funeral herald's fees / Torn down betimes i' the morning, though hangest fitly / To grace those sins that have no grace at all" (II.ii.133–35).

22. See for instance *The White Devil*, V.i., where Webster builds on the proleptic ironies by having Francisco and his fellow conspirators enter *"bearing their swords and helmets"* and hang them up (as Brachiano announces) "For monuments in our chapel" (ll. 43–51); on the black-draped stage they will irresistibly recall the achievements hanging above a hearse of tomb in a funeral church—the funeral being announced is, of course, Brachiano's own. One would like to know how the stage was dressed for the mixed genre of tragicomedy, and what variations may have been introduced to cater for the special needs of a play like *King Lear*, part of whose emotional effect depends on its playing against the existing expectations of the audience, created by the old *King Leir* with its romance ending. Conceivably different sets of hangings may have been used within a single play.

23. Sir Philip Sidney, "An Apology for Poetry," in *English Critical Essays (Sixteenth, Seventeenth and Eighteenth Centuries)*, ed. Edmund D. Jones, 2d ed. (London: Oxford University Press, 1947), p. 46. The plausibly balanced antitheses of Claudius's opening oration in *Hamlet* create a tragicomic paradigm in which "marriage" and "funeral" have the same metonymic function:

> with a defeated joy,
> With an auspicious and a dropping eye,
> With mirth in funeral, and with dirge in marriage,
> In equal scale weighing delight and dole.   [I.ii.10–13]

Tourneur crowns his *Atheist's Tragedy* with an enacted version of such "dirge in marriage" by combining the funeral of D'Amville and his sons with the marriage of Charlemont and Castabella, while "The drums and trumpets interchange the sounds / Of death and triumph" (V.ii.296–97; quoted from Irving Ribner's Revels Edition, [London: Methuen, 1947]). Except where otherwise indicated, all citations from Shakespeare are to *The Complete Works*, ed. Peter Alexander (London and Glasgow: Collins, 1951).

24. The quoted phrase is from York's rebuke to the king in *Richard II* (II.i.199).

25. In *The White Devil* Brachiano comes to see the whole course of his liaison with Vittoria as though it were the sacrificial procession of some pagan funeral (IV.ii.87–95).

26. See Frank Kermode, *The Sense of an Ending: Studies in the Theory of Fiction* (New York: Oxford University Press, 1979), pp. 25–28. For discussion of the way in which the individual's death came to be regarded as a private Day of Judgment, see Ariès, *The Hour of Our Death*, pp. 106–10.

27. *1 Tamburlaine*, V.i.472; all citations from Marlowe are to *The Plays of Christopher Marlowe*, ed. Roma Gill (New York: Oxford University Press, 1971). The pageantlike nature of the play, frequently remarked on, is emphasized by the incantatory repetition of words like "pageant," "triumph," and "progress." Nashe

turns the metaphor to especially brilliant effect in *Summer's Last Will and Testament*, a pageant play for the end of summer, which concludes in the season's funeral rite.

28. Tamburlaine's gesture with Zenocrate's hearse is less extravagant than it might appear: the melancholic earl of Essex, commanding a parliamentary army in the Civil War, chose "to encumber the baggage train of his already sufficiently discouraged army with his own coffin" (Mercer, *English Art*, p. 245). For Tamburlaine as Death, see D. H. Zucker, *Stage and Image in the Plays of Christopher Marlowe* (Salzburg: University of Salzburg Press, 1972), p. 48. *Soliman and Perseda* (ca. 1589–92), another tragedy of extravagant oriental tyranny written (perhaps by Kyd) to vie with *Tamburlaine*, turns Marlowe's metaphoric play with the Triumphs of Love, Death, and Fame to didactic explicitness: at the end of the play, after the corpse of Soliman has been carried silently from the stage, there ensues a formal debate among Love, Fortune, and Death, in which the latter demonstrates that "powerfull *Death* best fitteth tragedies." The language of Death's triumphant litany suggests that the dramatist intended to end with a spectacular realization of the Triumph of Death:

> And now, to end our difference at last,
> In this last act note but the deedes of Death.
> Where is *Erastus* now, but in my triumph?
> Where are the murtherers, but in my triumph?
> Where Judge and witnesses, but in my triumph?
> Where's false *Lucina*, but in my triumph?
> Where's faire *Perseda*, but in my triumph?
> . . . .
> And where's great *Soliman*, but in my triumph?
> Their loves and fortunes ended with their lives,
> And they must wait upon the Carre of *Death*.
> . . . .
> I, now will *Death*, in his most haughtie pride,
> Fetch his imperiall Carre from deepest hell,
> And ride in triumph through the wicked world.   [V.v.15–26]

Quoted from *The Works of Thomas Kyd*, ed. F. S. Boas (Oxford: Oxford University Press, 1941).

29. For a discussion of the iconographic resemblances between funeral pageantry and the Triumph of Death, see Ariès, *The Hour of Our Death*, in the Siena Triumph (figure 6), where the chariot is surmounted by a gigantic funerary urn, a formal analogy is established between the triumphal procession of King Death in the foreground and the funeral procession winding into the church in the background. The presence of the funeral, together with the prominent coat of arms on Death's chariot, may suggest that this painting was commissioned (like the Unton portrait) as a memorial; conceivably the deceased is among those who ride in front of Death's car.

It is worth noting that the Tamburlaine's symbolic colors (white, red, and black) dominate the color schemes of both the Unton portrait and the Siena

Triumph; their ultimate source is probably in the white, red, and black horses of the first three Horsemen of Revelation 6; every Triumph of Death is, of course, an Apocalypse in little, and the triumphant Tamburlaine combines aspects of all four Horsemen.

30. The motto is inscribed on the supposed portrait of Marlowe in Corpus Christi College, Cambridge.

31. While portable tomb properties were often used in funeral scenes of this kind, the implicit stage directions here show that the twin columns and tiered façade of the *frons scenae* could be used to evoke the grander forms of triumphal monument; cf. also my discussion of Antony and Cleopatra below.

32. See Spencer, *Death and Elizabethan Tragedy*, p. 184, for a suggestion that funerals were conventionally placed early in the action; Spencer takes no account, however, of the funereal aspect of the final "Exeunt with a dead march."

33. Cf. also the way in which the special intention of that unique history, *Henry V*, was to be signalled by the substitution of a wedding for the expected funeral at the end of the play (I am indebted to my colleague Sebastian Black for this observation).

34. Marcus's speech, later in the scene, spells out the double nature of this pageant:

> Long live Lord Titus, my beloved brother,
> Gracious triumpher in the eye of Rome!
>
> . . . .
>
> But safer triumph is in funeral pomp
> That hath aspir'd to Solon's happiness
> And triumphs over chance in honour's bed.   [I.i.169–78]

35. Although only one coffin is specified in the S.D. the action properly calls for several; at l. 149 the folio text emends the S.D. to read "*coffins*"; actual stage practice was probably contingent on that "as many as can be."

36. Passages that establish an imaginative association between the "blood-drinking pit" and the grave include II.ii.176–77, 198–202, 210, 222–24, 226–36, 239–40; the association would be visually reinforced by the conventional use of the stage trap as a grave.

37. See my "Remembrance and Revenge: *Hamlet, Macbeth,* and *The Tempest*," in *Jonson and Shakespeare,* ed. Ian Donaldson (London: Macmillan, 1983).

38. The two halves of Tourneur's *Atheist's Tragedy* are similarly marked by funeral endings—the obsequies of Montferrers and the supposedly dead Charlemont in III.i, being balanced by those of D'Amville and *his* dead sons in V.ii.

39. Ariès (*The Hour of Our Death,* p. 31) discusses the survival of this pagan belief in Christian eschatology. It is probably reflected in the formulaic curse protecting Shakespeare's own tomb from disturbance. Cf. also Pericles' distress at his failure to give proper burial to Thaisa (*Pericles,* III.i.58–64), and the emotional climax of Kyd's *Cornelia,* where the heroine condemns herself to unwanted life solely to ensure the decent interment of her father and husband (*Cornelia,* V.431–65). In neither case is the classical setting sufficient to explain away the intensity of

emotion attaching to proper performance of the burial rites; indeed in Massinger's *The Fatal Dowry* with its contemporary setting the plot is set in train by the heroically filial Charalois's preferring to commit himself to prison rather than see his father denied burial in the monument of his noble ancestors (I.ii.211–13). The care with which the scholars reassemble Faustus's "scattered limbs" for burial is also worth noting in this context. I am indebted to John Kerrigan for pointing out the element of mock funeral in Titus's banquet; Davenant repeats the "coffin" (casket/pie-crust) pun in *The Wits* where the Elder Palatine, undergoing his mock burial in a chest, feels "coffin'd up, like a salmon pie."

40. Cf. also III.ii.92–93; V.iii.50–51, 167–68; V.vi.153–57.

41. Cf. also *The Revenger's Tragedy* I.iv, where Antonio's elaborately formal tableau or mourning around the corpse of his wife (presumably in a fixed "hearse") contrasts with his perfunctory dispatch of the royal corpses at the end ("Bear up / Those tragic bodies," V.iii.127–28).

42. A casual pun in Dekker's *Lanthorne and Candlelight* (1608) suggests that black costumes may have formed an expected part of the funereal decor of tragedy: "And now, when the stage of the world was hung with blacke, they *jetted* up and downe like pround tragedians" (quoted in Chambers, *The Elizabethan Stage*, 3:79).

43. In the Players' dumb show Gertrude's infidelity is telescoped into the wooing-over-the-corpse motif already encountered in *Richard III* and used again by Webster in *The White Devil*. That this may have been part of the old *Hamlet* play is suggested by its recurrence in another *ur-Hamlet* offspring, Marston's *Antonio's Revenge*, where Piero successfully woos Maria over the tomb of her murdered husband, Andrugio (III.i.1, S.D.). Marston went on to rework the episode a second time in the opening scene of his *The Insatiate Countess*, where (in an episode full of echoes of *Hamlet*) the opening tableau of mourning gives way to the countess's passionate courtship of Roberto: "What thinkst thou of this change? / A Players passion Ile believe hereafter, / And in a Tragicke Sceane weepe for old *Priam*, / When fell revenging *Pirrhus* with supposde / And artificiall wounds mangles his breast. . . . The tapers that stood on her husbands hearse, / *Isabell* advances to a second bed" (*The Plays of John Marston*, ed. Wood, 3:8). Chapman carries the device to marvellously parodic extremes in the tomb seduction of his *The Widow's Tears*.

44. The strict theoretical order governing the place and mode of burial is analyzed by Ariès (*The Hour of Our Death*, pp. 45–62, 71–92): "There was a hierarchy of honour and devotion that extended from the confession of the saint or the high altar to the edge of the cemetery" (p. 50). Although Ariès suggests that this was less rigidly observed in England than in France, Weever (*Ancient Funerall Monuments*, pp. 10–11) certainly thought in terms of a stern gradation of rank that encompassed not only the place of burial but the style of monument to which the deceased was entitled. Properly speaking a "living monument" (*tombe animée*) was a tomb with effigies (Ariès, *The Hour of Our Death*, p. 229), but such structures did not belong in open cemeteries: Gertrude seems to be speaking rather of the coming "hour of quiet" (peace between the feuding families) as a memorial to Ophelia's sweetness.

45. For further discussion of the idea of the play-as-monument, see my "Monuments and Ruins"; and Spencer, *Death and Elizabethan Tragedy,* pp. 42ff. D. J. Gordon's outstanding essay "Name and Fame: Shakespeare's *Coriolanus*" in *The Renaissance Imagination,* ed. Stephen Orgel (Berkeley and Los Angeles: University of California Press, 1975) is also relevant. It is partly the familiar association of tragedy and fame that Hamlet has in mind when he describes the players as "abstracts and brief chronicles of the time," and warns that "after your death you were better have a bad epitaph than their ill report while you live" (II.ii.517–20). Compare also the ending of Massinger's *The Duke of Milan* where the villain Sforza falls silent just as he is about to speak his epitaph.

46. See John Kerrigan, "Hieronimo, Hamlet, and Remembrance," *Essays in Criticism* 31 (1981): 105–26; James P. Hammersmith, "*Hamlet* and the Myth of Memory," *ELH* 45 (1978): 597–605; Richard Helgerson, "What Hamlet Remembers," *Shakespeare Studies* 10 (1977): 67–97; and my "Remembrance and Revenge." Marjorie Garber, " 'Remember Me': Memento Mori Figures in Shakespeare's Plays," *Renaissance Drama* 12 (1981): 3–25, sees the Ghost's "Remember Me" as a deliberate recollection of the speaking skull of the *memento mori* tradition, and thus "directly proleptic to Hamlet's literal interview with a skull in the graveyard, and later transmuted to his dying request to Horatio . . . 'To tell my story'" (p. 4).

47. On this point, see Kerrigan ("Hieronimo, Hamlet, and Remembrance," pp. 113–14), who notes that "Hamlet never promises to revenge, only to remember" (p. 114). Cf. also the terms of Francisco's self-dedication as Isabella's revenger in *The White Devil*: "Believe me, I am nothing but her grave, / And I shall keep her blessed memory / Longer than thousand epitaphs" (III.ii.341–43); "What have I to do / With tombs, or death-beds, funerals, or tears, / That have to meditate upon revenge" (IV.i.110–12).

48. Whether or not we accede to the tempting possibility that the "dozen or sixteen lines" which Hamlet promises to contribute to the play are to be found in the Player King's big speech, "The Mousetrap" is Hamlet's "version" of *The Murder of Gonzago* if only because the context to which he has transferred it endows the play with completely new meanings.

49. The motif of an untellable tale whose astonishing power, if told, might transform its audience is an important one in the play, from Hamlet's vision of the Player whose "horrid speech" would "amaze indeed the very faculties of eyes and ears" (II.ii.553–59), to Ophelia's "document in madness" (IV.v.175) of which the Gentleman remarks that "the unshaped use of it doth move / the hearers to collection" (V.v.8–9) to the unspoken jests of Yorick's skull ("tell here . . . make her laugh at that," V.i.184–90), and Hamlet's enigmatic aposiopesis ("I could tell you— / But let it be," V.ii.329–30). The Ghost, in this context, becomes a presiding spirit of inarticulate nostalgia.

50. The play is full of repellently literal reminders of mortal decay; from the first appearance of the Ghost and Horatio's recollection of the broken cemeteries of Caesar's Rome (I.i.115–16), Elsinore is overhung with that stench of putrefaction which routinely filled every sixteenth-century church and cemetery (see

Ariès, *The Hour of Our Death*, pp. 56–59, 481–83; and Stone, *Family*, p. 78).
Hamlet's charnel vision of the world as a "foul and pestilent congregation of
vapours" (II.ii.291–309); his invocation of "the very witching time of night, /
When churchyards yawn, and hell itself breaths out / Contagion" (III.iii.379);
his mockery of the dead Polonius as a cadaver already in advanced decay (IV.ii.6;
IV.iii.20–37)—these are all images that give a brutally literal dimension to that
sense of "something . . . rotten," beneath the state and majesty of Denmark,
which the Ghost stirs. Significantly, the Ghost of Andrugio in *Antonio's Revenge*
introduces himself in terms that suggest a similar repulsive physicality: "Thy
pangs of anguish rip my cerecloth up; / And lo, the ghost of old Andrugio /
Forsakes his coffin" (III.i.32–34).

51. Ariès, *The Hour of Our Death*, p. 173.

52. See above, n. 21.

53. The force of the emotional claims exercised by the dead in this drama,
together with such documentary evidence as Jonson's desolating grief at the death
of his son, should act as a caution against uncritically accepting Stone's bleak
account of sixteenth- and seventeenth-century family life (*Family*, chap. 6). Cf.
also the large number of wills studied by Ariès whose terms suggest a longing to
extend the affection of family and friends beyond the grave (*The Hour of Our Death*,
pp. 75–77). One reason for the exceptional nineteenth-century popularity of
Hamlet, among all Shakespeare's tragedies, was its prophetic anticipation of those
Romantic attitudes towards death and bereavement described by Ariès (pp.
409ff.). In their violent repudiation of those rituals of mourning which "instead
of allowing people to express what they felt . . . acted as a screen between man
and death" (p. 327), both Hamlet and Laertes anticipate the intense affectivity of
a culture in which "One person is dead and the whole world is empty" (p. 472).
Ophelia's death (that favorite subject of Victorian painters) anticipates, in
Gertrude's idyllic description, the idealized "beautiful death" of the nineteenth
century—she literally "floats away."

54. Sir Thomas Browne, *Religio Medici and Other Works*, ed. L. C. Martin
(Oxford: Oxford University Press, 1964), p. 8.

55. See G. K. Hunter's introduction to his Regents Edition of the play (London: Arnold, 1965), pp. xvii–xviii.

56. *Duchess of Malfi*, IV.ii.156–62; John Weever's complaint that contemporary monuments were becoming vain pattern books for the latest fashions in dress
(*Ancient Funerall Monuments*, p. 11) is directed against the same worldly individualism. It was "the discovery of the individual . . . the desire to be oneself
[that] forced tombstones to emerge from their anonymity to become commemorative monuments" (Ariès, *The Hour of Our Death*, p. 293). Panofsky, *Tomb Sculpture* (pp. 56–74), traces the emergence of "retrospective" monuments from their
beginning in the thirteenth century to the "purely commemorative" programs of
sixteenth-century humanist designs. Stone, on the other hand, claims that in
England realistic portrait sculpture "was introduced from abroad by Nicholas
Stone [in the 1620s]" (*Family*, p. 225). Examples of realistic portraiture can be
traced, however, at least as early as Torrigiani's Henry VII's tomb in Westminster
Abbey. The same individualist tendency can be seen in the increasing elaboration

of biographical epitaphs (Ariès, *The Hour of Our Death,* p. 223). Mercer, *English Art,* pp. 237–51, stresses both the increasing individualism and the enhanced emotional content of sixteenth- and seventeenth-century monuments.

57. See Ariès: "The survival of the dead man . . . was also dependent on a fame that was maintained on earth either by the tombs with their *signa* and inscriptions or by the eulogies of writers. . . . In common practice, in the sixteenth and seventeenth centuries . . . the commemoration of the living person was not separated from the salvation of his soul. Indeed, this is the fundamental meaning of the tomb" (pp. 202–3, 215). The fact that English funerals became the province of Heralds (where in France they seemingly remained in the charge of priests) suggests an intensification of the commemorative function in Protestant England. Mercer, *English Art,* p. 218, stresses the importance of "the universal display of heraldry, often of doubtful authority" on church monuments of the period.

58. Weever, *Ancient Funerall Monuments,* p. 3.

59. Compare the ending of Marston's *Sophonisba,* where a spectacular scene, beginning as a military triumph *all' antica* for the victorious Scipio (ii.61) is ritually converted into a funeral triumph for Sophonisba when Massinissa "all in black" transfers to his dead Queen "this crowne / This robe of triumph, and this conquests wreath, / This scepter" with which Scipio has invested him (ii.63; I quote from *The Plays of John Marston,* ed. Wood). Ford surely had both tableaux in mind when he composed the extraordinary ceremonial ending of *The Broken Heart,* a white-clad ritual of marriage-in-funeral that resolves itself as a monumental display of Love's triumph over Death.

60. See Kernodle, *From Art to Theatre,* p. 172: "The Elizabethan facade was one emblem, superimposing castle, throne, pavilion, tomb, altar and triumphal arch."

61. The trope is fittingly turned on its head in *Troilus and Cressida* where the "monumental mock'ry" of "rusty mail" (i.e., the knightly achievements hanging over a tomb) serves Ulysses as a metaphor for the ephemerality of fame (III.iii.151–53)—of which the play itself (as an antichronicle of infamy) constitutes a sardonic demonstration. For further comment on this motif, see Duncan Harris, "Tombs, Guidebooks, and Shakespearean Drama: Death in the Renaissance," *Mosaic* 15, special issue, "Death and Dying" (1982): 13–28.

62. A standard reversal-motif in comedy and tragicomedy—exemplified by such plays as *Much Ado About Nothing* (Act V), Marston's *Antonio and Mellida* (V.ii.), Chapman's *The Widow's Tears* (Acts IV, V), Fletcher's *The Knight of the Burning Pestle* (Acts IV–V), Middleton's *A Chaste Maid in Cheapside* (V.iv) and Davenant's *The Wits* (Acts IV–V)—is the mock funeral or entombment followed by a comic resurrection: "Hey, no, 'tis nought but mirth / That keeps a body from the earth," as Merrythought's final song has it (*Knight of the Burning Pestle,* V.369–70). The astonishing eruption of Fernando from Biancha's tomb at the end of Ford's *Love's Sacrifice,* when followed by his and Caraffa's double suicide, is a witty mannerist reversal of this kind of comic peripety. Cf. also the burial and mock resurrection of Charlemont in *The Atheist's Tragedy,* III.i, and his "haunting" of D'Amville in the charnel house, IV.iii.

Subjecting the Landscape in Pageants and Shakespearean Pastorals

James J. Yoch, Jr.

Many Renaissance English pageants related landscapes to power.[1] Civic celebrations for mayors and monarchs used triumphal arches to turn London into a new Rome. Within the antique images of military success, designers displayed vignettes of scenery from actual towns and countrysides as well as from distant paradises, such as the New World and Nova Faelix Arabia, to suggest dominion over realms of fact and dream. Courts summoned fabulous scenes for entertainments that displayed nature in the monarch's service. Mountains fought at the court of Henry VIII; "a moovable island, bright blazing with torches" floated up to Queen Elizabeth at Kenilworth; seas seemed to wash against the sets of masques for James I. The labor, expense, and artistry of such projects as the earl of Hertford's artificial lake and vast islands provided spectacular metaphors illustrating the crown's command over the external world.[2]

Besides the flattery of civic and courtly pageants, other political concerns encouraged artists to develop vocabularies for portraying and arranging landscapes. William Cecil was unsurpassed "in understanding of the geographical facts which govern policy"[3] and built up a large collection of maps. He also connected actual scenery with power in the decoration of his showcase house at Theobalds, built principally to entertain the queen. Painted on the walls of his Green Gallery were fifty-two trees, each containing the coats of arms of the nobility in an English province. Between the trees were pictures of "the towns and boroughs together with the principal mountains and rivers of each district."[4] Such paintings illustrated the particular scenery of England within the larger contexts of authority.

Similarly, across the body of England, the great houses of Elizabethan

Figure 1. The artificial lake and three islands the earl of Hertford built
to entertain Elizabeth I at Elvetham in 1591. (From John Nichols, *Progresses
of Elizabeth* [London, 1823], vol. 2).

courtiers rose "as tributes and as monuments of loyalty,"[5] and such prodi-
gies attempted by hilltop towers and attached gardens to display power
over the countryside and to direct the viewer to the monarch who made
them possible. Commemorating a visit by the ruler, owners labeled their
houses with royal badges and arms in stone, such as those at Compton
Wynyates and Charlecote. Gardens, too, had advertisements of authority:
Henry VIII put more than 150 heraldic devices in his gardens at Hampton
Court; William Cecil set out Roman emperors at Burghley and put chivalric beasts on the turrets at Theobalds; Sir Christopher Hatton's triumphal arches at Holdenby and Kirby waited to organize theatrically the
queen's progress into an imperial Roman perspective.

Such designs in which landscape becomes the major ground of a courtly
or civic drama might well seem alien to Shakespeare's stage, in which
scenery was minimal. Indeed, as vocabularies and skills for representing
the landscape improve by the early seventeenth century, particularly
through experiments in the masques and through the Jacobean importa-
tions of Italian artists and techniques, the spectacular representations of
the physical world on stage appear hostile to the best-loved drama of the

period. Taking the struggle between Inigo Jones and Ben Jonson as archetypal, Glynne Wickham muses that "Shakespeare was fortunate not to have lived so long as his great rival [Jonson], for it is hard to see how he could have adapted his interpretation of dramatic art to conform with the new tenets of landscape art which Jones had successfully championed into the life of the English theater." However, in contrast to this prediction of defeat, "the ultimate eclipse of poetic drama,"[6] this paper argues that Shakespeare adapted into the visions of his characters traditional landscape metaphors—forest, mountain, and island—in the new forms that current entertainments and pageants gave them.

The first part of the discussion considers Shakespeare's experiments with landscape description as part of characterization in two late Elizabethan pastorals, *A Midsummer Night's Dream* and *As You Like It,* and relates their mood-informed scenes to other fictions about power over the physical world, such as the entertainment of the queen at Elvetham in 1591. The second part analyzes the new, unifying image that Prospero, like the watching monarch at a pageant, gives to the scenery of *The Tempest.* Drawing in this play on native and imported continental designs that advertised grand political effects and the institutions of government in city and court, Shakespeare daringly celebrated in words on the public stage the strengths of individual character and imagination.

Like architects and painters, pageant designers developed visual images for the landscape and gave its elements voices. George Gascoigne's "imaginative improvisations in dialogue on the local environment" entertained the queen at Kenilworth in 1575. Inspired by this innovation were many scenes in which "pools, woods, streams and boscages were peopled with nymphs, satyrs and the wild men of the folk, and gave convenient cover for hidden choirs of naiads and dryads." Aided by these experiments in developing a vocabulary to image the landscape, dramatists drew extensively on the refreshingly new material of country life.[7]

Facilitating the exchange of images from street and progress entertainments to the theater, successful writers and performers (including Peele, Dekker, Munday, Middleton, Webster and Heywood) worked in both genres.[8] Actors from the theatrical companies performed in the increasingly scenic displays of the pageants; Richard Burbage mounted a dolphin to play Amphion, the genius of Wales, in the London pageant welcoming Henry as prince of Wales in 1610.[9] Through such minglings of writers and actors, developments in pageants and plays could enrich each other, and scenery is one of the most important contributions of the pageant to the regular theater.

Pageants, and the representations of landscapes in them, become more unified at the end of the sixteenth century. The sponsoring livery companies insisted in their commissions that playwrights prepare a production exclusively for an individual occasion rather than presenting a play available in repertoire.[10] Specific scenes with realistic and accurate topography suit the needs of such drama to concentrate on the here-and-now as well as on the political theme "pervasive in these shows . . . for the preservation of the unity of the state against those forces that would destroy it."[11] Accordingly, artists developed painted sets, descriptions, dramatis personae playing parts such as wild men to illustrate in the landscape the eventual triumph of calm order.

The emotional structure of fears and hopes that the pageant scenes expressed for the community takes more personal form in Shakespeare's drama. His characters reveal moods and values through verbal landscape figures. Unencumbered by the need to construct sets and undistracted by the need to have landscape function as background as it did in Italian and English court productions, Shakespeare could develop moral dimensions for the occasional prop of bush or tree planted on his stage as well as for the vistas of the imagination. Indeed, in a single play he often combined diverse methods: the old-fashioned emblem, ornamentally "set in" the text and momentarily illustrative, with a "maximum surface vitality"; the more forward-looking (in England) larger scene, so unified that all its parts relate to one another by proportion rather than by juxtaposition.[12]

Late Elizabethan landscapes are resolutely emblematic and focus on individual elements. Gardens were in small, unrelated divisions: kitchen, orchard, pleasure. At Theobalds, for example, there was little attempt to connect the parts or to organize elements within sections. Indeed Cecil, the most powerful of courtly builders, seemed indifferent to visual coherence. He did not even make his garden façade symmetrical.[13] Pageants in such gardens, as well as in towns, establish corresponding examples of discrete elements. Elizabeth had to go through five gates and watch a skit at each before dismounting at Kenilworth on the first eve of Leicester's most famous entertainment in 1575. In such arrangements, the items were soon passed by and, unconnected, could be eclectic.

Elizabeth continually encountered diverse performers who interrupted her progresses, such as the pilgrims, wild man, and angler at Cowdray in 1591. These figures focus on the immediate moment rather than the general picture. Thus the wild man began by shifting attention from an overview of the scene to a narrow concentration on the emblematic oak tree hung with the escutcheons of the noblemen and gentlemen of the district: "The whole World is drawen in a mappe; the Heavens in a globe; and this Shire shrunke in a tree." Similarly, Elizabethan theatrical scenery relied primarily on individual props—the stuff of Henslowe's diary—rather than on unifying vistas.[14] The audience, monarch, or Lord Mayor gave focus to the diverse illustrations in the political and moral rhetorics of these productions.

From the momentary notes and items of the late Elizabethan shows, which separate the perception of scene into individual units, Jacobean architects and designers move to controlling and presenting larger and more complex notes on the design of its elements: "a scaffolde richely furnished"; "a gorgeous and sumptuous arke"; a tree the designer labeled "a palme tree." In contrast to these minimal sets, "bewtified with pictures and sentences," the lavish arches of James include scenic compositions. After descriptions showing familiarity with the vocabulary of contemporary Italian architecture, such as the Tuscan columns surmounted by Doric architrave, frieze, and cornice, Thomas Dekker invited the reader to see the innovative connections in the scene: "And these were the nerves by which this great triumphall body was knit together." The drive toward the single, centrally unified, literal, and complete took visual form in the first arch, "the upper roofe thereof, one distinct gate, bore up the true moddells of all the notable houses, turrets and steeples, within the Citie."[15]

Ben Jonson's commentary emphasized the improvement over the devices of the preceding reign in which the pageants required interpreters, "the most miserable and desperate shift of the Puppits," to explain them. In contrast to the "ignorant Painter" who labeled the specific emblems of an Elizabethan scene with signs, such as "This is a Dog," Jonson recorded the more subtle and pervasive Vitruvian unity of the Jacobean arches: "The nature and propertie of these Deuices being, to present alwaies some one entire bodie, or figure, consisting of distinct members, and each of those expressing it selfe, in their own actiue sphere, yet all, with that generall harmonie so connexed, and disposed, as no one little part can be missing to the illustration of the whole." He concluded by denouncing the typical Elizabethan mode in noting "that the *Symboles* vsed, are not, neither ought to be, simply *Hieroglyphickes, Emblemes, or Impreses,* but a mixed character, partaking somewhat of all."[16] Thus the theme of political unity, so important to the monarch, finds expression in the total organization of the landscape images.

This significant extension of the range of artistic power, the result of a generation of experiments in pageants and of the importation of continental innovations, made visual harmony an important ingredient in some of the best early Jacobean work. Inigo Jones built double cube rooms at Wilton and the Banqueting Hall and laid out the totally organized piazza at Covent Garden for the duke of Bedford. Perspective staging at Oxford, at court, and on progresses related buildings and scenes to the viewpoint of the seated monarch; the Blackfriars provided the enclosure that made

Figure 2. Londinium arch, whose unified image of the city welcomed
James I to London in 1604. (From Stephen Harrison, *Arches of Triumph*
[London, 1604]; reproduced by permission of the Folger Shakespeare Library.)

Figure 3. Wollaton Hall (built 1580–88), surveying its park and Nottingham from its hillside position. (Author's photograph.)

possible more control over the scene.[17] By 1611, when *The Tempest* was first staged and Serlio's designs for the unified Vitruvian scene were popularized in Robert Peake's translation, competitive playwrights had markedly changed their habits of treating the landscape. The triumphant unity of the political theme, flattering to the observing monarch at pageants, came to be illustrated even in theatrical representations of the natural scene.

Consistently interested in showing how reactions to the landscape reveal character, Shakespeare moved beyond the individual figures, portable objects, and occasional descriptions in his work of the 1590s to adapt in *The Tempest* the most fashionable methods of organizing the entire visual scene. The revelation of a unifying moral vision informing a single place is a dream familiar in the pageants where rulers redeemed whole provinces. Shakespeare turned these subject landscapes from public contexts into illustrations of personal feelings and beliefs.

I

Performed for the pleasure of the watching monarch or official, the pageants made the appreciation of the political and institutional designs in the scene a sign of virtuous understanding in control of diversity. Thus, the productions in plan as well as in theme illustrated right rule. Elizabethan festivities often required interpreters as well as the queen's re-

Figure 4. Hardwick Hall (1590–96), its *piano nobile* elevated to the third floor for even more imposing authority on its hilltop position. (Author's photograph.)

markable patience to help bring the eclectic elements into a single sensible focus.

The earl of Hertford's entertainment at Elvetham in 1591 illustrates the Elizabethan fascination with elaborate surface detail unified in the attitude of the presenter and the response of the observer. The specific connections to *A Midsummer Night's Dream* have been much discussed;[18] whatever the relationship, the two editions of the description, including an illustration of the artificial lake and three islands, made it famous in its day. Threatened with a visit to a small property, the out-of-favor earl developed his tiny house and four-acre site with Disneyland-like complexity to give maximum variety to the small stage which the monarch would observe. The central feature was the lake, in which three islands—ship, fort, snail—stood in a row. To the events on these separate scenes the earl's desperate submission and the queen's reaction provided unity of personal vision. The minimum plot conventionally externalized his response to the visit in the joyful welcoming and sorrowful valediction speeches in which the landscapes voiced his emotions.

Most important, the scene's ships, choirs of nymphs, islands, all performed for the monarch. Elizabeth continually heard of her control over
the displays presented to her; indeed, the events had of course no other
purpose but to convince her of the earl's devotion. This rhetoric confirmed
its argument by extravagant landscapes: for example, the battle of sylvan
and marine gods that ended in the peace she brought them illustrated her
supposed dominion over natural forces, properly humble subjects (despite
the rain that broke into the pageant). [19] In such shows the monarch set the
example of individual interpretation, unifying the designs of the landscape, which had become since Kenilworth in 1575 the new secular stage
for illustrating power in action. Similarly, Shakespeare in the 1590s developed the power of the observer over the landscape in two plays which have
significant passages and images related to scenery and its elements: *A
Midsummer Night's Dream* and *As You Like It*.

A *Midsummer Night's Dream* contrasts characters who understand scenery
as merely composed of emblematic and literal elements, such as the moon
in the representations of the rude mechanicals, with other characters, like
Puck and Oberon, who perceive larger designs. The variation in points of
view suits the methods of indicating scene from the particularity of specific objects (sometimes ported on stage), to the spaciousness of descriptions
for places real and imaginary (topographia and topothesia), allusions to
scenery from literary sources, and descriptions challenged by other characters or undercut by ironies. Moreover, this diversity resembles the experi-
mental and eclectic approach to scenery in many late Elizabethan pageants, where the theme of political integrity did not yet fully organize all
the elements of the drama into the visual consistency of a single program.

Such variety takes advantage of the "chameleon-like quality" of the
stage, which had minimal sets and props. [20] Many scholars have studied
Shakespeare's descriptions of landscapes in the play: the embellishment of
stage properties, such as Titania's bank; the expansion of the play to the
margin of the sea and beyond through the use of what Harold Brooks calls
"the universal treasure-house of nature-imagery," and David Young, "panoramas"; the use of the moon to yoke together the main play and the
burlesque. [21]

To enforce order on these materials and to systematize them into the
drama, Shakespeare used descriptions to reveal a character, whose mood
determines the kind of landscape envisioned. Oberon and Titania each
accuse the other of adultery by describing vast mythological sites (II.i.64–
80)[22] informed with both the emotion and the elegant style of the speakers: their godlike associations, their all-seeing ability to discover infidelity
no matter how far away, and their heroic recollection of splendid antique
events. Titania grumpily portrays the spoiled countryside and concludes

by affirming that the natural disorders in the landscape are images of the dissension in the marriage at the center of power (II.i.81–117). In the second half of the play Shakespeare used for the daytime monarchs symmetrical arguments also relying on topographias. Hippolyta (teasingly, rebelliously?) recalls a hunt she has never heard matched (IV.i.111–17), and Theseus retorts by boasting that his dogs will surpass the ones she witnessed (ll. 118–26). Maneuvering images of the landscape to suit their own theses, the rulers in the play show Shakespeare's versatility and control, momentarily resembling that of the pageant designers who flattered the queen with landscapes that seemed to perform for her pleasure and to show the effects of her rule.

However, rather than organizing his material to support a single, public theme, such as the pageant writer's claims for order and Robert Greene's single-minded deflation of classical images in *Friar Bacon and Friar Bungay* in order to celebrate English ones,[23] Shakespeare's descriptions join diverse ingredients into unstable combinations[24] that make more subtle the dimensions of character and situation they reveal. The mix is often unexpected and requires leaping from the present to the past, from England to the continent, from the distant to the immediate. Thus, the play combines local scenes and fairies with the love affairs of Theseus and Hippolyta (II.i.164–80), the wild pansy with the spacious geographies of Cupid's attempt on Elizabeth in her role as Diana (II.i.155–68), the hunt with Hippolyta's recollected expedition with Cadmus and Hercules (IV.i.111–17). To these grand dislocations, the mechanicals add another set by jumbling Ovid's story with their own naïve concentration on individual props, beards, wall, scarf.[25] The particularity of their focus, like that of which Jonson later complained in his description of the ignorant and literal painter, is a joke in Shakespeare's theater, where dramatists handled verbal scenery with more dexterity.

Going well beyond the literal and simplistic, Shakespeare established patterns in scenery, such as the symmetries that arrange the descriptions of the two ruling couples and the Ovidian parodies of Pyramus and Thisbe's story. Appealing similarly to the audience's ability to recognize repeated designs despite the surface flux in scenery, many descriptions shift scale regularly. The pictures often begin in vastly mythological realms and end in local, individual elements: a child, a flower, the moon, hounds, the speakers themselves (II.i.117), "this hallowed house" (V.i.377), "dust behind the door" (V.i.379), "this palace" (V.i.407). After noting that Oberon's great speech (II.i.155–68) comes "to rest on something small and familiar, the pansy," Young suggests that the panoramas in the play offer escape from confinement.[26] But the final close-ups of these passages also illustrate the important role Shakespeare gave to emblematic figures in his Elizabethan pastoral designs, which resemble the pageant extension from political tracts to immediate occasion. His personal focus makes scenery expand rather than contain character, which ultimately brings spacious, mythological, and heroic beginnings to end in the readily recognizable, homespun, and vernacular scope of a single, cared-for detail.

The personalization of the landscape, which exists only by the grace of a character's perceptions of it, has a different design in the spacious matching passages where Puck and Oberon observe the coming of the dawn. The significant differences in their descriptions reveal contrasts in character and in rank. Puck quickly makes the first panel:

> My fairy lord, this must be done with haste,
> For night's swift dragons cut the clouds full fast,
> And yonder shines Aurora's harbinger.   [III.ii.378–80]

More elaborately, Oberon creates a processional picture, richer in color, as though the light had already become more vivid and complete, matching the greater power of his role:

> I with the Morning's love have oft made sport,
> And, like a forester, the groves may tread
> Even till the eastern gate, all fiery red,
> Opening on Neptune, with fair blessed beams
> Turns into yellow gold his salt green streams.   [III.ii.389–93]

In this diptych, Puck fittingly records the movement and the herald of light, Oberon the opulent display of power and prerogative. Other patterns support such subtle differentiations of character through scenery, such as the assignment of shorter descriptions (I.i.209–15, IV.i.186–87) to lesser characters and major visions only to the rulers.

The moon elicits responses from many characters, whose various reactions indicate their diverse powers of imagination. The descriptions amplify the range of possibilities in the scenery from mythical splendors (I.i.209–11) to the folksy rendition that Starveling gives his part. Bottom's energetic powers of translation, parodying the actual authority of Theseus and Oberon, paradoxically assign the moon "sunny beams" (V.i.265) and thank it for "shining now so bright" (V.i.266). Conflicting reactions to the moon—by the end Puck has restored it to the sky, where the "wolf behowls the moon" (V.i.361)—function as repeated and unifying structural elements in the play. Thus, Shakespeare wittily brought the great forces of the exterior world into the control of the performance, so sophisticated it spoofs its own devices and makes a virtue of its limited technical facilities. Requiring strength of imagination rather than of carpentry, the immense variety of landscape descriptions and elements support orderly patterns of characterization and design beyond the apparent melee of discordant points of view.

Similarly, the moods of characters in *As You Like It* figure the scenery into self-consciously artificial and eclectic shapes,[27] which the audience alone can turn into harmonious designs. Lodge may have inspired some of this diversity, for Geoffrey Bullough observes that *Rosalynde*'s "courtly language is touched with more homely idiom." Similarly, Shakespeare mixed Italianate and classical elements with English settings. The disparity matches the poses of the characters. For example, Shakespeare turned part of the story, which Lodge had Rosader himself tell, into a scene where Oliver, with more literary elegance than natural observation, comes looking for Rosalind: "Where in the purlieus of this forest stands / A sheepcote, fenced about with olive trees?" (IV.iii.77–78). Celia, more realistically, brings the scenery back to an English site with her answer: "Down in the neighbor bottom. / The rank of osiers by the murmuring stream" (IV.iii.79–80). Such descriptive notes playfully illustrate the significant differences in the characters. In his question about the landscape as well as in his stereotypical roles as evil and as reformed brother, Oliver is confined to formulas artful and Mediterranean; Celia is more naturally, even casually, aware of the native scene. Their choices of plants suggest the distance between them: the drought-loving and tender olive would not grow near the English marsh where willows flourish.[28] This unlikely mix uses minor landscape details to mirror the larger tensions in the drama between rigidity and freedom. The unstable, even nervous, surface in which the characters are enmeshed contrasts with the comfortable ease and confidence in triumphant order that the audience enjoys.

Moreover, when Shakespeare borrowed scenery from *Rosalynde* or invented figures to establish the country setting, he drew the landscape closely into character. For Lodge, scenery was background: "Passing thus on along, about midday they came to a Fountaine, compast with a groue of Cipresse trees, so cunninglie and curiouslie planted, as if some Goddesse had intreated Nature in that place to make her an Arbour." Through such descriptions, like the painted figures on the ceilings of Renaissance palaces, Lodge gave his readers distant perspectives on the action, made less intense within larger contexts. Such scenery distracts from characters. For example, "The ground where they sat was diapred with *Floras* riches, as if she ment to wrap *Tellus* in the glorie of her vestments. . . . *Phoebus* could not prie into the secret of that Arbour." In place of such passages, Shakespeare anthropomorphically established the pastoral setting partly by having messages from nature affect the characters.[29] Thus, they find "tongues in trees, books in the running brooks, / Sermons in stones, and good in everything" (II.i.16–17). As though in an Ovidian fantasy, the characters see themselves and others as animals and seasons: "the falcon her bells, so man hath his desires" (III.iii.80–81); "one of you will prove a shrunk panel, and like green timber warp, warp" (III.iii.76–77); "No, no Orlando; men are April when they woo, December when they wed" (IV.i.133–35). Rosalind even resolves to surpass "a Barbary cock-pigeon . . . a parrot . . . an ape . . . a monkey" and to laugh "like a hyen" (IV.i.137–39). Thus, like the wild men, pilgrims, and nymphs of the pageants, characters readily take on or get assigned roles in the theater of the landscape.

The repeated touchstone of the stag, like the moon in *A Midsummer Night's Dream,* enables the audience to see the organizing power of the author and the diversity within and among characters. The lords observe the tearful deer, and then recall Jaques weeping for it (II.i). Orlando retrieves Adam, like a fawn (II.vii.128); Lodge wrote only "feeble friend." The duke awards the antlers of the slaughtered deer to the best huntsman in a ritual (IV.ii) embellishing a short paragraph in *Rosalynde* where Ganimede teases the moping Rosader for not getting enough reward on a hunt (p. 422). Instead, Shakespeare's scene shows the flexibility of Jaques's passion. Once sad for it, he, perhaps mockingly, leads the men in the celebration of killing it. He organizes his comrades into an antique ceremony by hyperbolically describing the successful hunter as "a Roman conquerer" with the antlers decking his brows as laurel would a hero's. The revel mixes classical and English customs to show the range of Jaques's reactions from ritual idealism to the scorn by which he invites them to "make noise enough" (IV.ii.9). The stag, merely mentioned in Lodge's romance, by repetition reveals the unstable attitudes of a major character and simultaneously creates for the audience a unifying pattern throughout the design of the play.

To the various moods that haunt scenes within the play, Shakespeare added greater complexity through a fantastic blend of flora and fauna. In contrast to the jeweled formality of *Rosalynde*'s elegant woodland pictures, "handled in the Montemayor manner,"[30] Shakespeare used jaunty and jarring combinations of palms, lions, apes, and olives that blend together in landscape possible in the imagination only. Location is unstable, both inside and outside: on the skirts (III.ii.319 and V.iv.153) and purlieus of the forest (IV.iii.77) as well as within the "desert inaccessible" (II.vii.110). There are both farms and woods. Rather than a place such as the Ardennes or Warwickshire which readers have proposed as actual sites,[31] the play

Figure 5. The great arches of Sir Christopher Hatton's palace at Holdenby, which survive alone in a meadow to recall the line of the queen's triumphal progress into the basecourt. (Author's photograph.)

Figure 6. Hatton's later, less-decorated arches at Kirby Hall. (Author's photograph.)

suggests a location as unsure as that in dreams or as varied as that in pageants, where hopes for political order unified a broad range of sets and actors. Drawing varied responses and roles from characters, the deliberate jumbling of elements in the landscape and the indifference to visual unity show the advantages of a theater unlimited by painted sets.

In Shakespeare's early pastorals, mysterious woodlands include a procession of shapes drawn from local, classical, and biblical lore. The variety of images for the scene suits the Elizabethan and Flemish appreciation of abundant detail and complex interwoven linear patterning,[32] so confused by the end that the plots require at least superficial nudge from the fairies and Hymen to create final harmonies on stage. But such solutions, growing old by the early seventeenth century, would be unattractive in a period when major energies in painting and staging aimed at unifying the scene more explicitly within the single perspective the monarch gave to the pageants. Adapting to this change in taste and skill, Shakespeare invented in *The Tempest* verbal settings related to his earlier landscape sketches in which characters reveal themselves. In Prospero's island—the grand fresco of cave, woods, and marshes all within the mind's eye—Shakespeare established political and moral unities as absolute as those hoped for in the pageants. The scenery of the play, like a progress entertainment and like the grounds of a Renaissance villa, has shrines along a plot aimed at calling attention to the ruler and the rightness of his perceptions. The impregnation of setting with imagination, which the pageants verbalized in their flatteries of the monarch, was a concern of Shakespeare's first play and is also central to his last. Retaining the traditional pageant focus on a single, grand figure, his change from the eclectic detail of vernacular practice to the harmonious unity of neoclassical design displays Shakespeare's deft application of the most fashionable methods for presenting the landscape.

2

To the extravagance of Shakespeare's other romances and pastorals, *The Tempest* adds the singleness of Prospero's vision and the confining unity of the island scene. Landscape terms, familiar in the constructed sets of pageants and masques illustrating power in action, blend physical detailing with moral perceptions. The conclusion of the play shows the physical limitations on authority and affirms the primacy of spiritual dimensions in scenery, where moral elements—guilt, fear, forgiveness, charity—control designs. The scale is ultimately personal, within the imaginations of characters, who come eventually into more or less willing harmony with Prospero's understanding: and the audience even joins in his scene at the final moment by contributing their good hands and spirits.

In *The Tempest* the material framing the usual variety of accumulated details in the late Elizabethan manner is much more forceful than in the earlier plays. A sequence of allusions to the *Aeneid,* the absolutism of Prospero, the witty interpolation of scenic passages related to courtly landscaping and theatrical projects give the audience an additional—and new—appreciation of the scene as a visual whole in contrast to the characters' perceptions of it in pieces. Most important is the absolutism of Prospero, who within the play and especially in its conclusion controls the metaphor of the island. His repeated reminders of the overall scene and its design, so much more assured than the earlier notations in *As You Like It* and *A Midsummer Night's Dream,* establish a rhythm playing unity against the mazelike confusion that other characters experience.

Separation and loss are the lot of the shipwrecked. Like the many displaced characters Shakespeare created in a line beginning with the Antipholi of *The Comedy of Errors,* Gonzalo wonders in the final scene how all the characters have found themselves, "when no man was his own" (V.i.213). The familiar gardening and literary image of the labyrinth forms an important part of Prospero's plot to transform his enemies. Each sloughs off his old life by coming to a strange landscape and a different part of the island: Ferdinand is left alone in an odd angle (I.ii.223), the ship "in the deep nook" (I.ii.227). After a tiresome walk, Gonzalo describes his experience of the island: "Here's a maze trod indeed / Through forthrights and meanders" (III.iii.2–3). In the final scene Alonso resummarizes the action in the same terms: "This is as strange a maze as e'er men trod" (V.i.242). Such divisions and comments show the island as a place seemingly broken into pieces.

Supporting this divisiveness, characters see the island differently.[33] Caliban's descriptions are sensual and physical: the various foods he can dig up, the island's strange sounds, "fresh springs," "hard rock." Gonzalo is idealistic and would turn the island into a perfect commonwealth. In contrast, the scorn of Antonio and Sebastian reduces the island to a place Gonzalo will carry home in his pocket (II.i.86). Rather than the comfortable, unified background sets of the narrative sources,[34] the play's island or isle—the words occur more than thirty times—changes in the private theater of each character. Several arguments about the island dramatize the multiplicity of views. Gonzalo describes a possible ideal commonwealth over a rattle of insults. Similarly, Adrian, in a remark much interrupted by joking, optimistically says: "Though this island seems to be desert . . . Uninhabitable and almost inaccessible . . . Yet . . . It must needs be of subtle, tender, and delicate temperance" (II.i.35, 38, 40, 42–43). Perhaps drawing also on the association of royal temperance with utopias in the pageants and masques,[35] the ultimate triumph of order in these passages mirrors the larger patterns of the play where Prospero harmonizes the arrangements of scenery.

Scenery even provides the punishments for the guilty according to the place each holds in the social hierarchy. Ariel takes Caliban and his new masters through the mud where, "calf-like they my lowing followed, through / Toothed briers, sharp furzes, prickling goss, and thorns" (IV.i.179–80). In contrast, Alonso suffers in the landscapes of his dreams:

> Methought the billows spoke and told me of it;
> The winds did sing it to me; and the thunder,
> That deep and dreadful organpipe, pronounced
> The name of Prosper, it did bass my trespass.   [III.iii.96–99]

These penances and redemptions, scenes of suffering endured and of kingdoms regained, mirror in their complexity the personalities involved.

Larger in scale, indeed all-encompassing, Prospero's vision is most important to the scenery, which is all his. Often aloft, like an observer on a garden mount surveying the wanderings of those in the labyrinth below, he provides a sense of the whole scene in contrast to the characters, who see only a single aspect of it. He displays his power to summarize the entire world in a few lines, as when he recalls Ariel's missions:

> to tread the ooze
> Of the salt deep,
> To run upon the sharp wind of the North,
> To do me business in the veins o' th' earth
> When it is baked with frost.   [I.ii.252–56)

His control of weather and location is so absolute that all opposition is but a momentary distraction: his enemies' attempts to save their ship, Ariel's grumbling, Ferdinand's challenge to fight, Caliban's foul conspiracy.

As the play progresses from the violence of the opening storm, Prospero's designs of "insubstantial pageants" and images of the landscape become more important than physical power and actual place. Thus, he leads Ferdinand to believe the island is paradise (IV.i.124), an affected word to suit the masque which makes the place momentarily seem so. More important, Prospero brings about the rational clarity of the conclusion, in which the freeing of the characters from their dislocation takes form in landscape images. Just as he suppressed the tempest of his fury with his "nobler reason" (V.i.26), so he brings the other characters' interior landscapes into the sunlight of virtue:

> And as the morning steals upon the night,
> Melting the darkness, so their rising senses
> Begin to chase the ignorant fumes that mantle
> Their clearer reason. [V.i.65–68]

He continues the metaphor by turning it into a seascape:

> Their understanding
> Begins to swell, and the approaching tide
> Will shortly fill the reasonable shore,
> That now lies foul and muddy. [V.i.79–82]

From his control over the physical world, Prospero moves by the end of the play to become a designer of imaginations, where topography provides the metaphors for guilt, hope, and reason as it does in the pageants.[36]

To the structure of images leading in a crescendo from physical to spiritual scenes and to the character of Prospero, who designs the sets from storm to auspicious gales, Shakespeare added several other devices to unify with more than usual care the geography of this play. He defined precisely the physical elements of the place with consistency despite the variety of observers. The island's nooks, specific fruits, springs, birds, caves, and sounds are so harmonious that actual islands (Lampedusa, Pantalaria) have been found that contain most of them.[37] Eclectic elements such as the apes, hedgehogs, and adders that torment Caliban, unlike the lion and palm of *As You Like It,* are explicitly theatrical, merely roles that spirits play.

Amplifying this physical unity, a series of allusions suggest coherent mythological patterns. Epithets from Virgil's *Aeneid* can be heard in two greetings: when Ferdinand first sees Miranda (I.ii.422) and when Ceres welcomes Juno (IV.i.101).[38] These Virgilian echoes perhaps establish a connection between the virtuous Miranda, whom Ferdinand momentarily believes rules the island, and Juno, who provides order in heaven and stability in marriage. More obviously, against Gonzalo's dream of an ideal state and his geographical speculation about the identity of Tunis and Carthage, Antonio and Sebastian play off a distracting word game on the widow Dido (II.i). Thus, the three discuss and exemplify in the form of their conversation the play's theme that the ideal state is based on self-restraint, like the *pietas* that made possible the founding of Rome. In contrast to such stabilizing devotion, a sequence of allusions recalls the self-willed destructiveness of Medea.[39] By drawing closely on Ovid's portrait of her, Shakespeare emphasized his daring conversion of her negative force to good. A brief remark initiates the pattern, Antonio mocks Gonzalo's dream for the island: "And sowing the kernels of it in the sea, bring forth more islands" (II.i.88–89). Overwhelming such debasing energies, Prospero uses positive elements[40] from Medea's great speech (*Metamorphoses*, 7.191–214) about her control over the landscape to reveal his similar powers and, surprisingly, to announce his plan to surrender them (V.i.33–57). These variations on classical figures embellish the struggles on the island by implying a unifying structure that might be called the triumph of Aeneas over Medea were its incidents set in the garden of an Italian prince.

To emphasize the theme of Prospero's restraint that organizes the drama, Shakespeare parodied current theatrical devices in the courtly world. Many readers have studied the connections between Shakespeare's play and the masques;[41] yet the extravagant technology associated with these shows continually comes to naught in this play. The tempest, the most startling event for staging possibilities, occurs first, rather than as the culmination of the drama, and is followed by a scene so calm it raises yawns. Similarly witty in the abuse of machinery is the banquet that ultimately disappears. Disillusionment and let-down mar all these devices: Prospero tosses aside the parade of goddesses as an insubstantial pageant and truncates the songs and dances of the masquelike tableau in a manner that could only have been disappointing to those committed to such productions.[42]

Similarly, *The Tempest* inverts designs of symbolic mountains in order to support a unifying vision over its moral geography. Like the surveying ruler on a princely mount, Prospero often overlooks scenes in the play, and the stage directions once specifically site him "on the top" (III.iii). The figure of "mervelous mounts or mountayns" had long been available in court as well as civic entertainments: two came before Catherine of Aragon in 1501, and the Stuart masques continued such traditional emblematic staging to assert superiority, as in *The Vision of the Twelve Goddesses*. In his production, Daniel noted the first concern was "the hieroglyphic of empire and dominion, as the ground and matter whereon this glory of state is built." Within a few years there was a rage for mountains that so often rise on the stage of the Banqueting Hall that Plutus complains in 1613: "Rocks? Nothing but rocks in these masquing devices?"[43] Carrying these metaphors into other theaters, both Queen Anne and Prince Henry were building gardens which included large-scale mountains. Aided by Salomon de Caus, the queen began at Somerset House in 1609 a garden with "a huge grotto fountain depicting mount Parnassus." Even more grandly,

Figure 7. An artificial mountain that Roy Strong (*The Renaissance Garden in England* [London: Thames and Hudson, 1979]) believes de Caus designed for Prince Henry's garden at Richmond Palace.

Prince Henry at the same time was erecting at Richmond "a great figure . . . three times as large as the one at Pratolino, with rooms inside, a dove-cot in the head and grottoes in the base." Figures, such as Orpheus in the prince's project and the Muses enthroned on the queen's,[44] connected power and wisdom in the manner of the Italian models. At Pratolino, for example, the surviving gigantic figure of the Apennines was meant to be part of a series representing the geographies subject to the Medici grand dukes. Shakespeare used lofty position and magical power to give Prospero even more than ducal authority, joining the *grandezza* of absolutism and the claims of necromancers, and then moved him beyond such control in the Epilogue.

Shakespeare closed the play by tampering with expectations carried into his theater from pageants, which presented the community's best hopes of limitless power in the present. Unrestricted by the focus of deifying rhetoric, which varied sets rather than the mind of the ruler, Shakespeare humanized Prospero as the observing monarch by carrying him past the illusion of a world that performs at his command. The play seems to end like a final *intermedio*: someone in touch with ultimate powers strews blessings: "calm seas, auspicious gales" (V.i.314). Yet, giving a third of his thoughts to the grave and recognizing his confinement on this bare stage, Prospero in his descent to earth does not raise the house to the company of the gods or bring divine gifts, but instead asks for favors: without the wind he just promised, he must beg the audience, "Let your indulgence set me free" (Epilogue, l. 20). Through this parody of the total dominion and eternity promised in the swagger of the masques and pageants, Prospero maintains to the end his control over the play's landscapes, which he deliberately discards to unify the theater into an affective community. Writers had long eluded the necessity of having to stage in the public theaters the splendid emblems that the purses of the court and of the livery companies made possible.[45] But it is a special achievement in *The Tempest* that rather than merely avoiding dependence on lavish staging, Shakespeare boldly turned its physical devices into a contrary pattern in which landscapes are finally only imaginary and power illusory.

Prospero shifts the emphasis from the eclectic variety of detailing in the earlier staging of the 1590s to the perception of the scenes as part of a single, moral composition. Playing both the designer of pageants and the observing monarch, Prospero finally invites us to see an image of a place informed by right moral judgment. His last request joins the audience in a power analogous to his, for their applause generously improves the figurative climate of the isle. The strength of such a conclusion, in which spiritual unities prevail over material ones, shows a control over images of the physical world more Jacobean than Elizabethan. The different representations of geography for the secretaries of state of Elizabeth and James I illustrate the shift in perception. When William Cecil gathered maps, he commissioned them for specific areas to suit problems as they came along; thus the collection he left his family is remarkably heterogeneous. In contrast, his son Robert preferred maps of entire areas and "began the mapping by professionals concerned with coordination and continuity."[46] Such new designs, subordinating individual problems within larger aesthetic and political contexts, provide a key to Shakespeare's innovations in *The Tempest*, where unities in the landscape, used elsewhere to celebrate the extent of princely power, here enrich the dimensions of character.

Notes

1. I am indebted to many readers for their contributions to this paper; especially to David Bergeron and to Ronald Schleifer for generous help in editing and to Huston Diehl for her close reading and valuable questions.

2. R. Laneham, *A Letter* . . . , in John Nichols, *The Progresses and Public Processions of Queen Elizabeth* (London, 1823), 1:431. In their four introductory essays, Stephen Orgel and Roy Strong, *Inigo Jones: The Theatre of the Stuart Court* (Berkeley and Los Angeles: University of California Press, 1973), have studied most fully the politics of entertainment and its culmination in the masques of Jacobean and Caroline court drama. See also Stephen Orgel, *The Illusion of Power: Political Theater in the English Renaissance* (Berkeley and Los Angeles: University of California Press, 1975).

3. R. A. Skelton and J. Summerson, "The Maps of a Tudor Statesman," in *A Description of Maps and Architectural Drawings in the Collection Made by William Cecil, First Baron Burghley, Now at Hatfield House* (Oxford: Printed for presentation to the members of the Roxburghe Club, 1971), p. 3.

4. F. Gerschow, *Diary* (September–October 1602), in Sir John Summerson, "The Building of Theobalds, 1564–1585," *Archaelogia* 97 (1959): 117. The frieze around the Great Gallery had "correct landscapes of all the most important and remarkable towns in Christendom" (p. 124).

5. John Summerson, *Architecture in Britain, 1530–1830* (London: Penguin Books, 1977), p. 61.

6. Glynne Wickham, *The Early English Stages 1300 to 1660* (New York: Columbia University Press, 1959–), vol. 2, pt. 1, p. 275. Harley Granville-Barker, *A Companion to Shakespeare Studies* (New York: Doubleday, 1960), praised Shakespeare's handling of the sceneless stage: "He created out of the dramatic vagueness which he found, nothing so cut and dried as a *system* of diversity as against unity of place, but a supple means to a definitely dramatic end" (p. 63). See also Frances Yates, *The Theatre of the World* (Chicago: University of Chicago, 1969), p. 125; Clifford Leech, "The Function of Locality," in *The Elizabethan Theatre* (Oshawa, Ont.: Archon Books, 1970), p. 105; Alan Dessen, "Elizabethan Audiences and the Open Stage: Recovering Lost Conventions," *Yearbook of English Studies* 10 (1980): 9–11. Hallett Smith, *Shakespeare's Romances* (San Marino, Calif.: Huntington Library, 1972), distinguishes between "scenery," which is seen on the stage, and "landscape," which can only be seen in the imagination (pp. 145–74). My concern is primarily with the latter; I use the terms interchangeably.

7. Wickham, *Early English Stages*, 3:54–55.

8. David M. Bergeron, *English Civic Pageantry 1558–1642* (Columbia: University of South Carolina Press, 197), p. 131; see also Wickham, *Early English Stages*, 3:58.

9. Bergeron, *English Civic Pageantry*, p. 95; Wickham, *Early English Stages*, 3:55, notes that Gascoigne played Sylvanus at Kenilworth.

10. Wickham, *Early English Stages*, 3:56–57.

11. Bergeron, *English Civic Pageantry,* p. 138.

12. Wylie Sypher, *Four Stages of Renaissance Style* (Garden City, N.Y.: Doubleday, 1955), defines such unity (p. 33) and emblem (p. 91) in the perspective of European art history.

13. Nichols, *Progresses and Processions of Elizabeth,* 3:93; E. K. Chambers, *The Elizabethan Stage* (Oxford: Clarendon Press, 1923), 3:51–52, 88–89, discussed the need for properties like rocks and trees.

14. Summerson, "The Building of Theobalds," writes: "There was no attempt at symmetry and irregular fenestration seems likely" (p. 121). The elements of the gardens in the existing plates show diverse, usually rectangular, shapes without connection to each other or to the house. See, for example, plates 25b and 29 in Summerson's article. Roy Strong, *The Renaissance Garden in England* (London: Thames and Hudson, 1979), accounts for the disarray at Theobalds: "The building story, which is one of stops and starts, sudden alterations and retrenchments, followed by bursts of extravagance, parallels exactly that of the garden" (p. 104).

15. Nichols, *Progresses and Processions of Elizabeth,* 1:39, 41, 53, 46, and *The Progresses, Processions, and Magnificent Festivities of King James I* (London, 1828) 1:330, 351, 343. Visual awareness and concern superior to that in the days of Elizabeth's entry appears in the improved vocabulary for describing the arches and even for technically naming the details, such as the French terms and the "half pillars of rustic" (p. 342).

16. C. H. Herford, Percy Simpson, and Evelyn Simpson, *Ben Jonson* (Oxford: Clarendon, 1925–52), 7:90–91.

17. Inigo Jones worked to unify the eclecticism of the native style and the buildings he found. Orgel and Strong, *Inigo Jones,* 1:39, discuss the progression of Jones's work from the Gothic-classic combinations of the earlier masque scenery to a more purely Roman (*alla italiana*) style by mid-career. Perhaps Jones's most ambitious and revealing project is for the entirely new palace at Whitehall. Here he would have presented an enclosed, complete, symmetrical image of the crown and its power to arrange the physical world and to sweep away the untidy mess of past disorders.

18. See C. L. Barber, *Shakespeare's Festive Comedy* (New York: World, 1963), pp. 121–22; Alice S. Venezky [Griffin], *Pageantry on the Shakespearan Stage,* (New York: Twayne, 1951), pp. 139 ff.; E. K. Chambers, *Shakespeare Gleanings* (Oxford: Clarendon Press, 1944), pp. 63–64, suggested that the rude mechanicals' play spoofed the performance given at court by the earl of Hertford's provincial troupe.

19. Bergeron, *English Civic Pageantry,* p. 60, discusses Elizabeth's role as peacemaker.

20. Neil Carson, "Some Textual Implications of Tyrone Guthrie's 1953 production of *All's Well That Ends Well,*" *Shakespeare Quarterly* 25 (1974): 56; see Dessen, "Elizabethan Audiences," pp. 1–20.

21. *A Midsummer Night's Dream,* ed. Harold F. Brooks, Arden Edition (London: Methuen, 1979), pp. cxxvi, cxxix; David P. Young, *Something of Great Con-*

stancy: The Art of A Midsummer Night's Dream, (New Haven, Conn: Yale University Press, 1966), p. 76.

22. William Shakespeare, *The Complete Works,* ed. Alfred Harbage, Pelican Edition, rev. (Baltimore: Penguin Books, 1969). References are in the text.

23. For example, *Friar Bacon and Friar Bungay,* in *Drama of the English Renaissance,* vol. 1, *The Tudor Period,* ed. Russell A. Fraser and Norman Rabkin (New York: Macmillan, 1976), xvi.76.

24. Young, *Something of Great Constancy,* p. 33.

25. J. L. Styan, *Shakespeare's Stagecraft* (1967; rpt. ed., Cambridge: Cambridge University Press, 1975), p. 29.

26. Young, *Something of Great Constancy,* pp. 78, 80. Orgel and Strong, *Inigo Jones,* 1:25, 51–53, observe that later masques similarly conclude in the immediate and pastoral.

27. David P. Young, *The Heart's Forest: A Study of Shakespeare's Pastoral Plays* (New Haven, Conn.: Yale University Press, 1972): "Natural details are stylized and mannered to a degree that would distance them even for Shakespeare's audience" (p. 43).

28. Geoffrey Bullough, ed., *Narrative and Dramatic Sources of Shakespeare* (London: Routledge and Kegan Paul, 1957–75), 2:147. References are in the text. Similarly, Oliver's story of the green snake and the hungry lioness establishes a literary posture against which Shakespeare plays the reality of Orlando's bleeding and of Rosalind's swoon. For the convention of owls and lions in romances, see E. R. Curtius, *European Literature and the Latin Middle Ages,* trans. Willard R. Trask (New York: Pantheon, 1953), who notes that early in the Middle Ages they add an artifice that is part of "epic stylization" and a legacy from the "rhetorical school exercises of late Antiquity" (pp. 184–85).

29. *Rosalynde,* in *As You Like It,* ed. Richard Knowles, New Variorum Edition (New York: Modern Language Association, 1977), pp. 404, 406. References are in the text. Barber, *Shakespeare's Festive Comedy,* pp. 135–36, 143, discussed anthropomorphic nature in *A Midsummer Night's Dream.*

30. Bullough, ed., *Narrative and Dramatic Sources,* 2:146.

31. *As You Like It,* ed. Horace H. Furness, Variorum Edition (London, 1890), pp. 16–18.

32. Richard Wilbur, in Shakespeare, *Poems* (Baltimore: Penguin Books, 1966), summarized the aesthetic qualities of this period's art in his description of *Venus and Adonis* as "additive, linear, spasmodic, opportunistic" (p. 14).

33. Young, *The Heart's Forest,* p. 185; Leech, "Function of Locality," p. 114.

34. Carol Gesner, "*The Tempest* as Pastoral Romance," *Shakespeare Quarterly* 10 (1959): 531–39, cites convincing examples of Shakespeare's use of *Daphnis and Chloe* (531–39). However, his drama derives nothing from the extensive scenic descriptions of that source, which begins with the town of Mitelene, moves to a country manor and then to a thicket (trans. Angel Day [London, 1587], sig. A– Aᵛ). Bullough, *Narrative and Dramatic Sources,* 8:238–40, shows that the pamphlets about Sir Thomas Gate's expedition were useful to Shakespeare, but *The*

Tempest includes very few specific landscape details from them and adds two items specifically excluded: frogs and springs.

35. The use of scene to illustrate royal temperance is familiar in masques. In the *Masque of Blackness* (1605), the "temperate clime and royal power" of Britain cures the petitioning nymphs. Three years later, *The Masque of Beauty* presented "an island floating on calm water" to remind the audience of the advantages of temperance. See Bullough, ed., *Narrative and Dramatic Sources,* 8:263–64.

36. Using similar imagery, Thomas Middleton centered his Lord Mayor's Show for 1613 on London's Triumphant Mount, which he showed several times "shrouded over with 'a thick sulphurous darkness, it being a fog or a mist, raised from Error,' " until Truth has Zeal destroy Error in the finale (Bergeron, *English Civic Pageantry,* pp. 184–85).

37. *The Tempest,* Variorum Edition, ed. Horace H. Furness (London, 1892), pp. 1–3.

38. See *The Tempest,* ed. Frank Kermode, Arden Edition (New York: Random House, 1964), pp. 37, 100.

39. The play rejects not only the destructive power of Medea but also the self-will represented by Venus. Prospero regularly reminds Ferdinand that he must control his sexual urges until the marriage is celebrated. The prelude to the masque mentions Venus, whose company Ceres has forsworn. Moreover, Iris reveals that Venus tried to put "some wanton charm" on Ferdinand and Miranda "but in vain" (IV.i.95, 97).

40. *The Tempest,* ed. Kermode, p. 149. Besides his choice of good elements from Medea's speech, Prospero's purpose also differs from hers. She recalls her powers as part of a prayer as she gathers herbs to lengthen her father-in-law's physical life; Prospero uses his magical control of material things for spiritual ends.

41. Orgel and Strong, *Inigo Jones,* 1:10. Enid Welsford, *The Court Masque: A Study in the Relationship Between Poetry and Revel* (Cambridge: Cambridge University Press, 1927), pp. 336–39, saw Prospero as a masque presenter; Muriel Bradbrook, *The Growth and Structure of Elizabethan Comedy* (1955; rpt. ed., Baltimore: Penguin Books, 1963), p. 214. Young, *Something of Great Constancy,* pp. 57–58.

42. There seems to have been occasionally a similar, though unaimed-for, frustration in the splendid designs for court. Bad acting often spoiled the productions; the devices didn't always work well or on time: for example, a "violent storme of rayne, or other appointment of his Majestie" put off one fireworks battle in 1610; and Chamberlain observed in February 1613 that the "last Castle of fire, which bred most expectation, and had most devices . . . had worst success" (Nichols, *Progresses of James I,* 2:322, 587).

43. Wickham, *Early English Stages,* cites numerous examples of mountains in entertainments (1:84, 91, 98, 224), in miracle plays (1:167, 170, 394), in tournaments (1:42, 44). Bergeron, *English Civic Pageantry,* p. 267, reviews civic pageants with stage-property mountains. Strong, *Renaissance Garden,* pp. 97–103, neglects the possibility of these popular and native models for Jacobean garden

mounts. Samuel Daniel, *The Vision of the Twelve Goddesses,* ed. John Rees, *A Book of Masques,* ed. T. J. B. Spencer and Stanley Wells (Cambridge: Cambridge University Press, 1967), p. 26. *Masque of the Middle Temple and Lincoln's Inn,* in Orgel and Strong, *Inigo Jones,* 1:258; there were great rocky centerpieces in *Oberon* (1611) and in the *Masque of the Inner Temple and Gray's Inn* (1613). Kitty Scoular, *Natural Magic* (Oxford: Clarendon Press, 1965), pp. 154–56, discusses the emblematic significance of hills and mountains.

44. Strong, *Renaissance Garden,* pp. 87, 91, 98. Strong observes that in de Caus's *La Perspective* there is a design for a "vast mountain eighty-four feet square by fifty-five high to be built in the middle of the garden" (p. 101). Such works are familiar in Italian gardens and existed in Ferrara in the fifteenth century.

45. Richard Southern, *The Staging of Plays Before Shakespeare* (New York: Theatre Arts Books, 1973), pp. 324–25, 581, cites examples from *Wit and Science* (1539) and, in a humorous context, from *The Cobler's Prophesie* (1589). Wickham, *Early English Stages,* 2:256, 251–59, notes that noncourtly performances would have avoided expensive scenery.

46. J. H. Andrews, "Geography and Government in Elizabethan Ireland," summarized in Skelton, "Maps," p. 25.

Pageants into Play: Shakespeare's Three Perspectives on Idea and Image

Bruce R. Smith

> *What now ensues, to the judgment of your eye*
> *I give, my cause who best can justify.*
> —Gower's Induction to *Pericles*

When they are working up the garden scene, the actors in *Richard II* must bridge a sudden dislocation in sytle. "What sport shall we devise here in this garden / To drive away the heavy thought of care?" Queen Isabel asks her attending Lady. Bowling, the Lady proposes. " 'Twill make me think the world is full of rubs," replies the queen. Dancing? "My legs can keep no measure in delight." Telling tales, perhaps? "For what I have I need not to repeat, / And what I want it boots not to complain." Singing, then? " 'Tis well *thou* hast cause." Catching sight of the Gardener and his two Men entering through one of the rear doors, the queen draws her attending Lady to one side of the stage, or perhaps toward the rear. "Let's step into the shadow of these trees," she suggests, and overhear what the two men have to say. Suddenly the language in *Richard II* modulates into a new key. Though full of puns and other verbal tricks, the queen's dialogue with her Lady is nonetheless touchingly intimate: it gives us a close-up view of the human suffering that attends King Richard's downfall. When the Gardener starts to speak, however, he transposes the play's language—and with the language, us as audience—out of the privacy of the garden bower and into the arena of public declamation:

> Go bind thou up yon dangling apricocks,
> Which, like unruly children, make their sire

Stoop with oppression of their prodigal weight.
Give some supportance to the bending twigs.
Go thou and, like an executioner,
Cut off the heads of too-fast-growing sprays
That look too lofty in our commonwealth.
All must be even in our government.
You thus employed, I will go root away
The noisome weeds which without profit suck
The soil's fertility from wholesome flowers. [1]

If the words sound out of character—*would* a gardener orate so woodenly before an "audience" of two fellow workers?—it is because he is not so much speaking his own mind as declaiming the verses of one of the most popular Renaissance emblems for the right governing of a commonwealth. The garden/commonwealth conceit that the Gardener labors in his speech in effect dramatizes an emblem like that in Guillaume de la Perrière's *La Morosophie* (Lyon, 1553): the woodcut image becomes a tableau onstage, while the moralizing verses beneath it become the gardener's speeches (see figure 1).

The Renaissance dramatic occasion for such emblems-brought-to-life were pageants. A pageant on just this theme had, in fact, greeted Princess Elizabeth as she made her progress from the Tower to Westminster the day before her coronation in 1559. Awaiting her at the Little Conduit in Cheapside was a device of two contrasted mountains, the north one "cragged, barreyn, and stonye, in the whiche was erected one tree, artificiallye made, all withered and deadde," the south one "fayre, freshe, grene, and beawtifull, the grounde thereof full of flowres and beawtie." The differences between "*Ruinosa Respublica*" on the north and "*Respublica bene Instituta*" on the south was spelled out visually in tablets hanging from the trees ("Feare of god," "A wise prince," "Learned rulers," "Obedience to officers," "Obedient subjectes," "Lovers of the commonweale," "Vertue rewarded," "Vice chastened") as well as aurally in a speech made by a child positioned on a "standynge" in front of the flourishing hill:

> . . . since thou understandst the good estate and nought
> We trust welth thou wilt plant, and barrennes displace. [2]

The Gardener and his men mount just such a pageant in *Richard II*. In the queen and her Lady, hidden though they are, the workmen even have an onstage audience to hear and watch their device.

To introduce a pageant into the middle of a play is to confront actors and audience alike with an aesthetic challenge. Behind the superficial difference in the styles of the speeches stands a more fundamental difference in the very nature of the fiction in which the audience is invited to join. Pageant and play represent two distinctive ways of combining image and idea. As a didactic program dressed up in costumes and decked out with speeches, pageantry is particularly apt for being looked at in the terms Plato applies to art. Behind the appearances that sense takes in are the Ideas that intellect perceives. Thus, Thomas Dekker introduces the published text of his contribution to King James I's royal entry into London in 1604 by proudly differentiating between the "soul" of the pageants, supplied by poets like himself, and the "body," supplied by mere "Mychanitiens."[3] A painting brought to life and supplied with words, pageantry fascinated the Renaissance imagination because, unique among art forms, it turned Cicero's metaphorical ideal *ut pictura poesis* into a literal reality.

If Dekker seems to follow Plato and keep his eye on the *pictura* side of Cicero's dichotomy, Sir Philip Sidney follows Aristotle and trains his critical attention on *poesis*. From a poet's standpoint it is not mere physical appearances that body forth ideas but *praxis,* a human action. The "peerless poet," Sidney maintains, combines philosophy and history, in that "he coupleth the general notion with the particular example."[4] The *pictura* implicit in Plato's view of literature and the *praxis* that is central to Aristotle's view pose two different ways of relating philosophical idea and dramatic image onstage. Both views coexisted in the Renaissance; they collide in the garden scene of *Richard II.*

A slow but perceptible shift in sixteenth-century art from the "general notion" side of Sidney's dichotomy to the "particular example" side seems, at least to us looking back four centuries later, part of the "this-worldliness" of the Renaissance: its so-called "discovery of man" and of the physical laws of perspective that govern man's vision when he sets his sights on the substantial realities around him and not on the shadowy Realities of a distant "other world." One thinks of the paintings of Botticelli, Raphael, Titian, and Veronese, who render appearances with an immediacy that dazzles our senses even before we see through to the didactic *sentence.* Like their continental counterparts, Elizabethan Englishmen were increasingly conscious of how important the newly rediscovered science of perspective was in the sensible worlds of painting and building, if not of play-writing and acting. In a catalogue of all the books on art, architecture, and optics known to have been in English libraries in the sixteenth and early seventeenth centuries Lucy Gent has determined that works on perspective were surprisingly common, far more so than books on painting itself. Literary evidence, likewise, indicates a much wider understanding of the term than we might suppose,

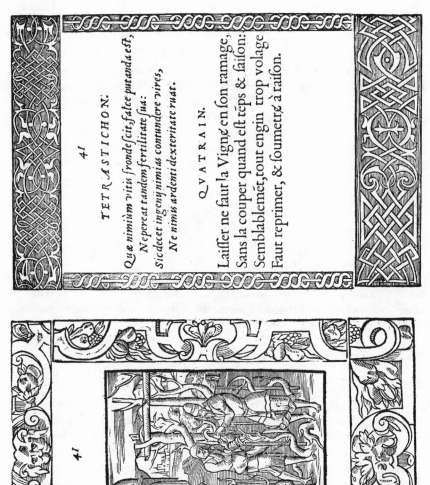

41

TETRASTICHON.

Quæ nimium vitis fronde sit, falce putanda est,
Nepereat tandem fertilitate suä:
Sicdecet ingeny nimias contundere vires,
Ne nimis ardenti dexteritate ruat.

QUATRAIN.

Laisser ne faut la Vigne en son ramage,
Sans la couper quand est tēps & saison:
Semblablemēt, tout engin trop volage
Faut reprimer, & soumetré à raison.

41

Figure 1. Woodcut of gardeners, with moralizing verses. (From Guillaume de la Perrière, *La Morosophie* [Lyon, 1553]; reproduced by permission of the Folger Shakespeare Library.)

especially when we consider the decidedly unprepossessing state of English painting at the time.[5]

These two principles of Renaissance aesthetics—the relationship between idea and image, and the perspective that governs how an audience sees an image—provide a revealing framework for considering how Shakespeare uses pageantry in his plays. In both the courtly and the popular pageantry of Renaissance England a simple two-dimensional relationship between idea and image persisted long after morality-play personifications had yielded the stage to personalities with so much lifelikeness as to require an actor not just to "play" a role but to "interpret" it. How did Shakespeare contrive to bring together stage figures that combined idea and image in two such different ways? As a translation of ideas into physical presence pageantry likewise involves perspective. What sort of relationship, figurative as well as physical, did Shakespeare set up between pageant devices and the audiences who watched his plays? In particular, what sort of perspective, figurative as well as physical, did he arrange onstage to relate pageant devices to the rest of the play? When we survey how Shakespeare confronts these artistic problems, we discover not one solution but three, and those solutions are different in Shakespeare's early, middle, and late plays.

I

To a fledgling dramatist like Shakespeare, setting out to write playscripts in the last decade of the sixteenth century, the traditions of pageantry did more than exemplify literary theory: They offered him some very useful devices for the stage. In the mumming devices that introduced holiday visitors into noble households, in the street shows that greeted royalty on their ceremonial entries into cities, in the speeches and spectacles that heralded dancing at court, in the debates and gift-giving devices that welcomed Elizabeth to the countryhouses she visited during her summer progresses over her realm Shakespeare found three things: (1) a repertory of stock subjects and stock sentiments for didactic speechmaking, (2) a widely understood visual vocabulary of characters, places, and props, and (3) a ready-made dramatic syntax for turning that vocabulary of words and images into theatrical events. Of these three, dramatic syntax may be the most important.

The show in Renaissance pageantry was always, in one way or another, a pictorial image brought to dramatic life by a "presenter." The characters within the image might pose in a tableau, or they might mime an action in dumb show, or they might sing, or they might even speak lines themselves, but the "presenter" remained an indispensable intermediary between image and audience. He introduced the show to the audience, sometimes by drawing aside a curtain and literally "dis-covering" the image, and he drew out of the scene the lesson to be learned.

As we are reminded by the devices for Elizabeth's London entry in 1559, Renaissance pageants were usually a show-within-a-show. Regardless of how many thousands of bystanders were looking on, the real audience for mummings, ceremonial entries, invitations to the dance, and country-house revels was the monarch himself. What the mass audience saw in Renaissance pageants was a "show" of the ruler watching a show. Built into the very social situation itself, then, was the juxtaposition of two planes of reality: the idealized world of the pageant and the real world of the human watchers. When we consider the pomp attending the monarch himself—dressed up in symbolic costume, wearing the crown as a "prop," playing the role of ruler, and (in the case of Elizabeth at least) speaking some extempore speeches to the pageant participants—we may even hesitate to label the world of the royal audience as "real," at least in the unceremonious terms of the twentieth century.

2

Even in his earliest scripts Shakespeare seems aware of the perspective problem posed by setting down two-dimensional pageants within a dramatic world of fully rounded heroes. In these earliest plays Shakespeare allows pageants to keep their separate identity; he brings them on as clearly defined set-pieces. In *Love's Labour's Lost* (1596), for example, the characters in the play put on two pageants themselves. Disguised as Muscovites and accompanied by musicians dressed as Blackamoors, the French lords attempt to flirt with the ladies in a mumming just like the surprise visits that Hall's *Chronicles* show Henry VIII and his courtiers to have relished. The stilted verses that Moth speaks as "presenter" for the Lords—verses so old-fashioned that John Lydgate might have penned them in one of his famous mumming devices for the court of Henry VI— draw from Boyet a barrage of mocking asides that serve to "frame" the pageant figuratively, just as physically Boyet must position himself between the mummers and the house audience to put his lines across.

A frame of watchers is likewise in place between audience and pageant when Holofernes and his companions answer Navarre's request for "some delightful ostentation, or show, or pageant, or antic, or fire-work" (V.i.99–100) by mounting—or attempting to mount—a "Pageant of Worthies." What bystanders in the streets of London were in 1559 the audience at the Globe was for *Love's Labour's Lost*: an audience watching a noble audience watch a show. The effect of this onstage frame is, physically and figuratively, to put the pageant into perspective, to make the house audience see the pageant as an order of reality different from that of the onstage audience of lovers. Likewise, the plodding verse and creaking artifice of Holofernes' device serve to distance the show, to place it "beyond" the frame of lords and ladies who watch it. News of the princess's father's death, however, produces a startling trick in perspective. The musical "dialogue . . . in praise of the owl and the cuckoo," intended originally to close the Pageant of Worthies, in fact closes the play itself, inviting the audience to stand back from the *entire* play and see the lovers' almost-successful quest for happy symmetry as a pageant debate between Spring and Winter. Hymen's descent during the denouement of *As You Like It* (1598) serves precisely the same function of forcing the audience to see the entire play as illusion.

Illusion is one of the metaphors Shakespeare introduces for pageant elements in his early plays; the other is dream. The Ghosts who appear to Richard III and Richmond on the eve of their battle may have their ultimate origins in Seneca's underworld, but they have made their way to Bosworth Field via the pageants that introduced Renaissance monarchs to their predecessors—biblical, legendary, and genealogical. Far more than the self-declared "illusions" in the early comedies, the "dream" in *Richard III* (1593) complicates the perspective order that relates pageant to play. Do the Ghosts possess metaphysical reality, or are they a projection of Richard's guilty conscience? Richard himself would like to believe the latter explanation. "What do I fear?" he asks himself when he first awakes. "Myself? There's none else by."

> My conscience hath a several thousand tongues,
> And every tongue brings in a several tale,
> And every tale condemns me for a villain.   [V.iii.183, 194–96]

And yet the Ghosts have a grip on his imagination—and ours—that no amount of rationalization can explain away. "O Ratcliffe, I fear, I fear!" Richard later exclaims.

> *Ratcliffe.* Nay, good my lord, be not afraid of shadows.
> *Richard.* By the apostle Paul, shadows tonight
>   Have struck more terror to the soul of Richard
>   Than can the substance of ten thousand soldiers
>   Armed in proof and led by shallow Richmond.   [V.iii.215–20]

"Shadows" or "substance"? A "tale" told by a guilty conscience or the agents of a moral universe physically intervening to right Richard's wrongs? That ambiguity turns what might have been a simple moral exemplum into a complex personal tragedy. Just such an ambiguity surrounds the three "Apparitions" of "an Armed Head," "a Bloody Child," and "a Child Crowned, with a tree in his hand" that the Witches "present" to the onstage "audience" of Macbeth before they produce the prophetic "show of eight Kings and Banquo" in Act IV, scene i.

"Illusion," "dream," or something far harder to define, pageant elements allowed Shakespeare to introduce into his early plays a second order of reality, "higher" than the human intrigue—a plane of reality where thematic ideas stand forth in unforgettable definition and declare their meaning with unmistakable clarity.

3

Even before he wrote *Macbeth* Shakespeare had begun to experiment with a second, subtler way of introducing the syntax of pageantry into the dramatic statements of his plays. The garden scene in *Richard II* represents something of a transition. Unlike the obvious set pieces in *Love's Labour's Lost, As You Like It, Richard III,* and *Macbeth,* the Gardener's speech in *Richard II* does, in its own way, fit into the plot. It is not set apart as show, "dream," or "illusion." Rather than labeling it a pageant, we would perhaps be more accurate to speak of such a scene as a "pageant moment" within the dramatized fable. That is to say, Shakespeare establishes a single fixed perspective on the human actors' plane of reality, but he accommodates pageant elements to that perspective in three ways: by transforming pageant spokesmen into dramatic characters with larger roles to play, by recasting didactic speeches as dialogue, and by turning the symbolic settings of pageantry into the fictional settings of the fable. A particular prop, a certain configuration of characters, a strategically placed speech can suddenly light up a scene with the emblematic meaning of a pageant.

If the strategy seems crude in *Richard II,* it has become so smooth and unobtrusive in Shakespeare's great tragedies that twentieth-century audiences, unfamiliar with the traditions of pageantry, are likely not to see the pageant elements at all. Take, for example, the fight between Edgar and Edmund in *King Lear* (1605). The brothers' combat is staged as a full-fledged tournament, complete with challenge read out by a herald, three soundings of the trumpet, and an onstage audience of Albany, Regan, and Soldiers. The allegory of the tournament, the thematic ideas it puts to debate, is made graphically clear at the combat's resolution. "But what art thou / That hast this fortune on me?" demands Edmund, lying wounded at his brother's feet (V.ii.165–66). What to Edmund is a happenstance of fickle Fortune is to Edgar a vindication of immutable moral law:

My name is Edgar and thy father's son.
The gods are just, and of our pleasant vices
Make instruments to plague us.
The dark and vicious place where thee he got
Cost him his eyes.   [ll. 171–74]

From the very start of the play Edmund has announced his own allegiance to the "goddess" Nature, not to that "fine word, 'legitimate'" (I.ii.1, 18). Now, prone in defeat before his "legitimate" brother, Edmund quite literally depicts an emblem of Fortune's wheel, and he acts as the presenter of the pageant himself: "Th'hast spoken right; 'tis true. / The wheel has come full circle; I am here (V.iii.174–75).

Like the Pageant of Worthies in *Love's Labour's Lost,* like the garden emblem in *Richard II,* like the dumb show in *Hamlet,* this "Pageant of Natural Fortune Against Moral Law" is framed for us by an onstage audience, but, unlike those more obvious set pieces, the combat of Edgar and Edmund is so fully "humanized," so fully integrated into the play's plot, as to pass unnoticed by twentieth-century audiences. The reason has less to do with twentieth-century insensitivity than with seventeenth-century artifice, for Shakespeare has established in the play a single fixed perspective in which men, not ideas, are the measure of things, and miraculously he has managed to adumbrate all the universal themes of the play without violating the human scale of that design. This technique of using unobtrusive "pageant moments" to illuminate the themes of the dramatic fable is perhaps best illustrated in the last two "middle" plays Shakespeare wrote before he turned to tragicomedy at the end of his career: *Antony and Cleopatra* (?1607) and *Coriolanus* (?1608).

Caesar's invasion of Egypt in Act IV of *Antony and Cleopatra* forces Antony to action—and to choices he has attempted to escape from the beginning of the play. The soldier whose eyes, Philo tells us in the first lines of the play, "have glowed like plated Mars" (I.i.4) must now become a soldier again. The choices he must make are emblemized in the way he puts on his armor.

> *Antony.* Eros! mine armor, Eros!
> *Cleopatra.* Sleep a little.
> *Antony.* No, my chuck. Eros, come; mine armor, Eros.   [IV.iv.1–2]

The character Antony summons in these lines is his squire—a supernumerary that Shakespeare did not find in Plutarch—but in the stage business of arming his master this "Eros" seems less a fictional character than an allegorical idea: watched by an onstage audience of "others" who, directed to enter with Antony and Cleopatra, are assigned no speeches and serve no other purpose but to be onstage and watch the pageant, the whole scene is less a preparation for battle than an ironic re-vision of the disarming of Mars by Eros and Venus, a *topos* that goes back to Plato's *Symposium* and Lucretius's *De rerum natura* and figured as one of the most popular subjects of Renaissance painting.[6] From the opening of the play Philo has disposed us to see Antony as Mars; Eros the squire is called by name five times within the first fifteen lines; and Antony's three flirtatious puns on "armor"-"*amor*"-"*Amor*" make the identification of Cleopatra with Venus complete:

> *Cleopatra.* Nay, I'll help too.
>   What's this for?
> *Antony.* Ah, let be, let be! Thou art
>   The armorer of my heart.   [IV.iv.5–7]

Antony's audacious sexual innuendoes make this military dressing up anything but a dressing down of passion:

> Thou fumblest, Eros, and my queen's a squire
> More tight at this than thou.   [IV.iv.14–15]

When an "armed soldier" enters ahead of Antony's waiting captains and their troops, the mortal Mars extends him greetings with a thrust that does not extend toward battle:

> Good morrow to thee, welcome.
> Thou look'st like him that knows a warlike charge.
> To business that we love we rise betime
> And go to't with delight.   [IV.iv.18–21]

The soldier who enters here is specifically an "armed soldier," perhaps to counterpose Cleopatra as Venus and to emblemize the ethical alternatives that confront Antony. Despite his armor, *amor* is Antony's choice.

The claims that compete for Antony's allegiance in this "Pageant of *Valor* and *Voluptas*" have in fact been suggested in the previous scene. There a "Company of Soldiers" are directed to enter and "place themselves in every corner of the stage," presumably leaving in the middle a conspicuous void. When "Music of the hautboys" is heard "under the stage," one of the soldiers questions whether it "signs" well.

> *Third Soldier.* No.
> *First Soldier.* Peace, I say!
>   What should this mean?
> *Second Soldier.* 'Tis the god Hercules, whom Antony loved,
>   Now leaves him.   [IV.iii.13–16]

One of the most popular subjects in emblem books all over Renaissance Europe, "Hercules at the Crossroads" portrays the great hero in the posture of choosing between the *voluptas* of Venus and the *virtus* of Minerva. In his version of the emblem Whitney identifies Venus with *vitium* and thus makes the choice hardly a choice at all[7] (see figure 2). Though no pageant materializes in IV.iii to fill the void in the middle of the stage, the oboes have hardly ceased before we see Antony himself "at the Crossroads" in IV.iv and watch him ignore the famous example of the god whom once he loved. The "pageant moment" that Antony enacts in IV.iv has all the trappings of the set piece in Shakespeare's earlier plays: an allegorical configuration of characters and iconic props, speeches that underscore the moral *sentence,* even an onstage audience to watch the pageant. Yet so smoothly does the event fit into the plot, so much in character are the speeches of Antony and the other figures that we have no sense at all of the pageant as an interruption in the human story. Like Botticelli, Veronese, and the other painters for whom the disarming of Mars was a favorite subject, Shakespeare has managed perfectly to fuse the thematic program of the play with the illusion of fully rounded character. Idea and image are aligned within a single perspective view.

Virtus is also the subject of a "pageant moment" in *Coriolanus,* likely the last play of Shakespeare's middle period. The most heroic episode in Plutarch's account of the life of Marcius Coriolanus occurs when the Romans are storming the city of Corioli. The Roman army has been divided for the assault, and the half who are entrenched in front of the city gates are attacked by a sally of Coriolans. Fired by Marcius's vehement speeches, the Roman soldiers drive the Coriolans back toward the city, yet they fear to pursue their attackers.

> Howbeit Martius being in the throng among the enemies, thrust himself into the gates of the city, and entered the same among them that fled, without that any one of them durst at the first turn their face upon him, or offer to stay him. But he looking about him, and seeing that he was entered the city with very few men to help him, and perceiving he was environed by his enemies that gathered round about to set upon him: did things then as it is written, wonderful and incredible, as well for the force of his hand, as also for the agility of his body, and with a wonderful courage and valiantness he made a lane through the middest of them, and overthrew also those he laid at: that some he made run to the furthest part of the city, and other for fear he made yield themselves, and to let fall their weapons before him.[8]

This is the deed that earns Marcius the appellation Coriolanus, and Shakespeare makes it a major episode near the play's beginning. In doing

Biuium virtutis & vitij.

WHEN HERCVLES, was dowtfull of his waie
Inclofed rounde, with vertue, and with vice:
With reafons firfte, did vertue him affaie,
The other, did with pleafures him entice:
    They longe did ftriue, before he coulde be wonne,
    Till at the lengthe, ALCIDES thus begonne

Oh pleafure, thoughe thie waie bee fmoothe, and faue,
And fweete delightes in all thy courtes abounde:
Yet can I heare, of none that haue bene there,
That after life, with fame haue bene renoumde:
    For honor hates, with pleafure to remaine,
    Then houlde thy peace, thow waftes thie winde in vaine.

But heare, I yeelde oh vertue to thie will,
And vowe my felfe, all labour to indure,
For to afcende the fteepe, and craggie hill,
The toppe whereof, whoe fo attaines, is fure
    For his rewarde, to haue a crowne of fame
    Thus HERCVLES, obey'd this facred dame

PENS

Virgil. in Fragm.
de littera y.
*Quifquis enim duros
cafus virtutis amore
Vicerit, ille fibi lau-
démque decúfque pa-
rabit.
At qui defidiâ luxúm-
que fequetur inertem,
Dum fugit oppofitos in-
cauta mente labores,
Turpis, inópfque fimul,
miferabilo tranfiget
avum.*

Figure 2. Whitney's version of "Hercules at the Crossroads." (From Geoffrey Whitney, *A Choice of Emblemes* [Leiden, 1586]; reproduced by permission of the Georgetown University Library.)

so Shakespeare makes perhaps the most inventive use of battlements in his entire career. Pursuing the Coriolans, "Martius follows them to gates and is shut in," the stage directions clearly state, and the cowardly Roman soldiers left onstage bear the directions out: "See, they have shut him in. . . . With them he enters, who upon the sudden / Clapped to their gates" (I.iv.47, 50–51). Perhaps these workable "gates" are simply one of the doors in the stage's back wall. If, however, we follow Glynne Wickham and take a liberal view of the stage properties available to Shakespeare's company, we may even imagine a stage mansion made like battlements.[9] In either case the gates function like the scenic device of a pageant. First Lartius, standing between us and the city gates with an onstage audience of Roman soldiers, presents a moralization of Marcius's exploits by quoting Plutarch almost verbatim and addressing Marcius rhetorically as if he were dead indeed:

> Thou wast a soldier
> Even to Cato's wish, not fierce and terrible
> Only in strokes; but with thy grim looks and
> The thunder-like percussion of thy sounds,
> Thou mad'st thine enemies shake as if the world
> Were feverous and did tremble.   [I.iv.56–61]

Having pronounced the moralization, Lartius then "discovers" Marcius, within or perhaps on top of the battlements, as if he were an allegorical figure in a pageant: "Enter Marcius, bleeding, assaulted by the Enemy." In this "pageant moment" Shakespeare has translated to the stage an emblem like Joannes Sambucus's device of "The Excellences of a Commander" (see figure 3). The commander interposed between his men and Fortune, say the Latin verses,

> teaches the leader to be swift in decision and powerful in argument, so
> that he can spur on the laggard and the war-weary, lead them, and
> sway them with persuasive speeches. When necessary he takes up his
> arms—idle delay makes matters worse—and with unbroken courage
> rushes ahead of the others into the midst of the enemy.[10]

Glowing in the audience's imagination through the rest of the play like a kind of afterimage, the tableau of Marcius in heroic isolation against the battlements presents not the moral lesson that Sambucus intends but, ironically, the very reason for Coriolanus's tragic downfall. And so it is with Edmund at the bottom of Fortune's wheel and with Antony armed by Cleopatra and Eros. Edmund reads his own downfall as the fickleness of Fortune, but that can no more stand as a complete explanation for events

Imperatoris virtutes.

Q v æ ratio belli fit, qua virtute Ducemque
Inftructum cupiam, fi præftet fortibus aufis,
Ni piget, en breuibus declarat fymbolon iftud.
Confilio celerem decet, eloquioue potentem
Effe Ducem vt caueat, tardos, Martisque perofos
Exacuat, regat, inflectat fermone fuaui.
Cùm proprium eft paret arma, nocet cunctatio vana,
Infractusque animo reliquis præcurrat in hoftem.
Anguibus & ftudium pacis, fœdusque notatur.
Nil tamen hæc profunt, vacua eftque fcientia belli,
Si fortuna nocet, pulchros confundat & orfus.

Abfit

Figure 3. Joannes Sambucus's device of "The Excellences of a
Commander." (From Joannes Sambucus, *Emblemata* [Antwerp, 1564];
reproduced by permission of the Georgetown University Library.)

in *King Lear* than Edgar's equally simple-minded conviction that the gods have punished Gloucester for his lechery. The moral lesson in "Hercules at the Crossroads" is the choice of *virtus* over *voluptas,* yet Antony's speeches betray his allegiance to love. In his middle plays Shakespeare not only accommodates pageantry to the verisimilitude of the dramatic illusion; he transforms the simplistic sermons of pageantry into something far closer to the complicated contingencies of human life.

4

If in his middle plays Shakespeare holds the mirror up to Nature and catches there a single unified image, in his late plays he has shattered the dramatic mirror; turning its fragments in different directions, he reflects such different kinds of images that the viewer must—in imagination, at least—move about to find a vantage point. *The Tempest* with its masque of Iris, Ceres, and Juno and its antimasque of the Harpies' banquet, *Cymbeline* with its spectacular descent of Jupiter, *Pericles* with its theophany of Diana all demonstrate how pageant elements, instead of being fused with the human story as they are in the middle plays, reassume the separate identity they have in the early plays. But the relationship between these pageant pieces and the plays in which they are set down is hardly so straightforward as before. Just as the plot motives of those early comedies and tragedies are combined into the far more sophisticated mode of tragicomedy, so pageants-within-the-play take on a theatrical and thematic importance far beyond their service in the early plays as entertainment, illusion, and dream. For in his tragicomedies Shakespeare grants the iconic world of pageantry a reality even *more* compelling than the human fable itself.

Rough studio sketch that it seems to be, *Pericles* (?1608) shows this new use of pageant elements in a more obvious way than the later tragicomedies. Among the plays' episodic scenes pageants and pageant moments stand out in glittering prominence. The protracted "triumphs" that celebrate Thaisa's birthday and emblemize her union with Pericles, for example, recall the self-contained pageants acted out in Shakespeare's early comedies. Though most modern editions present II.ii and II.iii of *Pericles* as two separate scenes (there are no act and scene divisions in the 1609 quarto and act divisions only in the third folio of 1664), the tournament parade in II.ii and the dance of the competing knights in II.iii in fact constitute one continuous action. There is no time lapse between the two scenes. Only the king's concluding lines in II.ii, "We will withdraw / Into the gallery" (II.ii.58–59), and the opening stage directions of II.iii,

"Enter the King and Knights from tilting," serve to demarcate one scene from another. What about the tournament that is supposed to take place in the meantime? Does the stage direction "Great shouts and all cry 'The Mean knight!'" indicate that the tournament takes place offstage? May it not just as well have been played out as a stylized pageant onstage, watched by the king and his retinue from the "gallery" above? Onstage or offstage, the procession of knights with their *imprese* in II.ii prepares us to see the tournament as a pageant display in which Pericles with his allegorical device, "In hac spe vivo," wins out over the ostentatious display of the other knights. As the six competing knights "pass by," Thaisa acts as pageant-presenter to the onstage audience of her father and at least three lords by narrating the knights' emblems and reading out their mottoes. It is the king who pronounces the moral lesson of the pageant when he answers the three lords' ridicule of Pericles' "rusty outside" (II.ii.50): "Opinion's but a fool, that makes us scan / The outward habit for the inward man" [II.ii.56–57].

A remarkably similar tournament scenario involving a "clownishly clad" knight had, in fact, marked one of Queen Elizabeth's Accession Day celebrations.[11] At the tournament's end the victorious "mean knight" is affianced to Thaisa, not in a scene of private conversation between the king and Pericles, but during the masquelike dance of the still-armed knights. In this iconographically rich context the conjoining of Thaisa ("beauty's child," the king has called her before the tournament) with Pericles becomes not just the union of two individuals but something like the "Union of Beauty and True Worth."

Pageant moments reminiscent of Shakespeare's middle plays are likewise part of the kaleidoscopic stage images of *Pericles*. The "music of the spheres" that sounds in the hero's ears during Diana's theophany (V.i.230) has been heard during an earlier pageant-within-the play when Cerimon, a lord of Ephesus, chances to find the sea-borne coffin of Pericles' wife and uses music, fire, and the mysterious contents of "boxes" fetched from his "closet" to bring Thaisa back to life. The onstage audience of, at the least, two Gentlemen and a Servant who witness the show express appropriate astonishment—and cannot fail to learn the lesson that Cerimon as "presenter" of the pageant pronounces for them. "Death may usurp on Nature many hours," he announces in the beginning, "And yet the fire of life kindle again" (III.ii.81–82). Afterwards it is again "nature" that "awakens" Thaisa's breath (III.ii.92). To see the emblem implied by these speeches we need only supply invisible capital letters when we hear the words "Death" and "Nature."

Thaisa's first words—"O dear Diana, / Where am I? Where's my lord?

What world is this?" (III.ii.104–5)—not only introduce the goddess of chastity as the dea ex machina of the play but suggest a possible iconographical connection between this pageant and yet another emblem in Sambucus's *Emblemata*. For in Sambucus's emblem of "The Difference Between *Physica* and *Metaphysica*" Nature is represented as the many-breasted Diana of the Ephesians (see figure 4). It is in Diana's temple at Ephesus, of course, that Thaisa becomes a priestess, and it is there that all the characters converge, at Diana's own direction, for the play's happy ending. The moral lesson of Sambucus's emblem is relevant, too, for it depicts Nature/Diana as the nexus between two realms of creation: on the lower right of the woodcut, the mutable physical world of darkness and vegetable decay that encloses the temple of Vesta, goddess of the earth, and, on the upper left, the immutable metaphysical world of light and soaring wings that open wide about the heavenly "temple of the foreseeing." Cerimon works his magic by translating powers from the metaphysical side of Nature/Diana's realm to the physical side, and he effects that translation of powers not just with fire and the contents of his mysterious "boxes" but with music. Music can form an "aural icon" in a pageant just as costumed characters against a scenic device can compose a visual icon. And the "idea" that is sounded in earthly music is the unheard "music" of cosmic order. Philosophically men of the Renaissance were still so well attuned to the music of the spheres as to believe that music had the power to transform physical reality. [12]

A figure like Sambucus's Diana may actually have presided over the final scene of *Pericles*. In the dream-vision Diana has commanded Pericles to proceed to Ephesus, enter her temple there, and "do upon mine altar sacrifice" (V.i.242). When Pericles does as she bids in the play's last scene, he addresses the goddess directly, as if she were physically present: "Hail, Dian! To perform thy just command, / I here profess myself the King of Tyre" (V.iii.1–2). In setting up this scene Gower has charged the audience to "see" three things: "At Ephesus the temple see, / Our king, and all his company" (V.ii.17–18). Cerimon, too, makes at least an imagistic gesture toward "Diana's altar" when he replies to Pericles' declaration (V.iii.16–18). If Glynne Wickham is right that the King's Men, especially after they took over the Blackfriars Theatre, had available the same kind of props that are inventoried for court productions, we may imagine a statue of Diana in a "temple" stage mansion as the focal point of this summary pageant moment in *Pericles*.

The triumphs that mark the union of Pericles and Thaisa, Cerimon's display of cosmic control in bringing the apparently dead Thaisa back to life, Diana's appearance as dea ex machina—the effect of these pageants

I. SAMBVCI

Physicæ ac Metaphysicæ differentia.

NATVRÆ *multa eft cognatio mobilis, atque*
  Prodiit æternis , illaque noffe monet.
Eft etenim fœtus veluti genitricis amic.e,
  Sed patitur, foluit tempus edaxque breuem.
Quidquid enim regitur, proprio nec nititur ortu,
  Compofitis abeunt partibus, atque iacent.
Illa fed excelfa manet, ☙ ftat fede perennis,
  Temporis ac nullis motibus obiicitur.
Ocia amat, mentem pafcit, non vtilis omni,
  Huius tu fobolem fed cole pr.ecipuam.
Vtque folent τ'ἤϑη vitam cumulare benignè,

                               Τοῖς

Figure 4. "The Difference Between *Physica* and *Metaphysica*."
(From Joannes Sambucus, *Emblemata* [Antwerp, 1564]; reproduced
by permission of the Georgetown University Library.)

and pageant moments set down among the generally episodic scenes of the play is to turn *Pericles* into a series of dramatic showpieces. With all due allowances for a corrupt text, Shakespeare seems deliberately to be destroying the single perspective that had unified his middle plays. Yet out of the fragments of *Pericles* a coherent dramatic image does emerge, and it is John Gower who composes it for us. Indeed, Gower offers us a perspective not only on *Pericles* but on the pageant variety of all Shakespeare's late plays. Gower's eight appearances in the play serve a variety of purposes. He bridges gaps in time and geography; with his three dumb shows he summarizes parts of the narrative that are not dramatized directly. But above all else he stands, figuratively and physically, between the audience and the play and tells the audience how to make imaginative sense of what they see.

The words that Gower himself uses to describe his relationship to the play are strategically chosen.

> To sing a song that old was sung,
> From Ashes ancient Gower is come,
> Assuming man's infirmities
> To glad your ears and please your eyes.   [I.Cho. 1–4]

Using archaic diction and speaking in the rhymed tetrameters that the historical Gower in fact favored, Shakespeare's Gower at first treats the dramatized fable as if it were a tale out of his *Confessio Amantis*: in singing his "song" (l. 1) he defers like the historical Gower to "what mine authors say" (l. 20), and he commends the tale by claiming that lords and ladies "have *read* it for restoratives" (l. 8). This curious sense of the dramatized action as a tale, not a play, has its most extreme statement in the last lines of the second interruption: "What shall be next / Pardon old Gower; this 'longs the text" (II.Cho.39–40). By the time of Gower's fourth and fifth appearances the "text" has begun to assume dramatic life as "our fast-growing scene" (IV.Cho.6, IV.iv.48). "Our story" (IV.Cho.19, IV.iv.9, V.Cho.2)—like "scene," a neutral term that can as easily refer to narrative as to drama—the fable remains until the final line in the script, when at last it becomes "our play" (Epilogue, l. 18).

Gower never uses the term "Chorus" for himself, and in fact the role he assumes is far more active and important than that of any of the characters Shakespeare himself labeled "Chorus." In narrative terms, Gower is the storyteller; in dramatic terms, he is more than anything else the "presenter" of a pageant. Just as he summons the three dumb shows and narrates them for us ("Like motes and shadows see them awhile. / Your ears unto your eyes I'll reconcile" [IV.iv.21–22]), so he sets up the play for us—

near the end he actually uses that technical stage term "discover" (V.Cho.24)—and pronounces the moral when the play is over. Gower's final speech is nothing like Shakespeare's usual epilogues with their coy appeal for applause; instead, Gower's verses, pentameter for once, summarize the action and underscore the moral lessons exactly as the verses do beneath a woodcut emblem:

> In Antiochus and his daughter you have heard
> Of monstrous lust the due and just reward;
> In Pericles, his queen, and daughter, seen,
> Although assailed with fortune fierce and keen,
> Virtue preserved from fell destruction's blast,
> Led on by heaven, and crowned with joy at last.   [Epilogue, ll. 1–6]

Gower's last speech has reference to more, however, than this final stage emblem of the Triumph of Justice, Truth, and Patience. It completes Gower's frame around the entire play. At the beginning of the play he has set that frame in place with two strategic words:

> What now ensues, to the judgment of your eye
> I give, my cause who best can justify.   [I.Cho.41–42]

"Judgment" and "justify"—for the original audiences of *Pericles* both words had precise technical meanings in the newly rediscovered science of perspective. To "justify" had a visual application that was not yet limited to typesetting: "to make exact; to fit or arrange exactly; to adjust to exact shape, size, or position" (OED 9). And "judgment" retains in modern English its specific sense as "that function of the mind whereby it arrives at a notion of anything" (OED 8). "The judgment of the eye," then, is the process of finding meaning and pattern in what one sees. As if to remind us of our task, Gower makes ever more frequent appearances in *Pericles* as "song" moves through "scene" and "story" toward "play": nearly five hundred lines separate Gower's first, second, and third appearances in the play; half that many lines his fourth, fifth, sixth, and seventh; and only eighty-four lines his seventh from his eighth. To judge and justify the disparate images of *Pericles* is to find a perspective that can accommodate several planes of reality at once. For rather than subordinating pageant elements to the plot, as he does in his early plays, rather than fusing pageant moments with the human fable, as he does in his middle plays, Shakespeare in his late plays positively insists on juxtaposing the disparate planes of reality in startling ways. Play-within-the-play, dream, illusion—none of these stage metaphors from Shakespeare's early plays is quite flexible enough to resolve the dizzying shifts in focus we encounter in *Pericles*. And pageant elements are far too intrusive for us to keep our eyes fixed on the plane of ideas to the plane of human action alone. Rather than subordinating the plane of ideas to the plane of human action, rather than fusing the two planes into one, Shakespeare has *coordinated* them. To see Shakespeare's tragicomedies aright is to "judge" and "justify" these two different planes of dramatic reality at once. Precisely because we are forced to find a perspective that relates these two kinds of images, precisely because we must "justify" the design, we are constantly reminded that the play is an imaginative construct and not merely a transcription of reality: a sophisticated strategy that relates Shakespeare's last plays to Mannerist painting.

Present in *Pericles* are all the pageant devices and perspective shifts we encounter in *Cymbeline* (?1609), *The Winter's Tale* (?1610), *The Tempest* (?1611), and *Henry VIII* (?1613): whole scenes are conceived as allegorical pageants, one or more presenter-figures stage-manage the procession of episodes and emblems, sharp intersections of one plane of reality with another challenge any easy perspective on the play and require that the audience "justify" what they see, first by placing pageant elements "beyond" the "foreground" of human action, then by observing how those distant visions of ideal truth transform to stark realities of the human scene closer at hand. After *Pericles* Shakespeare takes these juxtapositions between vision and fact and makes them less frequent but more strategic, just as in his later tragedies he learned to take the horrors upon horrors of *Titus* and focus them in a few crucial moments.

Thus in *Cymbeline* the shifts in fictional locale are as frequent and as casual as in *Pericles*, yet there is only one major shift from one plane of reality to another. As befits the king of the gods, Jupiter makes a pageant entry in *Cymbeline* that far outshines Diana's appearance in *Pericles*. Like that earlier intersection of the divine and the mortal planes, the pageant of Jupiter is discovered to Posthumus as a dream. Despite the spectacular effects of thunder and lightning and an eagle that apparently could move its wings and beak ("his royal bird," Sicilius observes, "Prunes the immortal wing and cloys his beak, / As when his god is pleased" [V.iv.117–19]), the didactic lesson of the pageant is as simple as that in *Pericles*: beyond physical appearances there is metaphysical order, and within that order human virtue is at last rewarded. "Whom best I love I cross," Jupiter declares (V.iv.101), sounding remarkably unclassical in his paraphrase of Paul's Epistle to the Hebrews: "For whom the Lord loveth he chasteneth" (12:6).

In *Cymbeline* metaphysical order is not quite so ethereal a matter as it is in *Pericles*. Just as Pericles' fortunes begin to turn when Cerimon rescues

Thaisa in the middle-most scene of the play, so in the middle of *Cymbeline*
the tragic directions of action in Saxon Britain, ancient Rome, and Renaissance Italy converge toward comic resolution in the natural utopia of
Wales. Belarius outdoes Duke Senior in finding tongues in trees and sermons in stones:

> O, this life
> Is nobler than attending for a check,
> Richer than doing nothing for a robe,
> Prouder than rustling in unpaid-for silk:
> Such gain the cap of him that makes him fine
> Yet keeps his book uncrossed. No life to ours.   [III.iii.20–26]

What Belarius later calls the country's "honest freedom" (III.iii.71) is
discovered in even more exuberant form in *The Winter's Tale* when Time
turns his hourglass upside down, and with it the tragic sifting down of the
plot. Unlike Diana in *Pericles,* unlike Jupiter in *Cymbeline,* indeed unlike
Time who "triumphs" in the play's source *Pandosto,* Shakespeare's pageant
figure of Time does not *cause* events to happen; by his own account, he
"witnesses" them:

> I, that please some, try all, both joy and terror
> Of good and bad, that makes and unfolds error,
> Now take upon me, in the name of Time,
> To use my wings.   [IV.i.1–4]

If it does not stretch the idea of a pageant moment beyond the critical
usefulness of the term, we may even regard Time as the "presenter" of the
"pageant" of the sheep-shearing festival in Bohemia. Perdita's own simile—"Methinks I play as I have seen them do / In Whitsun pastorals"
(IV.iv.133–34)—encourages us to view the scene as a play-within-the-
play, and in the persons of Polixenes and Camillo there is even an onstage
royal audience to watch the show and frame it for the house audience. This
"pageant" of Persephone scattering her flowers comes to an abrupt end
when Polixenes, the ruler for whose instruction the emblem is displayed,
rejects its lessons in time's regenerative force and in the transforming
power that human art "shares / With great creating nature" (IV.iv.87–
88). Prompted by the gap of sixteen years between Acts III and IV or by
the shift of scene to Bohemia or even by academic critics, most modern
directors have staged *The Winter's Tale* as if Time as Chorus were the
hyphen in tragi-comedy, but Ronald Eyre in his 1981 Royal Shakespeare
Company production left onstage throughout the play, even in Act IV, the
high constricting walls that had suggested tragic enclosure in Acts I, II,

and III, and so demonstrated what sound dramatic sense it makes to think of the revels in Bohemia as a self-contained episode, a bright parenthesis within the "sad tale" that's "best for winter." Certainly such staging gives the final scene even greater piquancy as a shift from tragic expectations to comic eventualities—and even sharper definition as a pageant-within-the-play.

Perdita prancing about the stage as Persephone is, in fact, a comic revision of an earlier pageant moment in *The Winter's Tale* when Hermione stands in tragic isolation at her trial and finally crumples beneath Leontes's injustice. As Time acts as presenter of the stage emblem in Bohemia, so the Officer reading out the indictment in III.ii "presents" Hermione to the onstage audience of Leontes and his Lords and Officers. The verses to the stage-emblem that they see are declaimed by Hermione herself:

> if powers divine
> Behold our human actions, as they do,
> I doubt not then but innocence shall make
> False accusation blush and tyranny
> Tremble at patience. [II.ii.27–31]

Again, all we have to do is mentally to capitalize Innocence and Patience in order to "see" the pageant that Hermione's trial represents. Like Claudius at "The Mousetrap," like Polixenes before the Pageant of Persephone, Leontes vigorously, even violently, rejects the lesson that he sees in this "Pageant of Innocence and Patience." His blindness is revealed at once, however, when an Officer—likely the same Officer/presenter who read out the indictment at the beginning of the scene—reads out the message from Apollo's oracle and articulates the precise, yet richly ambiguous conditions on which the happy ending ultimately turns: "if that which is lost be not found."

Elements from these earlier pageant moments in *Pericles, Cymbeline,* and *The Winter's Tale* itself are fused in the pageant of Hermione posed as a statue, a pageant far more complex than any of its predecessors seen by themselves: as soon as the statue is dis-covered we see, with a sharp sense of déjà vu, Hermione as the emblem of Innocence and Patience that we saw at her last appearance in Act II; in the music that Paulina summons to "awaken" the apparently lifeless form we hear an "aural icon," the concord of the physical with the metaphysical realms of creation that enabled Cerimon to recover Thaisa from Death's temporary "usurpation" and signaled the moments when Diana and Jupiter appeared to affirm the order and justice of the universe; in Paulina's two simple words " 'Tis time" we hear echoes of Time's speech as presenter of the Pageant and Persephone, as the "trier," the judge, of all things; when the statue answers Paulina's command "Bequeath to death your numbness," we witness a reincarnation of Persephone, an emblem of time's regenerative power; prompted by so many remarks on the lifelikeness of Julio Romano's handiwork, we witness, finally, the Pageant of Persephone in a more sophisticated way, as the triumph of the "art / That nature makes." We see all these earlier pageant moments, but we see something entirely new besides, for this time the pageant figure steps down out of the frame and brings its visionary force into the very midst of the astonished spectators.

Present in all the pageants-within-the-play in *Pericles, Cymbeline, The Winter's Tale,* and *The Tempest* is faith in the power of these iconic visions not just to reflect human reality but to transform it. That faith informs even *Henry VIII,* in which the elements of pageantry seem at first glance so gratuitous. The two great pageant pieces in the play, Anne Boleyn's coronation procession in Act IV, scene i, and Katherine's dream-vision of the heavenly banquet in the next scene, offer not only two occasions for spectacular stage effects but two visions of an order "higher" than ordinary human events—an order that turns suffering into triumph and tragedy into comedy. The coronation procession, passing over the stage "in order and state," as the stage directions specify, emblemizes a new political order—which is just the lesson that the onstage audience of three Gentlemen read out in what they see and hear. "You come to take your stand here, and behold / The Lady Anne pass from her coronation?" one of them asks another.

> *Second Gentleman.* 'Tis all my business. At our last encounter
>   The Duke of Buckingham came from his trial.
> *First Gentleman.* 'Tis very true; but that time offered sorrow,
>   This, general joy.   [IV.i.2–7]

In the next scene Katherine finds herself in a position remarkably like Hermione's as the cast-off wife. As she sits "meditating / On that celestial harmony I go to" (IV.ii.79–80), the celestial harmony in fact comes to *her* in a pageant of "six personages clad in white robes, wearing on their heads garlands of bays, and golden vizards on their faces, branches of bays or palm in their hands." These celestial "personages" quite literally *in-volve* the sleeping queen in their cosmic dance. The moral dimension of this stage emblem is perhaps suggested in the speech the usher Griffith whispers to Katherine's attending woman when the "sad and solemn music" begins to sound:

> She is asleep. Good wench, let's sit down quiet
> For fear we wake her. Softly, gentle Patience.   [IV.ii.81–82]

"Patience" is the attending woman's proper name, but this is the only time it is used in the scene, and in context it serves just as Eros's name does in *Antony and Cleopatra:* to point our attention to the moral emblem we see before us. In both Anne's coronation procession and Katherine's dream-vision the human actors actually become participants in the pageant: the iconic vision transforms the human story. Perhaps one of the reasons why *Henry VIII* seems so unsatisfactory when read in the study but so imaginatively convincing when seen in performance is that in reading the text we miss this power of the pageantry to cancel the old order and establish the new.

Anne's coronation procession and Katherine's celestial vision are as thematically crucial to *Henry VIII* as Hermione's statue is to *The Winter's Tale* and the wedding masque is to *The Tempest.* Extraordinary examples though they be, these scenes are altogether typical of how centrally important the traditions of Renaissance pageantry are in Shakespeare's dramatic art. To appreciate that importance when we read Shakespeare's scripts and when we produce them onstage, we must not only *read* the text but *see* the text. And seeing requires perspective. The perspective that we must find on Shakespeare's pageants-within-the-play is both physical and figurative. Physically, as we have seen, two planes of reality were juxtaposed when Renaissance Englishmen watched pageants in city streets, in country-house parks, and in the great halls of castles. Bystanders not only watched the pageant: most often they watched royalty or nobility watch the pageant. It is remarkable how often Shakespeare's scripts preserve this physical arrangement. The French lords and ladies watch Holofernes' Pageant of Worthies, Richard's queen and her attending Lady watch the Gardener and his Man, assorted "others" watch Eros and Cleopatra as they arm Antony, the entire cast of *The Winter's Tale* watches Paulina unveil Hermione's statue, three Gentlemen watch Queen Anne Boleyn's coronation procession, Griffith and Patience wait aside while Katherine has her celestial vision in *Henry VIII.* In every case this onstage audience "frames" the pageant for the house audience; the onstage audience, quite literally, "puts" the pageant "into perspective." But there is the subtler matter of *figurative* perspective. In all his scripts Shakespeare has confronted the problem of combining the flat two-dimensional world of the pageant with the three-dimensional world of the human fable, and he has experimented with three successive solutions to that problem. In his early plays Shakespeare brings on pageants as clearly defined set-pieces within the play. As entertainments, as illusions, as dreams he *sub-ordinates* pageants to the play. In his middle plays Shakespeare *fuses* pageant and play, so that both occupy a single "human" plane of reality. In his late plays, finally, Shakespeare *co-ordinates* pageant and play. They are juxtaposed as two equally compelling planes of reality. Indeed, there comes a moment in all the last plays when the three-dimensional foreground of the play recedes into a two-dimensional far distance where characters are ideas and dialogue is philosophy.

Notes

1. My quotations from Shakespeare's plays come from *The Complete Works,* ed. Alfred Harbage, Pelican Edition, rev. (Baltimore: Penguin Books, 1969). Added italics are mine. Future quotations are cited in the text.

2. *The Quenes Majesties Passage Through the Citie of London to Westminster the Day Before Her Coronacion* (1559), ed. James M. Osborn (New Haven: Yale University Press, 1960), pp. 46–50 (fols. C3ᵛ–D1ᵛ).

3. "Many dayes were thriftily consumed, to molde the bodies of these Tryumphes comely, and to the honour of the Place: and at last, the stuffe whereof to frame them, was beaten out. The Soule that should give life, and a tongue to this *Entertainment,* being to breathe out of Writers Pens. The Limmes of it to lye at the hard-handed mercy of Mychanitiens." Quoted in David M. Bergeron, *English Civic Pageantry 1558–1642* (Columbia: University of South Carolina Press, 1971), p. 244, where Dekker's distinction is made the basis for an analysis of English Renaissance pageantry in general.

4. "The philosopher, therefore, and the historian are they which would win the goal, the one by precept, the other by example. But both, not having both, do both halt. For the philosopher, setting down with thorny arguments the bare rule, is so hard of utterance and so misty to be conceived, that one that hath no other guide but him shall wade him till he be old before he shall find sufficient cause to be honest. For his knowledge standeth so upon the abstract and general, that happy is that man who may understand him, and more happy that can apply what he doth understand. On the other side, the historian, wanting the precept, is so tied, not to what should be but to what is, to the particular truth of things and not to the general reason of things, that his example draweth no necessary consequence, and therefore a less fruitful doctrine. Now doth the peerless poet perform both: for whatsoever the philosopher saith should be done, he giveth *a perfect picture* of it in someone by whom he presupposeth it was done, so as he coupleth the general notion with the particular example. *A perfect picture* I say, for he yieldeth to the powers of the mind *an image* of that whereof the philosopher bestoweth but a wordish description, which doth neither strike, pierce, nor possess the sight of the soul so much as that other doth" (italics mine). Quoted from Sir Philip Sidney, *Miscellaneous Prose,* ed. Katherine Duncan-Jones and Jan Van Dorsten (Oxford: Clarendon Press, 1973), p. 85.

5. Lucy Gent, *Picture and Poetry 1560–1620* (Leamington Spa, U.K.: James Hall, 1981), p. 74.

6. Edgar Wind, *Pagan Mysteries in the Renaissance,* rev. ed. (New York: Harper and Row, 1968), pp. 86–96.

7. For a full discussion of this *topos* and its various moral interpretations see Erwin Panofsky, *Hercules am Scheidewege und andere Bildstoffe in der neueren Kunst* (Leipzig and Berlin: Teubner, 1930). In addition to inspiring many Renaissance and baroque paintings, "Hercules at the Crossroads" provided J. S. Bach with the subject for one of his birthday cantatas (BWV 213) for the Electoral House of Saxony.

8. Plutarch, "Life of Coriolanus," trans. Sir Thomas North, in *Plutarch's Lives of the Noble Grecians and Romanes* (1579), ed. Paul Turner (Carbondale: Southern Illinois University Press, 1963), 1:120.

9. Glynne Wickham, *Early English Stages 1300 to 1600* (New York: Columbia University Press, 1959–), vol. 2, pt. 1, pp. 206–29.

10. Compare Plutarch: "For he was even such another, as Cato would have a soldier and a captain to be, not only terrible, and fierce to lay about him, but to make the enemy afeard with the sound of his voice, and grimness of his countenance" ("Life of Coriolanus," p. 119).

11. Frances A. Yates, "Elizabethan Chivalry: The Romance of the Accession Day Tilts," *Journal of the Warburg and Courtauld Institutes* 20 (1957): 4–25.

12. On music as cosmic language see John Hollander, *The Untuning of the Sky* (Princeton, N.J.: Princeton University Press, 1961); Wilfred H. Mellers, *Harmonious Meeting: A Study of the Relationship Between English Music, Poetry, and Theatre, c. 1600–1900* (London: Dobson, 1965); and Victor Zuckerkandl, *Sound and Symbol,* vol. 1 (New York: Pantheon, 1956). Renaissance faith in the physical power of music is revealed nowhere more clearly than in Cordelia's imprecation "O you kind gods, / Cure this great breach in his abused nature! / Th'untuned and jarring senses, O, wind up / Of this child-changed father" (IV.vii.14–17) while actual music sounds to soothe Lear's sleep.

Contributors

DAVID M. BERGERON, professor of English at the University of Kansas, is the author of *English Civic Pageantry 1558–1642, Shakespeare's Romances and the Royal Family,* and numerous articles on Renaissance drama.

JAMES BLACK is professor of English at the University of Calgary, Alberta, Canada.

GERARD H. COX, associate professor of English at the University of Washington, has published essays on Marlowe, Donne, Jonson, and Milton.

GORDON KIPLING, professor of English at the University of California, Los Angeles, is the author of *The Triumph of Honour* and is completing a study of the medieval civic triumph.

LEAH SINANOGLOU MARCUS, professor of English at the University of Wisconsin, Madison, is the author of *Childhood and Cultural Despair: A Theme and Variations in Seventeenth-Century Literature* and is completing a book to be entitled *The Politics of Mirth*.

MICHAEL NEILL, associate professor of English, University of Auckland, New Zealand, is the author of articles on Renaissance drama and has co-edited an edition of Marston for Cambridge University Press.

STEPHEN ORGEL, professor of English at Johns Hopkins University, is the author of *The Jonsonian Masque* and *The Illusion of Power,* and coeditor with Roy Strong of *Inigo Jones*.

BARBARA D. PALMER, Buhl Associate Professor of English at Chatham College, has published on Shakespeare, medieval drama, and *Piers Plowman* and has a forthcoming volume on West Riding art.

GAIL KERN PASTER, associate professor of English, George Washington University, is coeditor of the Variorum *Romeo and Juliet* and has published several essays on Renaissance drama, especially on the concept of the city.

BRUCE R. SMITH, associate professor of English at Georgetown University, is the author of essays on Queen Elizabeth's countryhouse entertainments and on Shakespeare's dramatic uses of Renaissance sculpture, and he has completed a book on the staging of Greek and Roman plays in England between 1500 and 1700.

JAMES J. YOCH, JR., professor of English at the University of Oklahoma, is the author of several essays on the relationship of literature and setting in the Renaissance.

Index